BRAZIL
AS AN ECONOMIC SUPERPOWER?

BRAZIL
AS AN ECONOMIC SUPERPOWER?

Understanding Brazil's Changing Role
in the Global Economy

Lael Brainard

Leonardo Martinez-Diaz

Editors

BROOKINGS INSTITUTION PRESS
Washington, D.C.

Library of Congress Cataloging-in-Publication data
Brazil as an economic superpower? : understanding Brazil's changing role in the
global economy / Lael Brainard, Leonardo Martinez-Diaz, editors.
    p.   cm.
Includes bibliographical references and index.
Summary: "Scholars and policymakers from Brazil, Europe, and the United
States examine the present state and likely future of Brazil's economy. Their
analysis focuses particularly on five key topics: agribusiness, energy, trade,
social investment, and multinational corporations"—Provided by publisher.
  ISBN 978-0-8157-0295-5 (cloth : alk. paper) — ISBN 978-0-8157-0296-2
(pbk. : alk. paper)
  1. Brazil—Economic policy—2003– 2. Brazil—Commercial policy. 3.
International business enterprises—Brazil. I. Brainard, Lael. II. Martinez-Diaz,
Leonardo. III. Title.
  HC187.B86584 2009
  337.81—dc22   2009003633

Typeset in Sabon with Strayhorn

Composition by Circle Graphics, Inc.
Columbia, Maryland

Printed by R. R. Donnelley
Harrisonburg, Virginia

Contents

Foreword

Brookings is giving new and sustained priority to Latin America and to emerging powers in the world like Brazil. In 2008 we launched our Latin America Initiative and convened the Partnership for the Americas Commission, which, under the chairmanship of Ernesto Zedillo and Thomas Pickering, made recommendations to the Obama administration. This volume is further evidence of our commitment to the region in general and to the importance of Brazil in particular.

Brazil is once again in the international spotlight, even as the world reels in economic crisis. For the past decade, Brazil's role in the world economy has been changing in important ways, and today the country occupies key niches in global energy, agricultural, service, and some high-technology markets. For this reason, Brazil may play an important role in helping the world economy recover. At the same time, Brazil still struggles with endemic problems of poverty and inequality and retains a deeply rooted ambivalence toward opening its domestic markets to foreign competition. How did Brazil come to occupy this position in global markets? What are the foundations of its economic success? How resilient will they prove in the future? And what are the politics and policies that underpin them?

To address these questions, Brookings's Global Economy and Development program commissioned papers from scholars and policymakers from Brazil, Europe, and the United States and brought the authors together in Washington, D.C., in April 2008. The debate at the conference centered around five topics: Brazil's role in world agribusiness and energy markets, its trade policy, its key social programs, and the performance of Brazilian multinational corporations.

This volume, edited by Lael Brainard—who has been the director of the Global Economy and Development program—and Leonardo Martinez-Diaz, includes chapters by Ricardo Sennes and Thais Narciso of Prospectiva Consultoria, André Nassar of ICONE, Geraldo Barros of the University of São Paulo, Pedro da Motta Veiga of CINDES, Mauricio Mesquita Moreira of the Inter-American Development Bank, Ben Ross Schneider of Northwestern University, Edmund Amann of the University of Manchester, and Marcelo Neri of the Fundação Getulio Vargas.

Julia Guerreiro provided valuable research assistance and coordination for this project. Amy Wong, Ann DeFabio Doyle, Anne E. Smith, and Michael Barnard provided valuable fundraising, communications, and administrative assistance. The editors also wish to thank Alfred Imhoff for timely and high-quality editing and Janet Walker of the Brookings Institution Press for her help in bringing the manuscript to publication. The authors remain responsible for the content of their respective chapters, including any errors and omissions.

This publication was made possible by generous support from the Alcoa Foundation, Citi Brazil, and Vale, with additional support from Liberty Mutual Group and an anonymous individual donor.

STROBE TALBOTT
President
The Brookings Institution

February 2009
Washington, D.C.

BRAZIL
AS AN ECONOMIC SUPERPOWER?

CHAPTER ONE

Brazil
The "B" Belongs in the BRICs

LEONARDO MARTINEZ-DIAZ AND LAEL BRAINARD

Brazil's economy has yet again become an object of fascination and speculation for international investors, academics, pundits, and policymakers in the United States and Europe. As a country replete with natural resources, endowed with a large internal market, and home to dynamic and increasingly global corporations, Brazil has been famously anointed as a "BRIC"—thus identified along with Russia, India, and China as one of the four very large, rapidly emerging economies that are key growth engines of the global economy.[1] Yet, coming only months after the International Monetary Fund provided a large loan to stabilize Brazil's economy in 2003, Brazil's inclusion alongside China and India in the BRICs was initially greeted with skepticism. Five years later, in April 2008, as the scholars who produced this volume gathered to debate Brazil's prospects, the world's major credit-rating agencies promoted the country's sovereign debt to investment grade, an assessment that would be tested later that year by financial turmoil emanating from the United States and Europe. In Brazil itself, the confluence of strong global demand for the country's major products, global successes for its major corporations, and steady results from its economic policies have strengthened confidence and even revived dreams of *grandeza*—the greatness that has proven elusive in the past. These dreams have been dampened

---

1. Goldman Sachs (2003).

somewhat by the global economic crisis, but many experts believe that Brazil will be one of the engines that will help pull the global economy out of recession in the coming years.

Brazil's economic potential has been on display in the past. Between 1947 and 1962, the country grew at an average rate of 6 percent annually and was seen as one of the brightest stars in the world economy.[2] During the so-called Brazilian miracle period (1968–73), the country enjoyed economic growth of more than 10 percent a year—among the highest in the world. Its industrial sector grew at almost 10 percent a year, and its agricultural exports almost doubled between 1962 and 1971.[3] Yet the country's star faded with the debt crisis in 1982 and the "lost decade" of the 1980s. Years of macroeconomic instability and high inflation followed.

In comparison with the Brazilian miracle of the 1970s, the country's bright prospects appear to rest on a more solid foundation this time around. The country is now a stable, vibrant democracy—not a military dictatorship. It has enjoyed a sustained period of low inflation and conservative macroeconomic management, in contrast to the external-debt-fueled 1970s. The 2002 election and the subsequent leadership of President Luiz Inácio Lula da Silva have demonstrated that a left-wing candidate can win the presidency, navigate a sound macroeconomic course, and open the country's economy to global trade and investment. Today, Brazil is more deeply integrated with the global economy than at any time in the past forty years. As figure 1-1 shows, trade now accounts for 25 to 30 percent of Brazil's national income, up significantly from the 15 to 20 percent share of previous decades.

Brazil's status among the world's rising economic powers emanates from an auspicious conjuncture of external forces and internal strengths. The entry of hundreds of millions of people into the middle class in China and India has boosted demand for many of Brazil's key agricultural and commodity exports, and Brazil's resource wealth appears destined to grow with new oil finds. In parallel, a growing premium on reducing and sequestering carbon emissions to mitigate the adverse effects of climate change is increasingly favoring Brazil's biofuel and hydropower sectors and may ultimately generate major transfers to preserve its environmentally crucial rainforests.

However, Brazil is not only benefiting from historically high commodity prices, which have proven to be fleeting. It is also benefiting from

2. Baer (2001, 63).
3. World Bank (1973, 2).

F I G U R E   1 - 1 . Brazil's Trade in Goods and Services as a Percentage of Gross Domestic Product, 1970–2006

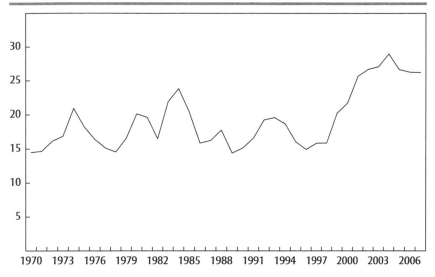

Source: Ipeadata (www.ipeadata.gov.br).

its sustained commitment to sound macroeconomic policies; from the strength of its corporations, which are achieving global success across a variety of sectors; and from the legacies of its policies on alternative energy and agricultural self-sufficiency, which were put in place in the 1960s and 1970s but are now delivering unanticipated benefits. For Brazil to capitalize on these advantages both during and beyond the current global financial crisis, it will need to address two main challenges. The first is to ensure that the benefits from its natural resource wealth translate into effective investments in education, infrastructure, and technology that will enable it to establish a foundation for sustained long-term growth. The second is that to achieve continued growth, it will need to steer a more consistent course on economic integration and on the governance of international markets. Brazil's ambivalence on these issues manifests itself in an inconsistent and uneven position, especially on trade policy, which limits its ability to influence global rules and institutions in its favor.

External Forces: Climate and Commodities

Brazil's growing economic heft in part reflects its ability to capitalize on two long-term global trends: strong commodity demand, driven by the swelling ranks of the global middle class; and the imperative of stabilizing the Earth's climate. In recent years, commodity prices have soared, reflecting a combination of increased demand for food and raw materials from China and other emerging economies, strong energy demand from the United States and other advanced economies, and medium-term supply constraints. Brazil has emerged as a major exporter of many of these commodities, including soy (where Brazil has a global market share of almost 40 percent), chicken (30 percent), coffee (30 percent), beef (20 percent), orange juice (80 percent), and tobacco (20 percent).[4] Brazil is also benefiting from the rising prices of iron ore and steel, because it is a leading producer of both, and it is poised to take advantage of rising energy prices.

Though commodity prices have softened in the current global financial turmoil, experts project strong demand over the horizon for the medium term. According to projections by the Brookings economist Homi Kharas, the ranks of the global middle class will swell by as many as 1.8 billion people over the next twelve years, so that by 2020 just over half the world's population will enjoy greater disposable income than the previous generation.[5] As more and more people adopt a middle-class lifestyle, sustained demand will be generated for those commodities and manufactures for which Brazil has a competitive edge, ranging from beef to regional aircraft.

In parallel, the imperative to stabilize the Earth's fragile climate means that the world will increasingly put a premium on carbon-efficient energy sources and carbon sequestration. Brazil is well positioned to capitalize on this trend, with the continued evolution of its biofuels industry, and its vast rainforests may become a magnet for significant international transfers when given their justly high value in a post–Kyoto Protocol climate framework.

Brazil is well positioned to benefit from these two medium-term trends, in part due to a favorable resource mix. The country contains the world's largest and most biodiverse rainforests and has one of the largest renewable reserves of freshwater. Its vast territory and varied climate allow for livestock farming and commercial agriculture on a large scale. Its mineral wealth is also considerable, particularly in iron ore. And if its recently discovered offshore oil and gas fields meet expectations, it will become one of the world's largest producers of hydrocarbon fuels.

4. These numbers are from the Economist Intelligence Unit (2008), and from chapter 3, by André Nassar, in the present volume.
5. Naím (2008).

Internal Choices: The Policy Legacy

Yet, sustained growth and ascension to the ranks of the global economic powers has eluded many resource-rich countries. Why might Brazil succeed where others have failed? One possible answer is that the country is reaping the benefits from its legacy of policies that were intended to advance its self-sufficiency and autonomy from international markets but are now paradoxically conferring important advantages for engaging with the world economy as its leadership seeks to seize opportunities in globalizing capital, product, and energy markets.

The state has historically loomed large in Brazil's economy. The country had one of the largest public sectors outside the former Communist bloc. In 1985, Brazil's public sector accounted for just under half of the net assets of its 8,000 largest firms, for about a quarter of their sales, and for a fifth of their total employment.[6] As late as 1990, before the administration of Fernando Henrique Cardoso began to privatize state-owned assets, 38 of Brazil's 100 largest firms were still government owned.[7]

Also prominent was the state's role as business manager and economic planner. As manager of state-owned businesses, the Brazilian state has a mostly typical record, but one punctuated by prominent successes, especially in aircraft manufacturing, biofuels, and petrochemicals. In sectors such as informatics, the state played the role of what Evans calls a "midwife," trying "to assist in the emergence of new entrepreneurial groups or to induce existing groups to venture into more challenging kinds of production."[8] This role was facilitated by a range of instruments, including protective tariffs, subsidies, targeted credit, and government help for local entrepreneurs negotiating with foreign investors.

For Brazil's leaders, starting with Getulio Vargas in the 1930s, the animating motivation for state-led development policies was the drive to make the country self-sufficient and independent. In the manufacturing sector, the drive for autonomy was motivated by the idea that any country destined for modernity had to develop an indigenous capacity in certain industries, particularly in the heavy manufacturing and chemical sectors. In agriculture and energy, the oil and food price shocks of the 1970s provided an urgent impetus to diminish reliance on foreign

6. Baer (2001, 281).
7. Baer (2001, 291).
8. Evans (1995, 13).

suppliers. During this time, Brazil's military government saw the drive toward self-sufficiency as a national security imperative, as a way of protecting the country in a world perceived as dangerous and uncertain.

The state-led development project came at considerable cost to the public purse and introduced ultimately debilitating economic distortions. The massive public financing of key sectors contributed to chronic inflation, which for decades would be the scourge of Brazil's poor and middle classes. The state's import-substitution industrialization strategy also involved extensive foreign borrowing, which created balance-of-payments pressures and often resulted in duplicative or excess investment. In the process of developing new products and technologies, the costs of failed experiments were often "socialized" and passed on to the public. The overall net cost of these policies, though difficult to quantify, was considerable.

Starting in the late 1980s, the Brazilian government began to dismantle many elements of the import-substitution industrialization policy framework.[9] Trade was liberalized in a series of rapid, unilateral tariff reductions in the period 1988–89, and the removal of nontariff barriers followed in 1991–93. Average nominal tariffs fell from 57 percent in 1987 to 32 percent in 1999.[10] At the same time, the Cardoso administration began a major privatization drive. Between 1991 and 2001, the government sold about $110 billion worth of assets, including the giant telecom Telebrás, and Brazil was dubbed "privatization's poster child."[11] Nonetheless, the state has retained an important foothold in the economy; 13 of the top 100 firms are still state owned, including the largest company, Petrobrás.[12]

Although Brazil's past state-led development policies to promote self-sufficiency were costly and counterproductive in many ways, the legacy of some of these policies is now paradoxically providing a strong foundation for the country's current generation of outward-looking political and business leaders as they pursue its global competitiveness. Policies put in place in the 1960s and 1970s helped to stimulate the agribusiness and biofuels sectors and to develop strengths in selected manufacturing areas. Through entrepreneurial vision, a number of Brazilian producers have been able to translate this policy legacy into competitive advantages in

9. On this policy shift, see Amann and Baer (2005).
10. See chapter 5, by Pedro da Motta Veiga, in this volume.
11. Smith (2001).
12. *Exame Melhores e Maiores,* July 2008.

global markets now that the country's policy orientation has turned outward and global demand has shifted favorably.

Technological Capacity

Several chapters in this volume highlight the notable involvement of the Brazilian state in technological development through investments in research centers and institutions. In chapter 4, for example, the University of São Paulo economist Geraldo Barros notes the importance of the Brazilian Agricultural Research Company (Embrapa), established in the 1970s, in contributing to develop the technologies that have helped Brazilian agribusiness double its total factor productivity since the 1975 and take advantage of new opportunities in global markets for agricultural products.[13] In chapter 7, Northwestern's Ben Ross Schneider credits two centers of engineering research and training (the Aeronautics Technology Center, or CTA, and the Aeronautics Technological Institute, or ITA) with setting the foundations for Embraer's commercial success in aircraft manufacturing. In chapter 8, Edmund Amann of the University of Manchester highlights the role of the Petrobrás in-house research center, CENPES, in helping the company develop the offshore oil exploration and production technologies that are likely to make Brazil a leading oil producer.[14] More broadly, these research centers are underpinned by a wider network of publicly funded state and federal universities and research institutes. However, it is difficult to know whether globally competitive producers would have emerged in these or other sectors that have proven less successful if the market had determined investment allocations.

From Self-Sufficiency to Export Strength in New Sectors

A second legacy came from the Brazilian government's deliberate attempts to push firms into sectors they might not otherwise have entered, perhaps most importantly the energy sector. In response to the oil price shocks of the 1970s, the Brazilian government put in place a series of policies to pursue higher levels of energy self-sufficiency. As Ricardo Sennes and Thais Narciso of Prospectiva Consultoria put it in chapter 2, "It was not merely the case of adjusting the national economy to the international price shock; it was also an effort to render the development and security strategy sustainable within an increasingly hostile international

13. See chapter 4, by Geraldo Barros, in the present volume.
14. See chapter 8, by Edmund Amann, in the present volume.

environment where energy was vital. So crucial was the country's strategy of development and industrialization to national security that it justified a thorough political, financial, institutional, and technological mobilization."[15]

As a result, the government invested heavily in hydroelectric power and undertook the Programa Nacional do Álcool (the Pro-Alcohol Program) to harness Brazil's plentiful sugarcane harvests to the production of an indigenous, renewable, and relatively inexpensive energy source. These initiatives succeeded in significantly reducing Brazil's reliance on oil imports and, over time, allowed the country to develop a qualitatively different energy matrix compared with those of countries belonging to the Organization for Economic Cooperation and Development (OECD) and other developing economies. Today, Brazil derives 46 percent of its energy from renewable sources, compared with a world average of 13 percent and an OECD average of just 6 percent.[16] It also has the world's largest infrastructure for the production and commercial distribution of ethanol. The unintended consequence of this policy originally designed to protect Brazil from oil-price shocks was to give the country a singularly strong comparative advantage in the production and export of sugarcane-based ethanol, a commodity now in high demand in a world of expensive oil and environmentally costly carbon emissions.

Triumphs and Limitations

A key question is what Brazil's firms and sectors are doing and will do with this policy legacy and these corporate strengths. Here, experts highlight both the triumphs and limitations of the country's key productive sectors. On the triumphalist side, Schneider applauds the former state-owned mining giant Vale for leveraging its legacy of scale and competent management to diversify geographically and along product lines after its privatization in 1997. Amann explains how Odebrecht, a construction services conglomerate, has used its innovative internal organization to mount a successful internationalization strategy. More broadly, in chapter 3 the Institute for International Trade Negotiations' director-general, André Nassar, illustrates how Brazilian agribusiness has leveraged its legacy of investments in productivity to penetrate world

---

15. See chapter 2, by Ricardo Sennes and Thais Narciso, in the present volume.
16. See chapter 2 in the present volume.

markets,[17] while Sennes and Narciso explain how Petrobrás has mobilized its legacy of deepwater exploration and production technology to mount a major international strategy with operations in twenty-six countries.

Yet important obstacles remain. In agriculture, Brazil faces challenges from poor transportation infrastructure, inadequate ethanol pipelines, and an uncertain legal framework governing genetically modified crops and land ownership. Amann worries about the country's ability to continue building on its technological legacy at a time when government spending on science and technology is at its lowest level in more than a decade and the private sector is not increasing its own spending to fill the gap. As a percentage of gross domestic product, Brazil's investments in science and technology now trail behind those of other emerging economies, including China, Russia, and South Korea.

Challenges of Deeper Integration

Brazil's future role in the global economy will in large measure depend on whether and how it chooses to integrate further into world markets. This choice, in turn, depends centrally on the country's domestic politics, which reflect its enormous ambivalence on the question of openness and contribute to a posture on trade that many agree is shortchanging its economic potential.

In chapter 6, Mauricio Mesquita Moreira of the Inter-American Development Bank highlights three dimensions of Brazil's trade policy that are inconsistent with the country's economic self-interest.[18] First, Brazil's emphasis on South-South trade agreements with countries like India and South Africa rather than on trade deals with major developed economies makes little sense from an economic standpoint. These South-South deals are of little economic consequence, whereas trade agreements with major developed economies would deliver far greater economic benefits to Brazil. Second, Brazil's leaders have tended to oversell the benefits of Mercosur while showing reluctance to address its major flaws, which are undermining its political support. Third, Brazil's high transportation and regulatory costs, along with its high tariff barriers, especially on capital goods—on average triple the level in rival emerging markets—harm the country's competitiveness.

17. See chapter 3, by André Nassar, in the present volume.
18. See chapter 6, by Mauricio Mesquita Moreira, in the present volume.

How can one make sense of these incoherent trade policies? Moreira points to the resilience of entrenched groups in key sectors that were protected during the period of import-substitution industrialization. Successful lobbying by these groups may explain why islands of hardened protectionism remain in Brazilian trade policy, even while the country overall has moved toward greater openness. The momentum of liberalization will be maintained only if powerful export interests emerge and mobilize in favor of greater openness. These "liberalizers" are most likely to appear in the dynamic agribusiness sector.

There is also another, more ideological, reason for the resilience of trade protectionism in Brazil. As Pedro da Motta Veiga, the director of the Centro de Estudos de Integração e Desenvolvimento, argues in chapter 5, the "national-developmentalist" paradigm of the 1960s still has a powerful hold on how Brazilian policymakers think about deepening integration. Its central tenets are that (1) trade policy should be subordinate to the political objectives of foreign policy, (2) international economic policy should be conducted in a way that maximizes the degree of autonomy and "policy space" available for industrial and other national development policies, and (3) international economic policy should be conducted so as to "neutralize" external factors that might jeopardize national economic development and the consolidation of domestic industrial capacity. The prominence of this paradigm receded during the Cardoso administration but has returned with the Lula administration.[19]

In practical terms, the continued influence of these principles can be seen in at least two important tenets of Brazil's trade policy. First, the country retains a "zero tolerance" position on linking trade with labor and environmental issues in trade negotiations, and it has adopted a minimalist approach to international disciplines in services, investment, and procurement. Second, it has downgraded trade negotiations with the European Union and the United States—including negotiation of a Free Trade Area of the Americas—while vigorously pursuing a South-South trade agenda. Bilateral negotiations with the major Northern economies are shunned as a potential source of vulnerability, in favor of a focus on multilateral negotiations through the World Trade Organization and regional and bilateral negotiations with other developing economies. However, Brazil's current trade policy strategy is not simply a return to the consensus of the 1960s. Veiga points out that, for the first time, the

19. See chapter 5, by Pedro da Motta Veiga, in the present volume.

strategy includes a significant "offensive" component: the quest to open some of the world's largest agricultural markets to Brazilian agribusiness. As it enjoys growing competitiveness in global markets, Brazilian agriculture is challenging the confines of the country's traditional policy framework and political economy.

Ensuring Broadly Shared Prosperity and Opportunity

Brazil's deeper integration into the global economy is creating social dislocation and tension, which are likely to escalate as global economic conditions deteriorate. Less competitive industries and firms are shrinking, workers are being laid off and require retraining, and income has often grown more unequal. Social investment and the creation of robust social safety nets are therefore critical ingredients for ensuring that the country's economic opening delivers benefits broadly, particularly given its highly unequal social structures.

In assessing Brazil's recent record in chapter 9 of this volume, the Fundação Getulio Vargas economist Marcelo Neri concludes that the country's income policies have had a beneficial effect on income distribution. Targeted income policies have resulted in significant and sustained reductions in poverty and inequality, particularly between 2001 and 2004. This is especially notable because inequality had remained extremely high and stubbornly persistent in previous decades, even during periods of positive economic growth.[20]

However, Neri argues that there is still room for strengthening income policies. The new generation of well-targeted conditional cash transfer programs—including the well-known Bolsa Família—exists side by side with a relatively ineffective set of income policies inherited from the past, which should be phased out. In addition, Neri recommends rethinking Bolsa Família's redundant conditionalities, whereby the government is paying recipients to do what they were doing without cash transfers.

Brazil as an Economic Superpower?

What can we conclude about Brazil's role in the global economy? Is it already an economic superpower? Will it become one? Naturally, this depends on what we mean by "economic superpower." In sheer size

20. See chapter 9, by Marcelo Neri, in the present volume.

and growth, Brazil today ranks among the world's ten largest economies in nominal gross domestic product, narrowly beating Russia for ninth place.[21] According to projections by Goldman Sachs, Brazil would have to grow by about 4 percent a year from 2005 through the middle of the century to become the world's fourth-largest economy. Whether these growth rates will come to pass will depend, among other things, on whether Brazilian firms are able to capitalize on new opportunities in the global economy and Brazilian policymakers pursue deeper global economic integration. The hill will become steeper for Brazil with commodity prices stabilizing and, in some cases, declining.

If by "economic superpower" we mean a country that can exert significant influence in the global economy—one that is a significant force as a rule maker, not just a rule taker—then Brazil is already well on its way. It already has the necessary material conditions to have economic influence globally, and it is a dominant player in many commodity markets and can exercise market power in some of them. Its role in energy markets—as a producer of ethanol and, eventually, oil and gas—is large and growing. Its vast rainforests and high utilization of renewables, such as sugarcane-based ethanol and hydropower, put it in a strong position to be a major player on climate change.[22] And its leading companies are aggressively investing abroad, tapping new markets and acquiring assets and technologies. This phenomenon may accelerate as Brazilian companies venture abroad and acquire cheap, crisis-affected foreign assets and companies.

Finally, Brazil has influential roles in some of the world's most important established and emerging bodies for economic decisionmaking. It was the designated leader for the finance Group of Twenty when that body convened at the leaders' level for the first time in October 2008. It plays a leadership role in the Group of Twenty caucus of developing economies in the World Trade Organization, and it enjoys growing voting weight on the International Monetary Fund's executive board. Brasília is also pursuing seats in other influential global forums, including the OECD and the Organization of the Petroleum Exporting Countries, and it has been joining new forums, such as the India–Brazil–South Africa initiative.

Whether Brazil is able to exercise more influence in global economic governance will depend on whether it can leverage its growing economic

---

21. Goldman Sachs (2008).
22. Sotero and Armijo (2007).

weight to set agendas and shape the debate in key international forums in collaboration with other emerging economies. But in areas ranging from climate change to trade, Brazil's ability to exercise leadership internationally will also depend centrally on whether its political leaders are able to build domestic support for outwardly oriented strategic policies.

References

Amann, Edmund, and Werner Baer. 2005. "From the Developmental to the Regulatory State: The Transformation of the Government's Impact on the Brazilian Economy." *Quarterly Review of Economics and Finance* 45: 421–31.

Baer, Werner. 2001. *The Brazilian Economy: Growth and Development.* London: Praeger.

Economist Intelligence Unit. 2008. *Country Profile 2008, Brazil.* London: Economist.

Evans, Peter. 1995. *Embedded Autonomy: States and Industrial Transformation.* Princeton University Press.

Goldman Sachs. 2003. *Dreaming with BRICs: The Path to 2050.* New York: Goldman Sachs.

———. 2008. *Ten Things for India to Achieve Its 2050 Potential.* Global Economics Paper 169. New York: Goldman Sachs.

Naím, Moisés. 2008. "Can the World Afford A Middle Class?" *Foreign Policy,* March/April.

Smith, Tony. 2001. "Flush from Sell-Offs, Brazil Is Privatization's Poster Child." BC Cycle, Associated Press, January 16.

Sotero, Paulo, and Leslie Elliott Armijo. 2007. "Brazil: To Be or Not to Be a BRIC?" *Asian Perspective* 31, no. 4: 43–70.

World Bank. 1973. "Appraisal of an Agro-Industries Credit Project—Brazil." June 1, Washington.

PART I

Brazil as an Agricultural and Energy Superpower

CHAPTER TWO

Brazil as an International Energy Player

RICARDO UBIRACI SENNES AND THAIS NARCISO

Brazil has been rapidly modifying its international strategy and insertion into world energy markets during the course of the last two decades. This outcome has been partly planned and state oriented and partly the result of pressures exerted by market forces and civil society at large. And it has also been a response to a multidimensional scenario that is imposing qualitative changes on the country's foreign policy and international outlook.

Several features have shaped these developments. In the first place, Brazil presently relies upon a relatively solid and stable macroeconomic context. In this manner, it enjoys a favorable balance of payments and, for the first time, its foreign reserves are larger than its foreign debt. In addition, from 2006 onward, Brazil became a liquid capital exporter. Following the global commodity boom, the country's agribusiness sector grew at extraordinary rates, while the internationalization process of a series of large and successful national firms contributed to creating the new "trans-Latins" category. Firms such as Gerdau, Vale, Petrobrás, Totvs, and Odebrecht gave the country unprecedented regional and international leverage. Contributing to this favorable picture, arguably, has been a degree of political consolidation of domestic institutions, whereas in the regional sphere, Brazil's presence has grown considerably. In this context, the country's relative prominence in the energy sector constitutes an additional positive factor among many others.

Yet this context only partially accounts for what Brazil is currently experiencing, because part of this phenomenon is rooted in policies adopted during the 1970s and 1980s. Energy is part of a favorable set of multi-dimensional features, as opposed to being an isolated phenomenon. Consequently, the Brazilian experience is markedly distinct from that of only-oil-exporting countries.

This chapter's central hypothesis is that, since the 1990s, Brazil has been moving toward substituting an energy strategy based on the pursuit of self-sufficiency (basically through the maximization of state control) for one of greater energy security and efficiency founded on domestic, regional, and international factors. Though state control is still important, it is no longer the determining factor. Still, the presence of the Brazilian state in this domain is fundamental for both oil and gas strategies.

Thus, this analysis argues that the country's new energy cycle is associated with a new foreign policy for energy. This policy is by no means unique; it has considerable differences related to the geographical scope, priorities, tactics, and alliances adopted in each of the different energy segments. It follows that not only do the oil, natural gas, biofuels, and hydropower domains have different market and political dynamics, but also that Brazil's strategies in these subsectors are partially constrained by such dynamics.

Following this introduction, the chapter is structured in six sections. The first one briefly outlines some structural characteristics of the international political economy of energy while positioning the Brazilian experience in this setting. In the second section, the recent evolution of the Brazilian energy matrix is qualified in absolute and relative terms. The third section assesses Brazil's energy matrix vis-à-vis developments since the 1970s oil shocks. The fourth section puts in perspective claims that Brazil is now an international energy player. In the fifth section, some tentative conclusions regarding the new oil and gas discoveries are drawn. The final section presents concluding remarks.

The International Political Economy of Energy

Energy is one of the most politicized sectors of Brazil's economy. The sector's strategic importance for the country's economic development and national security, the highly oligopolistic nature of the market, the sector's tendency to form natural monopolies, and the historically strong presence of states in both domestic and international markets are some of the contributing factors. At the same time, the energy market is strongly conditioned by economic and technical restrictions as well as by the obvious constraints of resource availability. These restrictions limit, to a great extent, political options and available country strategies concerning this theme, both domestically and internationally.

At least five key factors inform the definition of an efficient and secure energy strategy: (1) the quantity and quality of reserves or natural energy resources; (2) technological capacity, which corresponds to the entire energy chain, encompassing extraction, refining, hydroelectric power stations, transportation, and the like;[1] (3) capital availability, because it is a capital-intensive sector and scale capacity is fundamental in this market; (4) the energy transportation infrastructure (mainly ducts and cables); and (5) access to consumer markets.

Countries with all five of these factors simultaneously available are rare; these include the so-called major energy powers and the big oil- and gas-exporting countries. Most other countries are forced to seek part or all of these resources in the international market. Though self-sufficiency strategies are feasible, most of the time they imply extremely high economic costs. Therefore, factors are highly influential in a country's international strategy. The relative standing of a country vis-à-vis each of these five factors is the basic variable for understanding and evaluating its options and strategies.

Table 2-1 synthesizes some of the conditions and restrictions imposed by these five factors. As seen in the table, the key energy-related factors also shape the international dynamics of markets. Technical and economic restrictions in the electricity and gas sectors have rendered those international markets primarily regional, while those for biofuels and oil are global markets. Brazil's international strategy has been shaped by some of these factors, including technological and economic conditions, combined with political and geopolitical variables related to the country's relations with African, Middle Eastern, and South American countries. In addition, these conditions play a role in Brazil's performance in the multilateral sphere, whether at the World Trade Organization, at the United Nations, or in environmental forums.

---

1. Technology may render the exploration of a river's hydraulic potential economically viable, or the exploration of oil in deep waters, or even the exploration of natural oils to be used as fuel.

TABLE 2-1. The Energy Market from the Political and Economic Points of View

Energy source	Production	Transportation	Storage	Market
Oil	Resource availability	Easy (oil pipelines, land and naval)	Viable	Global
Gas	Resource and technology availability	Difficult and of regional reach (basically gas pipelines)	Viable, but expensive	Basically regional
Electricity	Vast array of sources (gas, oil, hydropower, nuclear, etc.)	Difficult and of regional reach	Impossible	Essentially regional
Bioenergy	Agribusiness economic viability (natural resources and technology)	Easy (oil pipelines, land and naval)	Viable	Global

Source: Designed by the authors.

The Recent Evolution of the Brazilian Energy Matrix

The Brazilian energy matrix is the result of strategies pursued during the military period (1964–84) and of regulatory reforms and privatizations in the 1990s. The changes during the 1990s did not redirect established tendencies in the country's energy policy, though there were some exceptions, most notably the introduction of the use of gas. By and large, previous policies were further developed, taking advantage of the maturation of earlier investments, as was the case for ethanol and oil. The reforms of the 1990s seem to be much more market oriented and economically efficient than previous options. Nevertheless, it is very likely that such developments would not have been made possible without earlier investments and policy options.

Even though these strategies were not significantly altered, important changes occurred in their international dimensions. For example, the strategies' content was altered both in the multilateral spheres—the UN, the International Atomic Energy Agency, and the like—and in terms of the country's international role, as it went from being an oil importer to being an oil, capital, technology, and ethanol exporter.

As was the case in the previous phase, the external dimension of the new energy cycle maintained strong state participation in the oil, gas, and electricity sector. With biofuels, conversely, there emerges an unusual participation of the private sector parallel to that of the state. A further

F I G U R E 2 - 1 . Domestic Energy Supply

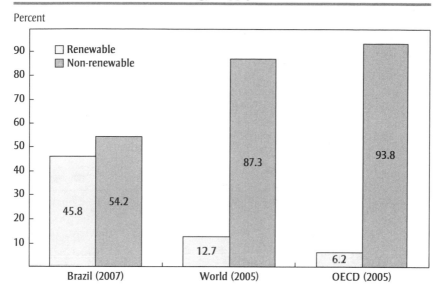

Percent

Source: Ministry of Energy and Mining, *Brazilian Energy Matrix Report 2007.*

important contrast to the previous period is that current strategies are greatly in tune with international tendencies to be more market and environmentally friendly.

In terms of the structure of energy supplies, the Brazilian energy matrix is different from that of most developed and developing countries' matrices in several respects. As shown in figure 2-1, Brazil is positioned considerably above the world average in terms of the use of renewable energy resources, especially when compared with the countries belonging to the Organization for Economic Cooperation and Development (OECD). Brazil's relatively high use of renewable resources is primarily due to its intense use of biomass and hydroelectricity, which, combined, accounted for 45.8 percent of its energy matrix in 2007. Conversely, as can be seen from table 2-2, the Brazilian matrix uses natural gas, coal, and uranium at significantly lower rates than the world average, although the use of natural gas has increased substantially in recent years (ranging from 0.4 to 9.3 percent participation in the matrix) and will increase further, given new discoveries off the Brazilian coast.

Over the course of the past thirty years, Brazil has followed a different path than most countries. It has invested heavily in hydroelectricity; while

TABLE 2-2. Internal Energy Supply
Percent and units of thermoelectric power

Specification	Brazil		OECD		World	
	1973	2007	1973	2005	1973	2005
Oil and derivatives	45.6	37.4	53	40.6	46.2	35.0
Natural gas	0.4	9.3	18.8	21.8	16.0	20.7
Coal	3.1	6.0	22.4	20.4	24.4	25.3
Uranium	0.0	1.4	1.3	11.0	0.9	6.3
Hydraulic and electricity	6.1	14.9	2.1	2.0	1.8	2.2
Biomass	44.8	30.9	2.4	4.2	10.7	10.5
Total (percent)	100.0	100.0	100.0	100.0	100.0	100.0
Total, millions of tep	82	238	3.762	5.548	6.128	11.434

Source: Ministry of Energy and Mining, *Brazilian Energy Matrix Report 2007*.

the world has maintained this energy source at around 2 percent of its matrix, Brazil went from a level of 6 percent in 1973 to around 15 percent in 2007. In addition, Brazil's use of biomass is also comparatively high. Although its use has decreased in relative terms, from 45 to 31 percent, it has maintained itself at drastically superior levels compared with the world average. Moreover, in spite of the maintenance of firewood and coal participation at surprisingly high levels of around 15 percent, the participation of biofuels is noticeable at an equal 15 percent rate. This last development can be seen as the direct result of a governmental program launched in the 1970s named Pro-Alcohol—a program that promoted sugarcane-based ethanol with the purpose of substituting large-scale oil derivatives consumption, and that was originally developed to restrict dependence on foreign currencies and pursue energy self-sufficiency in the event of oil shocks.

In this context, it is worthwhile noting that 64 percent of energy consumption in Brazil is derived from the industrial and transportation sectors; in OECD countries, these two sectors correspond to 52 percent of energy use, and in the rest of the world to 47 percent, as shown in table 2-3. These two energy-intensive sectors are also the main consumers of biomass energy sources, as will be further discussed below.

Furthermore, heavy industry is the main energy-consuming sector in Brazil; its participation in the matrix's final consumption went from around 30 percent in 1973 to 38 percent in 2007. Thus, on top of a participation

TABLE 2-3. Energy Matrix: Consumption
Percent and units of thermoelectric power

Specification	Brazil		OECD		World	
	1973	*2007*	*1973*	*2005*	*1973*	*2005*
Industry	29.8	37.8	30.8	20.8	35.8	27.5
Transport	25	26.7	23.3	31.3	23.4	19.7
Energy sector	3.3	9.7	8.3	7	6.9	7.9
Other sectors	38.7	19	30.4	31.5	29.7	37.6
Non-energy use	3.1	6.8	7.1	9.3	4.2	7.2
Total (percent)	100.0	100.0	100.0	100.0	100.0	100.0
Total, millions of tep	76.3	215.1	3,097.40	4,144.20	1,478.30	4,215.50

Source: Ministry of Energy and Mining, *Brazilian Energy Matrix Report 2007*.

rate well above the average for both OECD countries and the rest of the world, over the past thirty years this sector has increased its participation in Brazil's energy consumption, while its relative consumption has been drastically reduced in the rest of the world.

In terms of the relative use of energy for transportation, figures have increased substantially in OECD countries, have fallen in the rest of the world, and have remained constant in Brazil. Assuming some energy efficiency gains in transportation equipment, the data indicate the importance mobility acquires as countries develop. In Brazil, transportation has grown in proportion to the rise in transportation-energy efficiency; this development has been accompanied by a marked reduction in the share of other sectors (which includes home consumption) in the energy matrix. In other countries, efficiency gains seem to have been larger than the increase in overall energy use.

As shown in table 2-4, Brazil presents a relatively low pattern of oil and gas consumption for transportation. This is the result of the fact that energy originating from biomass is destined to substitute oil derivatives in the transportation sector, amounting to around 15 percent of total demand. Only recently has biomass begun to be used for energy generation. However, one should note the extremely low use of electricity for transportation, which is well below the world average and contrasts with the weight of hydroelectricity in the country's general energy matrix.

The program for ethanol use as fuel has regained greater force in recent years. At least three factors have contributed to this: the vertiginous

TABLE 2-4. Energy Matrix for Transportation: Total
Percent and units of thermoelectric power

	Brazil		OECD		World	
Specification	1973	2007	1973	2005	1973	2005
Oil derivatives	98.9	80.9	95.9	96.7	90.9	92.1
Natural gas	0.0	3.9	2.4	1.7	0.2	5.7
Coal	0.0	0.0	1.0	0.0	7.5	0.5
Electricity	0.3	0.2	0.7	0.8	1.5	1.5
Biomass	0.9	15	0.0	0.9	0.0	0.2
Total (percent)	100.0	100.0	100.0	100.0	100.0	100.0
Total, millions of tep	19.1	57.4	720.6	1,298.80	346	833.2

Source: Ministry of Energy and Mining, Brazilian Energy Matrix Report 2007.

increase in the international price of oil; the development of biofuel motors (and later on, flexfuel, which allows users to adjust the proportion of gasoline and ethanol every time they fill up their tanks); and finally, the development of technology that allows sugar-based alcohol factories to become more productive by using waste originated from their production to generate thermoelectric energy. This waste is then used at smaller factories connected to the traditional ones. Additionally, it can be sold on the wholesale market. In more recent projects of ethanol plants, the sale of electricity tends to correspond to around 35 percent of the projected profit.

The intense substitution of oil derivatives for industrial use experienced in Brazil, which brought figures down to 15 percent (more in accordance with international averages), is primarily explained by the fourfold increase in the use of energy deriving from biomass, which presently sits at 40 percent, compared with a 7.4 percent world average (see table 2-5). By contrast, the increase in the industrial use of electricity is very small. Though OECD countries started from the international pattern of around 18 percent of industrial electricity usage in the 1970s, doubling the relative use of electricity in its industry by 2005, the rest of the world experienced a 50 percent increase, while Brazil saw a relative rise of around 15 percent. The industrial use of gas energy sources was significant in Brazil, particularly during the 1990s, and was accompanied by a relative increase in the use of coal.

As table 2-6 indicates, Brazil's energy matrix does not depend much on international resources, with the exception of coal, which is almost

T A B L E 2 - 5 . Energy Matrix for Industry
Percent and units of thermoelectric power

Specification	Brazil		OECD		Others	
	1973	*2007*	*1973*	*2005*	*1973*	*2005*
Oil derivatives	61.2	15.7	32.6	16.7	23.9	14.7
Natural gas	0.1	9.5	26.6	29.6	20.1	14.7
Coal	10.9	14.3	18.8	12.4	32.6	34.2
Electricity	17.4	20.4	17.7	33.7	19.7	29.1
Biomass	10.3	40.1	4.4	7.6	3.7	7.4
Total (percent)	100.0	100.0	100.0	100.0	100.0	100.0
Total, millions of tep	14.6	81.3	954.6	860.5	538.1	1,158.8

Source: Ministry of Energy and Mining, *Brazilian Energy Matrix Report 2007.*

completely imported, and natural gas, of which one-third of the supply is imported. In the case of oil, the greatest part of the country's internal supply comes from local production, with its import volume (light oil) similar to its export volume (heavy oil). The fundamental difference between heavy and light oils lies in their quality. In recent years, there have been some changes in this picture, particularly concerning growth projections for gas, oil, ethanol, and biofuel production. In all these four cases, there are projects with international effects. In the case of gas, changes are related to reducing dependence on Bolivian gas, and in the remaining cases, the projection is of an increase in exports.

In sum, Brazil has a rather atypical energy matrix in comparison with both OECD countries and the world average. Key features of this matrix are not only the intensive use of biomass for transportation and industry but also the robust utilization of hydroelectricity for domestic consumption. Over the past thirty years, some significant changes in the matrix can be observed in terms of both energy-producing sources and their final use. At the same time, the country's dependence on imported inputs has fallen drastically, and in recent years it has increasingly become a net energy exporter.

This process has not only distanced Brazil from the average profile of OECD countries and from the energy matrices of other countries; it has also distinguished Brazil's matrix significantly from that of other South American countries, as will be detailed below. This reality reflects the legacy of policies that sought self-sufficiency and a reduction of foreign dependence.

TABLE 2-6. Consolidated Energy Balance, 2007

Thousand units of thermoelectric power

	Oil	Natural gas	Coal	Coal metal	Uranium	Hydropower	Wood	Sugarcane	Others	TOTAL
Production	90,670	18,025	2,268	119	0	32,197	28,635	40,051	7,626	219,589
Imports	20,971	9,093	0	10,821	0	0	0	0	0	40,885
Stock variation	−270	0	20	11	3,263	0	0	0	−20	3,003
Total offer	111,371	27,118	2,288	10,951	3,263	32,197	28,635	40,051	7,626	263,478
Exports	−21,813	0	0	0	0	0	0	0	0	−21,813
Rejected	0	−1,783	0	0	0	0	0	0	0	−1,783
Reinjection	0	−3,096	0	0	0	0	0	0	0	−3,096
Gross domestic offer	89,558	22,239	2,288	10,951	3,263	32d,197	28,635	40,051	7,626	236,786

Source: Ministry of Energy and Mining, *Brazilian Energy Matrix Report 2007*.

The Present Energy Matrix's Profile and the 1970s Oil Shocks

In light of the 1970s energy crisis, Brazil sought to pursue an autonomous strategy to secure its economic growth, which relied upon very distinct characteristics in relation to the global average. The country made heavy use of biomass for transportation and industry, and it counted on hydro-electricity for domestic and economic use (which excludes transportation and industry).

Two national objectives were behind both aspects of this strategy: sustaining economic growth based on strong industrialization and reducing dependence on imported sources of energy. These efforts were carried out through state policies, not only in the hydroelectric realm but also in that of oil and biomass, with the latter particularly concerned with the use of ethanol fuel.

This concerted effort had a strategic character that surpassed economic and financial motivations. The initiative was a nonliberal adjustment to the shock produced by the international energy market. It was not merely the case of adjusting the national economy to the international price shock; it was also an effort to render the development and security strategy sustainable in an increasingly hostile international environment where energy was vital. So crucial was the country's strategy of development and industrialization to national security that it justified a thorough political, financial, institutional, and technological mobilization.

These lines of action had a strong international component, mobilizing diplomatic efforts, state-owned companies (Petrobrás, Eletrobrás, and Nuclebrás[2]), and the Brazilian private sector. The financial effort needed for such initiatives was, for the most part, made by the state, which deepened its pattern of foreign fund-raising to make its audacious projects viable.[3] These international strategies had a strong regional dimension (particularly in the Río de la Plata region), Atlantic and Middle Eastern dimensions (especially on the Western and Northern African coasts), and a multilateral dimension (principally in the UN and the Non-Aligned Movement).

Although these strategies had both internal and external limitations, they did not end up rendering unviable the implementation of the original

2. However, in the case of the decision to build the nuclear plants of Angra I and II, it is very unlikely that it had actual energy-related objectives or that the objective was to simply master the nuclear technological cycle and enable the country to operate with atomic energy.

3. Curiously enough, the country's greatest external vulnerability ended up occurring in the financial domain, as it came to be known as the external debt crisis of the 1980s.

programs—such as Pro-Alcohol, the construction of the Itaipu hydro-electric power station, and other extensive hydroelectric power stations. Nevertheless, as a consequence of these limitations, the programs experienced constant setbacks, reformulations, and adjustments. In addition, there was collateral damage in (among others) the financial cost involved; the delay in the maturation of returns; and the political, social, and environmental costs of implementation.

The Regional Question

Among the various themes that are part of South America's regional integration agenda, few demonstrate so much potential for economic gains and economic rationality as energy. The great availability and variety of energy resources, the relative proximity between producer sources and consumer markets, complementary seasons, and the existence of state-owned and private companies with business and technological capacity in this domain—all these make energy integration a rather attractive alternative for countries in the region. It is estimated that with energy integration, the region would save from $4 billion to $5 billion per year,[4] on top of expressive gains in energy security.

In the South American region,[5] there are both energy-exporting and energy-importing countries. Venezuela possesses the largest oil and gas reserves in the region, occupying the tenth position in the world scale of production of these hydrocarbons. Bolivia has the region's second-largest natural gas reserves and exports mainly to Brazil through the Gasbol pipeline, which is the region's main private investment in energy infrastructure. Argentina has the region's third-largest natural gas reserves and fourth-largest oil reserves. Brazil holds the region's third-largest oil reserves. Brazil imports electricity from Venezuela to cover its consumption in the extreme North, and it jointly owns two electric power conversion stations with Argentina and Uruguay. Chile is highly dependent on the import of energy inputs. Colombia is self-sufficient in oil and exports the remainder of its production. Peru has initiated the exploration of the Camisea complex, which will provide natural gas for internal consumption as well as for partial use by its neighbors. Ecuador is an

---

4. Linkohr (2006).
5. Regional data from the U.S. Energy Information Administration; official data from the U.S. government, including several *Country Analysis Briefs* from 2003 to 2006, available at www.eia.doe.gov.

important oil exporter, and Uruguay does not have oil or gas reserves, importing such inputs for internal consumption. Paraguay holds neither oil nor gas reserves, but it exports hydroelectric energy to Brazil and Argentina. Finally, it is important to note that no oil pipelines connect any countries in the region; neither Brazil nor any other South American country possesses the means for transporting oil to any other regional partner.

In light of this scenario, the relatively low degree of energy integration between countries in the region is surprising. In spite of the potential for economic gains from regional energy integration, there has been only a limited adoption of integration initiatives. Existing policies are basically focused on single connections between some countries, as opposed to structured long-term programs concerned with the formation of a regional market and the optimization of available energy inputs.

Brazil, as the key country in South America for making regional energy integration a reality, contributes considerably to the present state of affairs. But although the autonomy-seeking attitude of the country's energy strategy persists, prointegration impulses and interests have been advancing. The 1990s regulatory reforms, which occurred both in Brazil and in the region at large, contributed to improving the environment for market solutions with a regional scope. Yet these developments have not been enough to produce a significant shift toward regionalism. Moreover, economic and political crises, especially in Argentina and Bolivia in the early 2000s, have led to setbacks.

Until the early 1990s, the energy interchanges among South American countries occurred with strong participation by state-owned firms. The region's states took up the roles of entrepreneur, operator, and regulator for these projects; at times, the private sector would play a secondary role. But these projects were not the result of a joint-optimization strategy of the region's available resources. At most, they were the result of bilateral actions. It is worthwhile noting that these initiatives refer essentially to regional electricity and natural gas markets, which demand the construction of a physical infrastructure between countries in order for energy to be transported.

The consequences of this extremely low level of regional integration are reflected in the enormous asymmetry among the energy matrices of countries in the region. Given that energy markets do not communicate with one another, price formation and options available to consumers and firms are strictly conditioned to national supplies and conditions. The latter are,

TABLE 2-7. The Latin American Energy Matrix

Percent

Years	Country	Natural gas	Oil	Hydropower	Nuclear	Coal	Others biomass
2003	Argentina	46.0	34.0	13.0	3.0	1.0	1.0
2003	Bolivia	33.0	53.0	13.0			1.0
2006[a]	Brazil	9.6	37.9	14.8	1.6	6.0	30.1[b]
2003	Chile	23.0	42.0	22.0		10.0	1.0
2002	Colombia	17.0	44.0	29.0		10.0	
2003	Ecuador		81.0	19.0			
2004	Mexico	29.0	58.0	4.0	1.0		2.0
2002	Peru	2.5	60.0	31.7		5.5	0.3
2003	Paraguay		12.0	88.0			
2002	Uruguay	1.0	47.0	52.0			
2004	Venezuela	40.0	39.0	22.0			

Sources: U.S. Energy Information Administration; official data from the U.S. government; several *Country Analysis Briefs* from 2003 to 2006, available at www.eia.doe.gov.

a. Source for Brazil: Ministry of Energy and Mining, 2007.

b. Sugarcane products, 14.6 percent; wood, 12.4 percent; others, 3 percent.

in general, strongly conditioned to the state-owned firms operating in the sector.

Table 2-7 synthesizes the energy matrices of selected Latin American countries. In spite of the fact that they are all heavily dependent on oil, which oscillates from 34 to 60 percent of most their matrices (with the exception of Paraguay, with only 12 percent), the case of Ecuador is distinctive, for oil consumption corresponds to 81 percent of its energy matrix. If one turns to natural gas, Argentina, Bolivia, and Venezuela find themselves in the range of 30 to 46 percent, and Chile along with Colombia have a range of 15 to 25 percent. The remaining countries, including Brazil, have 0 to 10 percent natural gas participation in their energy matrices. All the other energy sources are secondary, including coal, nuclear energy, and renewable sources. As has been noted above, the Brazilian case is unique, for its matrix depends considerably on renewable sources; in this sense, the use of alcohol fuel originating from sugarcane is highlighted.[6] The region presents a picture of reasonable energy interconnections; however, this does not mean integration between markets. In other words, exchanges of energy

6. Although there is not yet any integration program based on renewable sources, manifestations in this direction have been growing. President Luiz Inácio Lula da Silva's special adviser on international affairs is one of the public defenders of this idea.

inputs between countries are predominantly bilateral, without involving any convergence between their markets.

Concerning electricity, electric integration initiatives in South America have amounted to an attempt at creating a common electricity market in the Andean Community, as well as the creation of four power stations and some electric interconnections in the Southern Cone. Thus, in comparison with the oil and gas sectors, the electricity sector is possibly the most advanced in terms of interconnectivity throughout South America. Additionally, this sector claims a reasonably installed infrastructure. Infrastructure bottlenecks do exist, yet they are of lesser prominence than in other segments of the energy market.

Before the 1990s, there was only one international gas pipeline in South America. It connected Bolivia to Argentina and began operating in 1988. The construction of gas pipelines is a direct reflection of the economic reforms implemented in the region's countries during the late 1990s. Since then, this domain has come to be characterized by the participation of private firms as they have constructed and operationalized gas pipelines. At present, there are gas pipelines connecting the following countries: Argentina and Chile (since 1995), Argentina and Uruguay (since 1998), Bolivia and Argentina (since 1996), and Brazil and Bolivia (since 1999).

In addition, there are projects in the works that plan to connect different countries in the region. Some of these follow the bilateral pattern, such as the Bolivia-Chile, Bolivia-Paraguay, Peru-Bolivia, and Peru-Brazil gas pipelines. Other projects still being studied plan to connect more than two countries; namely, the Mercosur Gas Pipeline, the Austral Gas Pipeline, the Mercosur Energy Ring, and the polemic Great Gas Pipeline of the South connecting Venezuela, Brazil, and Argentina.[7]

Nevertheless, in spite of the thickening in South American gas infrastructure, the nationalism of domestic regulatory marks still predominates, with a few exceptions, such as Chile. In effect, energy nationalism is intrinsically associated with strong state-owned energy companies, whose weight is considerable in both the political and economic spheres. These firms have not always focused on building efficient matrices but have often pursued other goals. At times, these firms have been primarily sources of revenue for their countries; at others, they have focused on helping to

---

7. According to the previous minister of energy, Silas Rondeau, this project is in its research phase. See the interview in *Abinee Magazine,* December 2006 (www.abinee.org.br/informac/revista/39c.pdf [August 2007]).

manage the balance of payments. State-owned firms are also used to finance special political programs in the form of domestic policies or as foreign policy instruments.

Brazil's Energy Strategy and South America

Recent conditions in the international energy market, as well as domestic factors in Brazil, have been rapidly altering the country's international competitiveness in the energy sector. The growth of Petrobrás' technological and managerial capacity, the continuous rise in oil and gas production and refining, and the leap forward taken by the national biofuel industry—all constitute the base for this potentially new pattern in Brazil's international insertion.

Brazil is still the seventeenth-largest country in the world in proven oil reserves (12.2 billion barrels), and its reserves have grown more than 40 percent in the past ten years in a context where world reserves have grown only 14 percent and most countries have seen their reserves shrink, apart from a few exceptions such as Kazakhstan and Angola. Brazil's total registered reserves—although not yet proven—amount to 18.2 billion barrels, according to the Agência Nacional do Petróleo of Gás Natural e Biocombustíveis (ANP, National Agency of Oil, Gas, and Biofuels).[8]

The same is the case for oil refining and production. With respect to production, Brazil is the sixteenth-largest country in the world, with 1.8 million barrels a day, a greater than 100 percent increase over ten years in the face of an 11 percent rise in global production capacity. ANP projections for 2020 point to a production capacity of 2.96 million barrels a day—in other words, a 65 percent increase. The country is the twelfth-largest in the world in refining capacity (1.9 million barrels a day), and the largest in Latin America.[9]

There are proven gas reserves of 350 billion square meters in Brazil (whereas total reserves are 588 billion square meters);[10] however, these have been increasing at a rapid pace over the past several years, especially with the recent discoveries of the Tupi and Jupiter oil and gas fields. In terms of gas production, the country ranks thirty-fifth in the world, with 12.7 billion square meters, having grown 95 percent in the past ten years compared with the world's production increasing only 22 percent.[11]

8. ANP, *Anuário Estatístico Brasileiro do Petróleo e do Gás 2007* (ANP 2007).
9. ANP (2007).
10. ANP (2007).
11. ANP (2007).

Brazil's biofuels production also took a leap forward over the past five years after experiencing a contraction in the latter half of the 1990s, increasing 70 percent since 2001 to around 17 million square meters. Brazil's installed capacity for biodiesel production is 638,000 square meters, although only 10 percent of its capacity was used in 2006.[12]

With regard to technically usable hydroelectric capacity, Brazil has the third-largest potential in the world, behind Russia and China only.[13] The Agência Nacional de Energia Elétrica (ANEEL, National Agency of Electric Energy)[14] estimates that the potential growth probability of this capacity is 225 percent relative to presently installed capacity. Some projections suggest that these numbers are likely to increase substantially over the following years.

The increase in Petrobrás' oil and gas finds in Brazil and its international enterprises are basically associated with exploration technology in the country's ultradeep waters. More than 92 percent of Brazilian oil reserves are found at sea, of which 82 percent are offshore. The same holds true for the gas sector, where 78 percent of reserves are located at sea.[15] Figure 2-2 illustrates Petrobrás' technological advancement in oil prospecting and production. The most recent finds—Tupi and Jupiter—are located in the pre-salt layers, which have between 5,000 and 7,000 meters in depth. The first oil well in the pre-salt layers took more than a year to be drilled and cost $240 million. At present, Petrobrás is drilling a similar oil well in sixty days, at a cost of $60 million.[16]

Brazil makes use of oil, gas, and their imported derivatives in its energy matrix, also exporting both oil and its derivatives. In 2006, the country attained a surplus in its oil and derivatives commercial balance for the first time in its history, a fact that was announced as the achievement of energy self-sufficiency.[17] Nonetheless, the actual case is that though Brazil produces an oil volume similar to what it needs for its internal consumption, its production (mainly of heavy oil) has a quality that is not entirely compatible with the country's refineries, as they are made to refine light oil. Brazil exports part of the heavy oil it produces and completes the refinery

12. ANP (2007).
13. World Energy Council (2004).
14. See the ANEEL website, www.aneel.gov.br.
15. ANP (2007).
16. "Definição de investimentos no pré-sal adia novo plano de negócios da Petrobrás," *Folha Online,* May 13, 2008.
17. ANP (2007).

FIGURE 2-2. Petrobrás's Deepwater Exploration Technology Capacity, 1977–2003

Meters

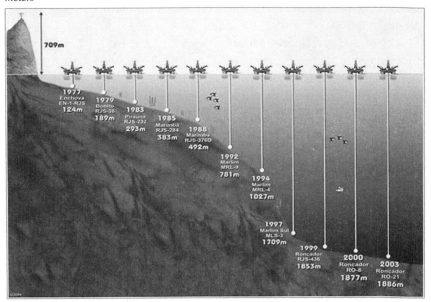

Source: Petrobrás (www2.petrobras.com.br/Petrobras/portugues/plataforma/pla_aguas_profundas.htm).

mix with imported light oil and its derivatives. Following this line of thought, in 2006 the country had a surplus in the sector of 10,000 square meters a day.

Table 2-8 shows the gradual reduction in Brazilian dependence on oil imports. It is interesting to note that Brazilian oil imports from other South American countries have been radically reduced, after having expanded in the 1990s, with its principal regional partners being Argentina and Venezuela. The latter had its sales to Brazil reduced to zero in 2006. A significant reduction also took place in relation to purchases from the Middle East. However, Brazil's trade operations with Africa, especially Nigeria and Algeria, have increased significantly.[18]

During the 1990s, Brazil's energy purchases from other South American countries were part of a regional policy of political engagement with its neighbors, which also served to counterbalance commercial agreements in other domains. Curiously enough, this trade has been drastically reduced

18. ANP (2007).

T A B L E 2 - 8 . Oil Imports, Selected Years
Millions of barrels

		1997	2001	2006
North America		0	2,076	3,445
South America		81,917	35,039	3,943
	Argentina	46,518	20,634	664
	Venezuela	34,481	10,828	0
Middle Orient		64,779	27,666	32,669
	Saudi Arabia	38,123	24,921	22,906
	Iraq	0	1,441	9,764
Africa		55,353	85,658	90,890
	Angola	1,918	5,988	6,890
	Algeria	21,401	29,349	21,830
	Nigeria	31,091	45,215	52,575
Total imports		**202,049**	**152,481**	**131,942**

Source: Agência Nacional do Petróleo, Gás Natural e Biocombustíveis, *2007 Annual Report.*

in recent years, even during the first term of the Luiz Inácio Lula da Silva government, in which rhetoric and statements favoring greater energy integration were very much present.

Yet South America will acquire a more prominent role in the international trade of Brazilian oil and its derivatives. In this case, South America constitutes Brazil's main exporting region, accounting for 35 percent of regional total imports. Attention should be drawn to Argentina, for it is the country of origin for 25 percent of Brazil's imports. Moreover, the region is also the main trade partner for Brazil's oil derivative exports, representing 32 percent of its total exports.[19]

Turning to natural gas, given that Brazil does not possess any significant internal production or any regasification plant, the central point for its integration with its South American neighbors is the construction of gas pipelines that are able to transport gas from producer to consumer markets. To this end, long-term agreements are fundamental. The integration problem here is not related to a lack of gas reserves (available in Bolivia, Venezuela, Argentina, and Peru) but to the low level of political and regulatory convergence between Brazil and the other countries in the region.

As was observed above, the 1990s saw the construction of gas pipelines in South America, among them Gasbol, the pipeline that transports natural gas from Bolivia to the most industrialized states of Brazil. Gasbol was

19. ANP (2007).

built as the result of a 1996 bilateral agreement and started operating in 1999. At this point, Brazil began to import increasing quantities of gas, going from 400 million square meters a year in 1999 to 9.3 billion in 2006.[20]

The first agreements that established the Brazilian use of Bolivian gas date to 1930, and there have been many attempts of this kind over the course of the subsequent decades. Brazil's decision to implement the construction of a gas pipeline, celebrating a gas supply agreement with Bolivia, and Petrobrás' massive investments in this country were considered a benchmark in bilateral relations, as well as of Brazil's new regional posture. The process of rendering these developments viable demanded internal and external political engagement from the government of President Fernando Henrique Cardoso (1995–2002), for it required intense action by Brazilian diplomats and faced a lot of resistance from Petrobrás' technical sectors.

The political crisis that followed Evo Morales's election in Bolivia and the nationalization of gas and oil reserves and production in Bolivia did not interrupt gas imports. Still, they generated important effects over costs and Brazilian strategies to this product. This process affected Brazil's average imported gas prices. From an average level of $80 per 1,000 square meters, the value went up to $98 in 2003 and 2004, $116 in 2005, and $159 in 2006. This amounted to a 37 percent increase between 2005 and 2006.[21]

As was observed above, this product was basically destined for industrial use—particularly in Brazil's Southeastern region—as well as for fuel use, predominantly in fleets of buses and taxis. Residual gas was allocated to thermoelectric power stations for use after the 2001 electricity blackout. In addition to the economic impact of price increases—only partially transmitted to consumers—the political impact was considerable. In the eyes of some Brazilian diplomats, Petrobrás, industry, and public opinion, the episode fanned historical fears of regional energy integration in the face of fragile long-term agreements with unstable neighbors. As a result, Petrobrás announced several years of investment in gas prospecting as a means of reducing dependence on Bolivian gas. The firm also launched studies for the construction of a regasification plant to make possible imports of liquid natural gas from other countries. Furthermore, negotiations and studies are in progress about importing gas from the Camisea region of southern Peru, where production should start soon.

20. ANP (2007).
21. ANP (2007).

As far as hydroelectricity is concerned, the present situation and future projections have a strong geopolitical element. Itaipu—a binational state-owned firm controlled by the Brazilian and Paraguayan governments—is central to bilateral relations between the two countries. This is partly explained by the history of this investment and by the format adopted in the deal. Itaipu's energy production is divided equally, and one country is conditioned to selling to the other the surplus from its own production. This first-generation utility started operating in 1984, and since then Brazil has imported electricity from Paraguay.

The hydraulic use of the Paraná River (Seven Falls plus Foz do Iguaçu) is an old and controversial theme. However, it was brought back to the fore during the energy crisis of the 1960s and 1970s. At the time, two alternatives involving neighboring countries—Bolivian gas and a hydroelectric power station with Paraguay—were considered for reducing dependency on oil imports. The Bolivian option was then considered to be too risky to ensure supply stability, so the Paraguayan one was pursued, generating a new geopolitical entanglement with Argentina. The Argentines pursued the project as a means of exerting significant influence over Paraguay and controlling the mouth of the Paraná River, located only a few kilometers away from the border between Paraguay and Argentina. This controversy was settled in 1979 with the Tripartite Agreement.[22]

According to the deal's format, which has been a central issue recently in the Paraguayan elections,[23] the project was entirely defined, structured, financed, and executed by Brazil.[24] Itaipu was planned to be the largest hydroelectric power station in the world in water volume, through a $14 billion project (value at the time). It again brought to light century-old border questions—among them the Paraguay War of 1865–70. Only in 1966 did the countries sign an agreement defining a cooperative pattern to settle their border and hydraulic disputes.[25]

The Itaipu project would flood a large part of the land under litigation, and the nonflooded part would become a binational ecological park to be

22. See the website for Itaipu Binacional (www.itaipu.gov.br).
23. In this year's Paraguayan presidential elections, the theme "renegotiation of the Itaipu Agreement" has been central. The newly elected candidate, Fernando Lugo, has used this theme intensively in his campaign, and he is expected to give it considerable attention in his mandate.
24. This work was partly funded by domestic funds and partly funded by international ones. In both cases, Brazil took responsibilities. The international funding will be in place until 2023.
25. See the website for Itaipu Binacional.

administered by Itaipu. In 1973, the Itaipu Treaty was signed, and in 1974, an international mixed-capital firm was created to manage operations and exploration. The power station started operating in 1984, but it only reached its integral capacity in 2007 with the installation of the last of the twenty planned turbines. Moreover, the station almost doubled Brazil's capacity to produce electricity, going from 16,700 megawatts of installed power capacity to almost 30,000 megawatts. In 1997, Itaipu represented more than 25 percent of the nation's electric production.[26]

Since then, there have been other large hydroelectric power station projects in Brazil, such as Tucurui and Balbina. Nevertheless, they have not had any significant regional or international notice. It was only recently that public tenders for the hydroelectric use of the Madeira River, located close to the border with Bolivia, provoked some noise, given that the course of the river enters the neighboring country.

In this manner, Brazil's international trade in electricity is still highly concentrated in Paraguay, as a result of Itaipu. However, after 2000, a series of ad hoc concessions for electricity imports and exports were authorized by ANEEL. This has been done on a limited scale with some neighboring countries, amounting to $80 million and 900,000 kilowatt-hours.[27]

Yet there are signs that Eletrobrás—the state-owned electricity firm partially privatized in the 1990s through the sale of a substantial part of its distributing and transmitter stations—is securing the space to expand its international presence. The Brazilian Senate recently approved a Provisory Measure (No. 396) authorizing both Eletrobrás and the concessionaries under its control to participate in projects and tenders outside Brazil.

Finally, private sector actions in the biofuels sector are widely influenced by state actors. Although Petrobrás has recently entered this sector, it remains principally controlled by the private sector. Annual sugarcane ethanol production has not been linear through the course of the past ten years; it suffered a significant decrease from 1997 until 2001, recuperating to growth again in 2001, and arriving at 17 million square meters of production in 2007—but the productivity gain has been constant.[28]

Yet the energy balance of sugarcane ethanol remains remarkably favorable. The relationship between produced and consumed energy throughout the process reveals this differential. In the case of ethanol,

26. See the website for Itaipu Binacional.
27. See the ANEEL website, www.aneel.gov.br.
28. ANP (2007).

this ratio is 9.3, whereas for beetroot and wheat it is 2 and for corn it stays at 1.4.[29] The Brazilian biodiesel program was approved in 2004 through Law No. 11,097, which establishes targets and deadlines for the introduction of this new fuel in the national energy matrix. Since 2005, the federal government has authorized the addition of 2 percent biodiesel to all diesel consumed. From 2008 onward, this 2 percent mix will be compulsory, enabling the market to expand.[30]

On March 20, 2008, an agreement was signed establishing the pursuit of technical viability studies for the construction of an alcohol pipeline connecting Campo Grande, the capital of Mato Grosso do Sul State, to the Paranaguá port, located in Paraná State and primarily focused on exports. The Brazilian target for ethanol exports is to surpass the present 500,000 square meters and reach 4.7 billion square meters by 2012.[31]

After much resistance, Petrobrás decided to enter the biofuels domain. Thus, the target of expanding the company's participation in the ethanol market is part of its 2007–11 business plan.[32] To secure the supply increase, partnerships are being studied in more than forty alcohol production projects. Petrobrás exported 80 million liters of alcohol in 2006 and is planning to multiply its sales abroad. To this end, the company will invest more than $1.6 billion in ethanol production, storage, transportation, and distribution. In addition, the state-owned firm is implementing its first industrial biofuel production units, which will generate 171 million liters of alcohol per year. Two of the units were inaugurated in mid-2008 in the municipalities of Candeias (state of Bahia) and Quixadá (state of Ceará); a third unit, located in Montes Claros (state of Minas Gerais), is to be inaugurated in 2009. Petrobrás is also studying other projects in various regions of the country in partnership with different types of investors, ranging from big economic groups to rural workers' cooperatives.

Ethanol exports have amounted to an average of $1.6 billion since 2005, with the principal buyers being the United States (almost 25 percent of total exports), Japan, and Holland.[33] Contrary to what happens in the gas and electric sectors and to what partially takes place in the oil sector, biofuels do not relate to South American countries.

29. This unit represents the amount of energy contained in ethanol per unit of fossil fuel input.
30. Programa Nacional de Produção e Uso do Biodiesel (www.biodiesel.gov.br).
31. Petrobrás (2008).
32. Petrobrás (2007a).
33. See the website of the Ministry of Development, Industry, and Trade, www.desenvolvimento.gov.br.

Vectors of International Projection

As it has been noted above, Brazil's international performance in the energy realm is fundamentally centered on Petrobrás. This includes the oil, gas, their derivatives, and petrochemical sectors as well as the biodiesel and ethanol sector, although on a smaller scale. The electricity sector is the only one that follows international dynamics alien to Petrobrás, for it is under the influence of another state-owned firm, Eletrobrás.

Yet it would not be incorrect to say that Petrobrás is an arm of the Brazilian federal government, or even of the country's executive power. The company's lines of action, decision-making process, and strategies have reasonable autonomy in relation to not only the federal government but also ANP.

The 1988 federal constitution consolidated the Brazilian state monopolies over oil and gas exploration and production, as well as refinery, import, export, and transportation activities. Nonetheless, in 1995, a constitutional amendment liberalized the country's oil and natural gas regime, allowing the participation of national and international capital in the different spheres of this industry. In 1997, the Oil Law was enacted, creating ANP and regulating private participation in the oil and gas industry, thus putting an end to Petrobrás' forty-year monopoly. This law also allowed Petrobrás to take part in joint ventures and to create subsidiaries without congressional approval.[34]

The new Oil Law consented that the government should reduce its participation in the state-owned firm to 50 percent plus one additional share. Until 2000, the government possessed 84 percent of all preferential shares as well as 53 percent of Petrobrás' total capital. In August 2000, the federal government sold 180 million blocks of 100 shares for $4 billion. Of the total sum, 40 percent was sold in Brazil and 60 percent abroad through American Depository Receipts (ADRs) on the New York Stock Exchange. In this manner, Petrobrás' financial and management reports started to be analyzed and regulated by the Comissão de Valores Imobiliários (CVM, Brazilian Securities and Exchange Commission) as well as by its American counterpart, which supervises open capital firms. Petrobrás' ADRs figure among the principal types of paper traded on the international market.[35] At present, the federal government holds only 33 per-

34. ANP, Oil Law, 1997 (www.anp.gov.br/conheca/lei.asp).
35. Landau and Lohmann (2006).

cent of Petrobrás' capital; however, it keeps most of the preferential shares (56 percent).[36]

Even since the end of its monopoly in 1997, and the entrance of some private players in the sector, the giant Brazilian state-owned firm continues to have a dominant presence in the national market. In spite of the liberalization of private sector participation in different energy domains, Petrobrás still leads in all sectors, controlling 95 percent of crude oil production in the country.[37] Downstream, this leadership is also observed because Petrobrás was allowed to keep its existing refineries, and private companies intending to invest in new refineries need ANP's approval. In the transportation sector, Petrobrás is charged with the maintenance of the existing gas pipelines; nevertheless, it does so through its subsidiary Transpetro, which controls gas pipelines, maritime terminals, and oil pipelines. Private companies are allowed to build new gas pipelines, as well as use Petrobrás' existing pipelines, albeit through the payment of tariffs.

Furthermore, apart from Petrobrás, Brazil's international action in this field centers on a few private firms from the petrochemical sector, most notably Braskem. Grupo Ipiranga is the other important company doing business in the sector, both in petrochemicals and distribution. It was recently bought out by Petrobrás. Although Petrobrás is listed on the São Paulo and New York stock exchanges, the firm keeps an influential management and technical apparatus in relation to the Brazilian Congress, ministerial organs, and national public opinion. The company's recent efficiency gains and profits have made its influence even greater.

The firm's revenue in 2007 was $100 billion, with profits of $12 billion.[38] Additionally, it keeps 70 drilling rigs (43 of which are at sea), 12,395 oil- and gas-producing wells, 109 production platforms, 15 refineries, 23,000 kilometers of pipeline, and a fleet of 153 ships (54 of which belong to the company); it also has 3 fertilizer factories and almost 6,000 retail units.

Petrobrás, already active in twenty-six countries, is principally focused on exploration and production. However, it has been advancing its performance in gas and energy in general, as well as the refining stages and trade. After going through financial restrictions in the 1990s, the firm

36. Petrobrás (2007b).
37. ANP (2007).
38. Petrobrás (2008).

recovered its investment capacity, and from 2003 onward it decided to speed up its internationalization process. Today, around 8.5 percent of its proven reserves are located abroad, especially in Argentina, Nigeria, Peru, and Venezuela.[39] It holds a similar standard production capacity internationally, although its principal bases are in South America, most notably in Argentina. Its liquid receipts abroad in 2006 were worth $6.5 billion.[40]

Petrobrás has audacious international plans for the next several years, in various fields of action. Its 2008–12 investment plans foresee investments of $112 billion—around $22.5 billion per year—out of which 13 percent should be invested abroad.[41] The company's target is to arrive in 2020 as one of the world's five main integrated energy companies. Its 2012 target is to export around 770,000 barrels of oil per day through a combination of its international production and its domestic surplus.

Petrobrás' presence in South America is growing and is a central part of its strategic planning for the next ten years; while activities in Argentina, Uruguay, and Bolivia have a place of prominence in such plans, there have been intense discussions over Venezuela. In the latter case, projects also imply some participation by Petróleos de Venezuela (PDVSA, Venezuela's state-owned oil firm) in Brazil, whether through gas pipelines or investments in refineries.

On December 13, 2007, PDVSA and Petrobrás signed an agreement to create a joint company for the construction and operation of the Abreu e Lima Refinery, which will be located in Pernambuco.[42] The company's participation shares should be divided, with 60 percent for Petrobrás and 40 percent for PDVSA, and with staff from both state-owned firms operating the enterprise. By means of the same agreement, PDVSA has granted Petrobrás the right to take part in improved oil production in Venezuela, and the latter has already been participating in projects in the Orinoco Basin.

Out of all Petrobrás' international investments, exploration and production is the segment that will receive the greatest sum, totaling $15 billion in investments, of which $10.5 billion (70 percent) will prioritize projects in Latin America, West Africa, and the Gulf of Mexico.[43] Nevertheless,

39. Petrobrás (2008).
40. Petrobrás (2008).
41. Petrobrás (2008).
42. "Petrobrás e PDVSA fecham acordo para refinaria em PE," BBC-Brasil.com, December 13, 2007.
43. Petrobrás (2008).

TABLE 2-9. Oil Finds

Index	Tupi field	Jupiter field	Carioca field
Status	Official statement from Petrobrás	Official statement from Petrobrás	Unofficial statement
Starting exploration date	2012	2013/2014	Undetermined
Potential recoverable volume	5 to 8 billion barrels of oil equivalent		33 billion barrels of oil equivalent
Oil quality	Light oil of high aggregate value and natural gas	Natural and condensed gas	

Sources: Petrobrás data; "Petrobrás descobre megacampo, diz ANP," *Folha de São Paulo*, April 15, 2008.

if oil prices are kept at the current level, this picture could be altered in eight to ten years, the estimated time frame for the new oil and gas finds at the Tupi and Jupiter fields to become productive.[44] These new reserves, which were announced at the end of 2007, are located under the pre-salt layer—that is, at more than 5 kilometers depth (2 kilometers of water, with the remaining 3 kilometers being soil)—and contain an estimated 5 to 9 billion barrels of light oil. Such finds could represent a 50 percent increase in Brazilian proven reserves, considerably elevating the country's world ranking for the sector. Though these new reserves' technical viability for exploration does not seem to be a problem, their economic viability is questionable because exploration costs are significantly high.

An additional factor that could alter this scenario in an even more decisive fashion is the discovery of the Carioca oil and gas field. In this case, estimates are still extraofficial, but they point to reserves on the order of 33 billion barrels, as can be seen from table 2-9. Petrobrás defines itself as an integrated energy company that acts on six fronts: (1) exploration and production; (2) refinery, trade, and logistics; (3) distribution; (4) gas and other energy; (5) petrochemicals; and (6) biofuels. Though the exploration and production area has less of a geographical dimension, the refinery, trade, and logistic front focuses on the South Atlantic region, and the gas and other energy and petrochemical fronts are primarily attuned to South America. In the case of biofuels, activities center on the global market.

The clear definition of different geographical areas of action, according to a specific energy market segment, feeds the hypothesis that Petrobrás

---

44. "Definição de investimentos."

does not directly and automatically reproduce the federal government's priorities and policies. In many cases, their relationship is symbiotic and of mutual support; however, it can clearly be divergent in others. If there is no consensus or unique line of action within the federal government with respect to the international sphere, it is unlikely that there could be one within Petrobrás.

As has been seen above, the electricity sector's international articulation has a clear South American focus, particularly in the Southern Cone. Its project seems to be far less structured and advances at a slower pace than the oil sector. Eletrobrás is taking initial steps toward internationalization, but the very peculiarities of the electricity segment restrict the options of both the company and the state. Additionally, this is a less capitalized firm with less of a technological differential than Petrobrás.

Even if the electric sector does possess a wide array of interconnections and a binational power station, it does not make use of this condition to attain a regional projection. An additional distinction from the oil sector is that the electricity sector is not seen as an element that can articulate industrial policy and stimulate other production chains; thus, it mobilizes fewer interest groups and political segments.

As far as biofuels are concerned, the situation is even more dispersive in terms of strategic coordination. Only recently did the sugar-alcohol sector manage to articulate its strategies with public policies in a broad fashion that encompass the international sphere. Up until this point, the sector's traditional political influence was directed to price politics and had an oscillating relationship with energy policies that was always conditioned to the relative prices of sugar and alcohol.

The sector only started to act more broadly and in a reasonably coordinated fashion in the international sphere when it was able to associate production chain interests with those of the machinery and automobile industries, as well as to the country's energy needs and environmental rules. Without these conditions, a "left-wing developmentalist" government such as that of President Lula could not have incorporated biofuels' international agenda in such an integral manner.

As has been previously observed and in great convergence with Petrobrás' strategy in this sector, the biofuels market and international policies are global (a regional agenda on the theme is practically nonexistent) and affect the subsidy and other issues related to multilateral trade and environmental forums such as the World Trade Organization and the Kyoto Protocol.

Tentative Conclusions Concerning the New Oil and Gas Discoveries

Even though there are no exact figures about new discoveries in the Brazilian pre-salt layer, a contentious debate has already started concerning the political and economic consequences of this event. Let us look at this in detail.

Foreign Policy

The new discoveries in the Brazilian pre-salt layer may propel a paradigmatic shift in oil geopolitics that would probably entail changes in the country's foreign policy. If estimates prove to be correct, Brazil's reserves would figure among the ten largest in the world, falling behind only those of the Middle Eastern countries, Russia, Nigeria, and Venezuela.

It is also the case that Brazil does not offer the same political and economic risks as do other energy giants, most notably in Africa and the Middle East, whereas it can point to a safer and less politicized business environment. In this manner, and taking into consideration the reality that global demand for energy is growing at unprecedented rates—with oil being the main promoter of this trend—Brazil could make use of its advantageous position as an energy player to gain preferential standing in other areas. Thus, its energy status could potentially enable it to gain a more assertive political and economic presence in the world.

In effect, both President Lula and Energy and Mining Minister Edson Lobão have already publicly expressed the intention of joining the Organization of the Petroleum Exporting Countries (OPEC), arguing that Brazil could help bring a more conciliatory tone to the institution. Even if OPEC members have not extended any formal invitation to Brazil, the fact that the country was invited to OPEC's most recent emergency meeting—which took place in Saudi Arabia in late June 2008 and aimed to discuss the possibility of increasing output in the face of recent increases in oil prices—reflects its changing position in global energy politics. More to the point, not only is Brazil preparing itself to act as a major oil exporter, but the world is also recognizing that this should probably be the case.

In the regional sphere, with the new oil and gas finds, the gap between Brazilian and Venezuelan oil reserves should be considerably reduced. Venezuela's current reserves amount to 77 billion barrels, whereas the figure for Brazil is 11 billion barrels and could potentially reach 38 to

41 billion barrels. Moreover, it is a known fact that in the race for geo-political influence, energy politics plays a central role. Brazil's increased ethanol production and its effort to project this status internationally have already led many commentators to categorize it as an energy giant.

Although this enthusiasm should probably be tempered with caution given the challenges the country will face as far as exploration, production, and technological demands are concerned, it seems plausible to expect that the regional dynamics will be considerably altered. Oil is a central part of Venezuelan president Hugo Chávez's effort to gain diplomatic and political leverage in Latin America, and these new finds could possibly tip the regional balance of power toward greater Brazilian prominence, putting the integration debate in a new light.

Yet, with regard to the regional context, there is much speculation over sensitive issues in energy geopolitics given recent developments in Bolivia, Argentina, and Paraguay. The media and to a great extent opposition parties have been very keen on portraying Bolivia's effort to nationalize its gas sector as a major threat to Brazil's future energy needs that ought to be met with aggressive policies.

As was noted above, the gas imbroglio in Brazil can be synthesized in terms of an enormous dependency on Bolivian gas—which, in the light of recent events, has implied a vigorous search for a diversification of gas suppliers, an increase in national exploration efforts, and an effort to achieve greater efficiency. Additionally, the central challenges the Brazilian gas sector has faced so far include the need to expand domestic supply, optimize the supply of thermoelectric power plants, and render the price policy more efficient. In this sense, it is clear that preoccupations with short-term gas supply are not only valid but a pressing necessity.

However, the idea of a threat posed by Bolivia that deserves an aggressive response should be relativized. This neighboring country needs Brazilian demand to sustain its gas sector, its principal national source of revenue. And one could argue that the new Tupi and Jupiter discoveries will prob-ably alter the dynamics of gas consumption. The new finds are not only in tune with Brazilian needs in this sector, but they could also potentially lead to a restructuring of the regional balance of power as it relates to gas supply. In other words, it is possible that in the medium term, Brazil will become a central gas player in South America—a step that would defi-nitely substantiate its regional role and would give it leverage to exert more concerted regional leadership that would spill over into domains beyond energy.

As regards Brazil's relations with Argentina in the face of that country's current domestic political turmoil, Brazil has been adopting a conciliatory position when its involvement is requested. The Argentine government's recent raising of taxes on the agriculture and cattle sectors' exports, as a response to the increase in international prices, has led to considerable social unrest. Farmers have gone on strike and have been blocking roads, resulting in food shortages; there have been many public manifestations throughout the country; and the economy minister stepped down in late April. Among other things, variable export taxation is used to maintain the government's policy of controlling energy and fuel prices.

In addition, Argentina is also facing an energy shortage, which has forced it to rely on regional support to guarantee supply during the winter. Argentine president Cristina Kirchner's initial proposal was that Brazil would give to her country part of the 30 million cubic meters of gas that it imports daily from Bolivia. Although the Lula government was fiercely opposed to such a concession, it adopted a conciliatory approach to its neighbor's problem when both countries signed an agreement of bilateral understanding for the exchange of electric energy in early May. This agreement provides that from May until August 2008, Brazil was to deliver from 800 to 1,500 megawatts of electric energy to Argentina, the equivalent of 4 to 8 percent of internal demand. As a means of compensation, Argentina was to give an equivalent amount of energy back—which could have come as hydroelectricity, fuel, or even gas—by September–November 2008. The Brazilian provision is mostly coming from Petrobrás' thermal power stations in the state of Rio Grande do Sul.

As for Brazil's relations with Paraguay, though both countries defend conflicting interests regarding the binational Itaipu hydroelectric power station, Brazil is by no means indicating that it is closed to a conciliatory solution for the issue. During the course of the recent presidential dispute in Paraguay, the revision of the Itaipu agreement was a central element in all candidates' agendas. Besides, Fernando Lugo's election is a clear indication that the issue will loom large in bilateral relations, because he was the one who most fiercely defended changes in the contract. At present, the energy produced in the plant is divided equally between the two countries. However, Paraguay only consumes 5 percent of the energy generated and is obliged to sell 95 percent of its production to Brazil. Itaipu accounts for 20 percent of the Brazilian energy supply, providing most of the energy consumed in the country's Southeastern region, where the vast majority of its industrial and business activities are concentrated.

Lugo's electoral campaign centered on recovering "energy sovereignty" by putting an end to the exigency that obliges Paraguay to sell its excess production to Brazil and, more important, by renegotiating the price of the energy sold to Brazil. The Lula administration has not demonstrated any intention of altering the contract; however, it has been constantly affirming that Brazil is open for discussions over the price issue. In spite of the fact that public debate over this question has tended to present the Brazilian position as quite irreconcilable, one should stress that not only in relations with Paraguay but also with Bolivia and Argentina, Brazil simply cannot afford to adopt a unilateral position. In other words, regional relations are so intricate and multidimensional that a stance on an energy issue is connected to a series of other political and economic issues pertaining to regional or bilateral relations within the region. Therefore, energy politics is part of broader regional strategy, and negotiations over this theme are linked to a series of other issues. Consequently, and despite the fact that the new oil and gas discoveries may lead to greater regional prominence, one can expect Brazil to pursue a conciliatory approach to sensitive energy themes with its neighbors.

Domestic Implications

It is clear that the combination of new oil and gas discoveries in the Tupi field with the evidence that there are huge reserves under the pre-salt layer will have a series of domestic implications. Yet international experience signals that this situation should be treated with caution; Nigeria, Angola, Saudi Arabia, Russia, and Venezuela all own extensive reserves but are faced with the failure to transform the wealth generated by the commodity into benefits for their people. And it is a known fact that oil-producing countries have historically gained less from this resource than non-oil-producing ones as a result of taxes charged for the consumption of fuels.

In this context, speculation over whether Brazil will experience Dutch Disease is only to be expected as a consequence of new energy finds combined with the recent classification of the country as investment grade by the rating firms Standard & Poor's and Fitch. Dutch Disease is an economic phenomenon whereby a country's currency suddenly becomes overvalued as a result of increases in commodity prices, which in turn render other exportable goods less competitive in the external market.

The term is a reference to events occurring in the Dutch economy during the 1980s, when mounting gas prices led to substantial increases in export receipts, overvaluing the guilder (the former basic currency unit in the Netherlands) and thus knocking down the competitiveness of other exports.

On the one hand, it is quite plausible to expect that under a macroeconomic scenario that has already started to cause current account deficits for the first time in a long while, the investment-grade classification may only contribute to a greater strengthening of the real (the basic Brazilian currency unit). Given a greater inflow of foreign capital into Brazil, interest rates should probably be lowered, resulting in a larger rate of investment in GDP and, in turn, in a higher evaluation of the real, which, combined with energy finds, could strengthen the effects of a potential occurrence of Dutch Disease.

On the other hand, such considerations need to be treated with a considerable degree of caution. First, it is worthwhile bringing attention to the fact that the impact of being granted investment grade should not result in automatic and unprecedented changes in the economy. It ought to be stressed that though the classification improves the country's international image, it should mostly attract portfolio investment as opposed to foreign direct investment, thus amounting to a more volatile and restrictive contribution. Second, the acquisition of investment-grade status has been anticipated and expected for a long while. Third, it is essential to note that unlike most major oil-producing countries, Brazil does not have an economy exclusively based on oil. In this sense, it seems too early to nurture preoccupation with Dutch Disease.

Nevertheless, various issues arise concerning the management of these new discoveries—most notably, debates over whether it is better to use reserves now or leave them for the future, given that price increases may render oil and gas production more profitable at a later stage, or over the possibility of establishing production targets. However, the underlying question informing governmental discussions of the situation is: How can Brazil gain the most from this new reality?

The most obvious answer has been that in light of a scenario of drastically reduced exploration risks and booming oil prices, the present regulatory system will have to change in order to increase government levying. Yet, though it is certain that oil and gas taxation will increase in the near future, the scope of such changes is by no means clear and there is a fair amount of speculation over the situation. There seems to be some conflict in the perspectives of the Ministry of Mining and Energy, Petrobrás, ANP, and the private sector. Still, it is fundamental to note that beyond disputes over which is the best regulatory model, what seems to be in place is a renewed discussion concerning the centrality of the state in energy management.

At present, the regulatory system adopted by Brazil is the License or Royalty and Tax Agreement established by the 1997 Oil Law. According to this system, the government receives from 5 to 10 percent of oil and gas fields' production in royalties and from 10 to 40 percent of the profitability of giant fields by means of government takes, which are defined through presidential decrees. Though the government's preliminary reading is that these takes should be increased, a measure that would not amount to changes in the Oil Law, the introduction of the Production-Sharing Agreement model and the Risk or Services Agreement is also being discussed. Table 2-10 illustrates the key characteristics of such models and points to the main implications of adopting each one for Brazil.

ANP is in charge of studying the different types of possible regulations of the pre-salt area. The Ministry of Mining and Energy should formulate a policy, which will in turn be taken to the Conselho Nacional de Politica Energetica (CNPE, National Council on Energy Policy). In convergence with the private sector's position on the theme—most notably reflected through articulations by the Brazilian Oil Institute—the agency defends the view that the model presently in place is the best fit for the nation.

The central arguments underpinning this perspective are that the Oil Law was officially created with three main objectives: to stimulate competitiveness, to give incentives for private investment, and to regulate the government's takes from oil and gas exploration and production. Thus, if the aim is to carry on observing these imperatives, there is no need to change the law because greater taxation can be attained through presidential decrees. Moreover, it is argued that the present model is flexible and investment friendly because both government and companies of different sizes can benefit from it. This position sees the License Agreement as rather successful, given that from 1997 to 2007 the oil sector's participation in GDP went from 2 to 10 percent, production rose by more than 100 percent, and investments went from $4 billion to $25 billion a year. It is argued that without this model, the new discoveries would not have occurred and that a change in the law would imply legal instability and could hamper much-needed investments.

TABLE 2-10. Oil and Gas Regulatory Systems

| Index | Type of agreement | | |
	License or royalty and tax	Production-sharing	Risk or services
Countries	Most oil-producing countries, including Brazil and United States	Angola, Nigeria, Norway, United Kingdom	Iran, Mexico, Venezuela
Monopoly on natural resources	Host country	Host country	Host country
Premised on	High exploration risk and efficient attraction of investment	High exploration risk and low cost areas with great profitability	Low exploration risk
Ownership of find	Concessionary, but a clause on domestic supply may be imposed	Production is shared between host country and concessionary in a pre-arranged fashion.	Host country
Host-country compensation	Signature bonus (prices geological risk) Royalties Government take (charged over production and profitability) Charge over occupation and retention of areas All other national taxes	Taxation is based on concessionary's finds. Share in production	All agreements seek to maximize host country's participation in finds.
Implications for Brazil	No change in Oil Law (1997); legal stability Changes in government take through decree	New oil and gas legislation; long-term process Creation of a 100 percent state-owned national oil company	Model badly regarded by foreign investors.

Sources: various; designed by the authors.

Petrobrás' president, José Sérgio Gabrielli, contests this position, emphasizing the low exploration risk in the pre-salt area.[45] He maintains that the area deserves a special regulatory model and that the proposal for a new system should be taken to Congress. He does not, however, indicate which model would be best fit, arguing that both the Production-Sharing Agreement and Services Agreement should be seriously considered. It is interesting to note that the adoption of the Production-Sharing Agreement model entails the existence of a fully state-owned national oil company,

45. "Novas jazidas vão modificar regulamentação do petróleo," *Valor Econômico*, April 18, 2008.

and this is by no means Petrobrás' case. In this fashion, the adoption of this model would demand clear changes in the structure of the national oil and gas sector. In addition, there is speculation that some sectors within Petrobrás defend the view that the pre-salt layer should not be open to foreign investment at all and the reality is that CNPE Resolution 06/2007 has already taken all high potential blocs neighboring Tupi out of the bidding rounds annually promoted by ANP.

The minister of mining and energy, Edson Lobão,[46] had always been publicly defending changes in the Oil Law. He has recently manifested his preference for the Production-Sharing Agreement model and the creation of a new state-owned company to administer exploration efforts.[47] It is interesting to note that he defends this position not only in terms of new discoveries in the pre-salt area but also as a means of increasing government levying and better allocating profits between municipalities and states within the nation. He believes that the regulatory mark should be adapted, thus contemplating a more prominent position for the state.

An analysis of these different positions, as well as of debates being held throughout the country, indicates that state's control of the oil and gas sector seems to be the central issue once again. In this context, it is useful noting that in spite of an observed tendency to portray policy implementation in the oil and gas sector as stemming from low-quality policymaking, policies are more the result of an intricate, heatedly disputatious decision-making process.

Thus, policy implementation has tended to be the result of precarious consensus. Although there have been some considerable changes, such as the brake on the state monopoly in the oil sector and the creation of ANP, the latter remains relatively weak and Petrobrás' market power is still considerably greater than what is established by the law.

The decisionmaking process in Brazil is marked by fierce political clashes that surpass divisions between right and left. More to the point, the country's multiparty political arrangements, in which a considerable number of actors hold some relative power, have made policy implementation in the oil and gas sector the result of compromise solutions based on long-term, established cleavages. In this fashion, after the rearrangement of the sector in the 1990s, the old balance of forces between distinct groups came back to the fore.

46. "Lobão defende aumento da tributação sobre o petróleo," *O Globo,* April 17, 2008.
47. "Ministro quer nova estatal e partilha do petróleo," *Valor Econômico,* June 27, 2008.

Following this line of analysis, one should expect heated disputes over the country's energy situation in the near future. Nevertheless, if an effort is made to leave ideological readings of how the sector should be organized aside, it is clear that the imperative to transform the new oil and gas discoveries into a vector of national growth and development is faced with a major challenge: the need for technology to explore these deepwater fields. This new technology frontier demands unprecedented rates of investment, for the oil is found in high-pressure and high-temperature conditions and under extensive salt layers that make exploration operations extremely complex as well as capital and technology intensive.

Conclusion

Brazil's new energy cycle emerged in the 1990s, conditioned by marked changes in the international scenario as well as by domestic factors. Moreover, it is clear that this new cycle will lead to a reconception of the country's international performance and presence, as far as energy is concerned. Even if there are still references being made to self-sufficiency and a reduction of vulnerabilities, the new energy strategy has forcefully incorporated market standards and efficiency parameters. Certainly, this strategy has achieved the ends of preserving a strong state presence in the sector and, first and foremost, preserving the central role of the main state-owned energy firm, Petrobrás.

At the same time, efficiency gains and technological advancements, both in the biofuels domain (production, motor technologies, distribution logistics, etc.) and in oil prospecting and production in deep waters (feeding promising projections for the national oil and gas sector) have contributed to Brazil's new international role in the energy sector. On a smaller scale, bets on the country's hydroelectric potential have also ended up favoring this process.

In conclusion, in all these four Brazilian energy segments, the present context would not have been possible if it had not been for direct state intervention, whether through its firms or strong subsidies and regulations. These policies have had enormous costs for the country and contributed to deepening its economic crisis in the 1980s and 1990s, particularly the financial dimension. Nevertheless, since that period, some of the positive effects of this path of action have contributed to redefining Brazil's energy strategy under extremely favorable conditions.

References

ANP (Agência Nacional do Petróleo, Gás Natural e Biocombustíveis). 2007. *Anuário Estatístico Brasileiro do Petróleo e do Gás* (Annual Report 2007). Brasilia.

Landau, G., and J. Lohmann. 2006. "Relations between Oil-Producing Countries and Oil Companies in the 20th Century: The Case of Petrobrás in Brazil." Paper presented at the international conference organized by Identités, Relations Internationales et Civilisations de l'Europe (IRICE), Centre National de la Recherche Scientifique, Paris, September 18–19.

Linkohr, R. 2006. "La política energética latinoamericana: Entre el Estado y el mercado." *Nueva Sociedad* 204, July–August, www.nuso.org/upload/articulos/3367_1.pdf (September 2008).

Petrobrás, 2007a. *Plano de Negócios 2007–2011.* www2.petrobras.com.br/ri/port/apresentacoeseventos/conftelefonicas/pdf/planonegocios20072011_port.pdf (September 2008).

———. 2007b. *Relatório Anual 2007.* www2.petrobras.com.br/portal/frame_ri.asp?lang=pt&area=ri&pagina=/ri/port/ConhecaPetrobras/RelatorioAnual/RelatorioAnual.asp (September 2008).

———. 2008. *Plano Estratégico Petrobrás 2020: Plano de Negócios 2008–2012.* www2.petrobras.com.br/ri/port/ApresentacoesEventos/ConfTelefonicas/pdf/PlanoEstrategico2008-2012.pdf (September 2008).

World Energy Council. 2004. *Survey of Energy Resources 2004.* www.worldenergy.org/documents/ser2004.pdf (September 2008).

CHAPTER THREE

Brazil as an Agricultural and Agroenergy Superpower

ANDRÉ MELONI NASSAR

The world's population is facing new challenges in relation to the supply and demand for agriculture-based products. The rising prices of agricultural commodities indicate that the world market is not in the desirable equilibrium of agricultural raw materials for food, feed, and fuel. The world debate is evolving from a discussion about the effects of increasing commodity prices on costs to vocal manifestations from governments and supranational agencies with respect to the risks of high food prices for the political stability of food-importing countries. Neo-Malthusian theories are being touted by alarmists who insist on singling out biofuels as the main driver of the current food crisis. Of course, the fact that the world is facing a shortage of agricultural commodities has nothing to do with structural shortages of food. The food market is conjecturally tight; but we will see in the next few years countries with an availability of natural resources (like land and water), competitive agricultural sectors, and nonusers of discriminatory policies against agriculture (e.g., the use of export taxes) responding to the higher prices by increasing production. Brazil fits in this group.

A spike in world food prices also throws into question the concept of food security as we know it today. The creation of the special products (SPs) and the special safeguard mechanism (SSM) provisions in the context of the Doha Round of multilateral trade negotiations shows that food security, for many developing countries, is synonymous with food sovereignty and self-sufficiency. The underlying idea is that self-sufficiency is the necessary condition to guarantee food security because it allows countries to be less dependent on the world market. Both mechanisms, SPs and SSM, have been proposed to protect countries against a fall in prices that would negatively affect food security, livelihood security, and rural development. Under both mechanisms, consumers—those suffering from the high prices—seem to be of no importance.

High world prices, however, push up food prices everywhere, even in regulated markets with high tariff barriers like the European Union, on the developed side, and India, on the developing side. In the short run, the best way to tackle the current situation of food prices is to eliminate market distortions and tariff barriers, letting the production of competitive countries calm down the excess in demand worldwide. Trade, given the situation of the world market we are facing, is part of the solution. Food security, in this context of high food prices, is definitely something different from food sovereignty.

In the long run, the high prices will result in structural changes in the supply of agricultural commodities. To meet the increasing demand for food and other uses, the supply of agricultural commodities will need to be sourced from a greater variety of suppliers. The exports of agricultural commodities have been concentrated in a few supplier countries in recent years, either because developed countries such as the United States and the EU members are not capable of increasing production as they did in the past, or because many developing countries are still using policies that do not promote productivity gains and production efficiency. For many developing countries, agriculture is supposed to be the sector for maintaining people in rural areas, and raising efficiency is not part of the policy framework. However, in a context of short supply and high prices, policies that are production oriented are much more important than those that are employment oriented. If, until now, livelihood security was the priority for many developing countries' domestic policies, from now on the aim of the policies should be efficiency improvement.

Higher agricultural prices are surprising us not only because they are changing the concept of food security, but also because they are the result of an unexpected spillover effect of the rising price of oil. Many negative consequences of increasing oil prices have been predicted since they started getting higher. World economic recession, the more alarmist of those predictions, has not yet become a reality. Increasing agricultural commodity prices, however, are an unpredicted consequence. Short supply, rising demand, financial market globalization, and high fertilizer costs have contributed to promote a strong integration between oil and agricultural commodity prices. Though the supply of agricultural commodities keeps increasing at a lesser rate than that of demand, oil prices will nonetheless push up those commodity prices. Agricultural prices will be decoupled from oil prices, as they were until 2003, as long as production starts to increase faster than demand. Consequently, an interruption of this integration is only a matter of time.

Oil prices, however, do have a structural impact on agricultural prices. Due to higher energy and fertilizer costs, the price floor of agricultural products has shifted up. This means that the world markets will not face lower agricultural prices, such as those of 1999 to 2002—at least until new technologies are developed that lead to increases in productivity without higher levels of fertilizers. Bringing down oil prices, reducing demand in developing countries through economic depression, and reducing the globalization of financial markets are not the appropriate solutions to bring agricultural prices down to levels that are affordable for producers and consumers. Conversely, supply expansion and trade liberalization are reachable solutions. This chapter focuses on the role of Brazil as a world supplier of agricultural commodities.

The current rising prices of agricultural commodities are challenging Brazil. The recent harvests have shown that Brazil's capacity to respond to changes in world prices has not been as quick as was expected. Economic problems, such as high transportation costs and financial constraints due to the farming sector's level of indebtedness, are undermining the capacity of producers to expand production. Those short-term constraints, however, do not change the long-term picture; although not unlimited, Brazil has plenty of natural resources, compared with other big agricultural players, that form the base of the agribusiness sector's competitiveness in any part of the world. Unlike in the past, today natural resources are not used solely by the agricultural sector. These have to be shared with Brazilian society and, increasingly, with the world community.

It is hard to deny that Brazil is in a privileged position in the world debate on food versus fuel. With a fuel ethanol program that originated in the 1970s, and with an increasing consumption of ethanol from 2003 onward following the upward trend of flex-fuel cars sales, sugarcane production—the feedstock for Brazilian ethanol—has been demonstrating a capacity to increase without any harsh competition against cereals and oilseeds. Although this is not the case for all adopters of biofuels, the Brazilian experience can be replicated by many countries.

This chapter addresses these questions: Is Brazil ready to be an agricultural and energy superpower? Which obstacles must be overcome in seeking this position? What are the new challenges faced by Brazilian agriculture? Is Brazil prepared to handle them?

The Geography of Brazilian Agriculture

To understand the development of Brazilian agriculture, it is important to know how production is distributed around the country. The producing regions can be characterized in the context of the Brazilian biomes. Brazil is divided into six biomes, as can be seen in figure 3-1: South Grassland, Atlantic Forest, Savanna, Pantanal wetland, Steppe, and Amazon Forest. The South Grassland is mainly characterized by irrigated rice production combined with cattle. A typical production system in this region consists of the rotation of rice and grass-fed cattle. Grains and soybeans are also produced in this region, but rice is the predominant crop. The Pantanal is a region with cattle as the main agricultural activity and where the land floods during the rainy season. As with the South Grassland, the Pantanal is a region characterized by low altitude.

Figure 3-2 presents a set of maps pointing out the location of grain, sugarcane, and meat production in Brazil. Grains, oilseeds, and sugarcane are produced in the Atlantic Forest and Savanna regions. In the Atlantic Forest, land approaching the coast becomes increasingly less suitable for agriculture. Sugarcane production is concentrated more in São Paulo, northwest of Paraná, and southwest of Minas Gerais. However, this crop is also evolving in Goiás, Mato Grosso do Sul, and, to some extent, in Mato Grosso, three states that constitute the sugarcane expansion region. Sugarcane is also important on the coasts of Sergipe, Alagoas, and Pernambuco. Although the area of planted sugarcane in these regions is not expanding, production has been improved with the utilization of irrigation systems.

Corn and soybeans are located in similar regions. Both products are used not only for crop rotation but also for double-cropping systems. The second corn crop, cultivated in land used for a first crop of soybeans, represents around 30 percent of the total area of corn planted. Corn and soybeans are produced in the South region (Rio Grande do Sul, Santa

FIGURE 3-1. Brazilian Biomes and States

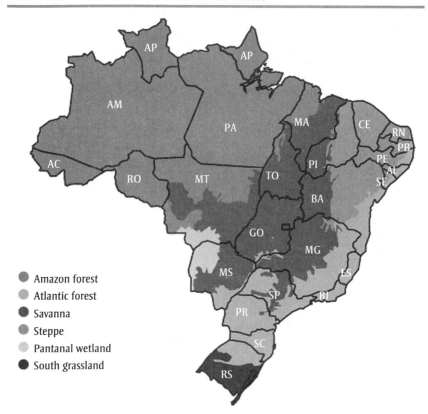

- Amazon forest
- Atlantic forest
- Savanna
- Steppe
- Pantanal wetland
- South grassland

Source: Instituto Brasileiro de Geografia e Estatistica, 2004.

Catarina, and Paraná), Southeast region (São Paulo and Minas Gerais), and the Center-West region (Mato Grosso do Sul, Goiás, and Mato Grosso). Though corn is more concentrated in the South and Southeast, soybeans are in the South and Center-West regions. The expansion areas for soybeans and corn are on the border between the Savanna and the Amazon biomes in the state of Mato Grosso, and in the savannas of Maranhão (in the south of the state) and Piauí (in the west of the state). The savanna in Bahia (in the west of the state) is also an important soybean- and cotton-producing region. This region and Mato Grosso State are the two most important cotton-producing regions.

Chicken and pork production follow corn and soybeans; both are concentrated in Santa Catarina, Paraná, and São Paulo. With the increasing

FIGURE 3-2. Geographical Distribution of Agricultural Production in Brazil

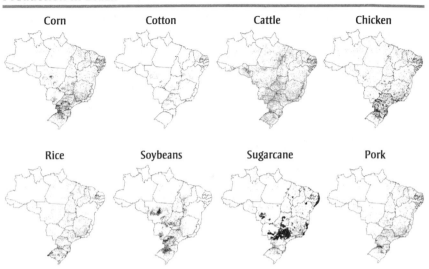

Source: Pesquisa Agricola Municipal, Instituto Brasileiro de Geografia e Estatistica (2007).

production of feed crops in the Center-West region, that region is the expansion area for chicken and pork production.

Cattle are spread all over Brazil, with different production systems found throughout the country. The most important of these systems are full cycle, calf rearing, and steer termination. The full-cycle system can be grass based (lower productivity) or grass based on pasture rotation and handling (higher productivity). In the second system, cattle are fed with corn silage during the winter. Calf rearing and steer termination are complementary systems; the former is grass based whereas the latter can be either grass based with pasture rotation or feedlots. Systems of production depend on a set of variables, such as the price of land (in regions with higher prices of land, more intensive systems tend to predominate), the availability of feed (feedlots are normally located in regions where feed is available), the level of professionalization of the rancher (grass based with pasture rotation systems requires use of improved pasture), and land suitable for agriculture (regions that are not well suited for agriculture normally have low-quality grass, and, therefore, cattle production tends to be based on extensive systems).

The regularization of land titles (property rights), transportation costs, regional land availability, environmental requirements, and illegal logging in the Amazon region are the four most important factors affecting the allocation and expansion of crops and cattle production in the region. Mato Grosso State is the most important tract of land in Brazil, but its competitiveness for crop production is lower than in Paraná and Santa Catarina due to the very high costs of transporting soybeans, corn, and cotton to consumer centers and ports. As long as transportation costs are not reduced by investing in railways and waterways, chicken and pork production and cattle feedlots will grow in Mato Grosso. Grain marketing in this region will be made more and more through meats.

Mato Grosso's production is also under pressure in the Amazon region. Although farmers are allowed to use 20 percent of the farm plot for agricultural uses in this biome, international consumers are concerned about importing soybeans produced on Amazonian land. Even if it is not the trigger for deforestation, soybeans from the Amazon are not welcome in developed markets such as the European Union.[1] For that reason, although there is an abundance of suitable land for agriculture in the Amazonian Mato Grosso, the environmental pressures associated with high transportation costs may reduce the attractiveness of investments in crop production.

Given that the Goiás and Mato Grosso do Sul savannas are more occupied in terms of land use, grain production will tend to grow vigorously over the next years in the Bahia, Maranhão, and Piauí savannas. That region has two advantages: transportation costs and distance to ports are lower than certain Mato Grosso regions; and it has vast amounts of land with low-productivity agriculture and cattle production that can be converted to high-productivity intensive agriculture.

Illegal logging and a lack of property rights in the Amazon biome determine the movement of the pastureland frontier. Once the timber is extracted, the remaining trees in the plot are set on fire and the wood is sold for the production of vegetable coal. The cleared land is then occupied with cattle. Although this is a simplified explanation of the factors contributing to the deforestation of the Amazon, it is clear that cattle are

---

1. Soybean companies and environmental nongovernmental organizations are dealing with this situation with the Soybean Moratorium Initiative. More information of the initiative can be found at www.greenpeace.org/brasil/amazonia/moratoria-da-soja (June 2008) and www.abiove.com.br/english/ss_moratoria_us.html (June 2008).

used to give value to lands with no alternative use. In the South, Southeast, and Center-West regions, cattle rearing is being intensified with more efficient systems of production. In these regions, cattle ranches are relinquishing land for grains and sugarcane production. Therefore, as a general trend, beef production will grow, but the cattle herd will not. In the Amazon region, we can expect to see cattle herds increasing, following the trends in deforestation.

It is important to note that the productivity of cattle raising is also increasing in the Amazon region. Many states of the region, such as Acre and Rondônia, are leading Brazil in terms of stock rate. Respectively, they have stock rates of 2.4 and 2.3 animals per hectare, which are above the 1.2 average for Brazil.[2] Both states have been showing a strong capacity to increase productivity using improved pastures and pasture rotation techniques. Cattle production in the Amazon regions has to be understood from both perspectives: as a specialized business and as a mechanism to increase the value of land and to promote land occupation.

The expansion of beef production in Brazil, therefore, will depend on three factors:

—*The expansion of grains and sugarcane.* Competition over pastureland leads cattle production to increase the stock rate (the number of animals per hectare). Higher stock rates lead to higher productivity, in terms of the slaughter rate (the number of slaughtered animals of the stock of animals per year) and the reproduction rate (the number of calves per cow). In the regions where the slaughter rate and reproduction rate are low, beef production will increase without cattle herd growth.

—*Market competition.* This will also determine the reallocation of cattle herds in the country. In regions where the opportunity costs for land are high and cattle production market returns are lower than grains and sugarcane, it is expected that cattle herds will move to other regions. This process is already taking place in São Paulo, Paraná, Rio Grande do Sul, and Mato Grosso do Sul. Similar trends are also expected to happen in Mato Grosso, Goiás, and Tocantins over the coming years.

—*The amount of land that will be available for cattle in the agricultural frontier.* The more land is available in the Amazon region, as a function of the deforestation process, the less significant will be the

---

2. These data are from the Instituto Brasileiro de Geografia e Estatística, "Pesquisa Pecuária Municipal," available at www.sidra.ibge.gov.br (June 2008).

intensification process in the nonfrontier regions. The availability of land resulting from deforestation is decreasing over time, because federal and state governments are improving the means to control illegal logging, but also because pressures from civil society and environmental nongovernmental organizations are becoming stronger. Therefore, we can expect that the productivity of cattle raising will certainly increase at a faster rate.

Brazilian Agriculture in the Context of World Agricultural Trade

The increased importance of Brazilian agribusiness, which has positioned Brazil as one of the world's most competitive producers of agricultural commodities, is the result of a number of factors. Today, Brazil is capable of expanding supply both horizontally and vertically, particularly in view of its previous investments in technology and research. Moreover, other factors were equally important in the current configuration of the country's agricultural sector, among them the reduction of government intervention through market deregulation, the opening of markets to foreign competition, and the stabilization of the economy.

Brazil is the fourth-largest agricultural exporter in the world, with $39.5 billion in exports in 2006, behind only the European Union–27, the United States, and Canada, as can be seen from figure 3-3.[3] This fact deserves attention not only because exports have been growing by 9.4 percent a year over the last ten years, but also because of the future role Brazil will play in supplying agricultural products to the entire world. The country ranks first and second place in world trade in many sectors, such as sugar, ethanol, chicken, beef, coffee, tobacco, orange juice, and soybeans, as can be seen in table 3-1. Table 3-1 also shows that Brazil has a diversified agricultural sector, comprising tropical products, temperate products, and meats. The country has soybeans, corn, and cotton varieties adapted for the savannas' weather conditions, which are distinct from conditions in the South. New varieties of sugarcane are also being developed for the savannas.

Brazil's overall market share in these products is also worth noting. The country's high market share demonstrates that export supply is

3. World Trade Organization, International Trade Statistics Database, http://stat.wto.org/Home/WSDBHome.aspx?Language=E (March 2008).

FIGURE 3-3. Performance of the Main Agricultural Exporters, 2006

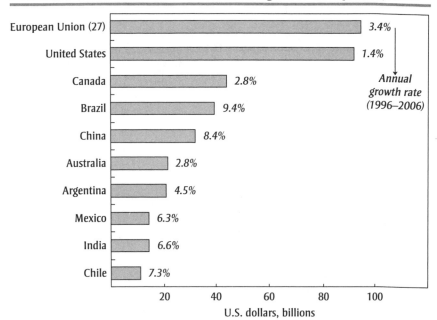

Source: World Trade Organization, *International Trade Statistics 2008.*

concentrated in a few suppliers, which is one of the reasons why today's agricultural prices are high. In a world of increasing demand, if suppliers are not capable of responding by expanding production at the same pace, prices tend to go up and become more volatile. Brazil's high market share helps to understand why Brazilian sectors in some industries are becoming internationalized. In the sugar, chicken, and beef sectors, Brazilian companies are investing overseas in manufacturing and distribution facilities. This is an indication that future growth is no longer associated only with increasing exports but also with vertical integration and value aggregation strategies.

Even more important than Brazil's past performance is its future performance in comparison with other countries. It is clear in figure 3-4 that Brazil presents the best performance in terms of the evolution of planted area and in the production of grains (cereals and oilseeds), in comparison with other large agricultural producers. Argentina's performance is also very good, but the lower relative availability of land in that country (in Argentina, the expansion of grain production is clearly competing with

TABLE 3-1. Brazilian Agrifood Exports, 2007

	Exports 2007 U.S. $ millions	Brazil / World (2005)		Annual growth rates (1996–2007)		
		Share	Ranking	Value	Volume	Price
Soy complex	11,386	38%	2	9%	10%	1%
Sugar/Ethanol	6,770	29%	1	13%	14%	0%
Chicken	4,626	29%	1	19%	19%	−1%
Beef	4,232	20%	1	28%	25%	−2%
Coffee	3,887	29%	1	6%	2%	−3%
Tobacco	2,262	23%	1	6%	3%	−3%
Orange juice	2,252	82%	1	5%	3%	−2%
Corn	1,943	2%	8	54%	42%	−8%
Pork	1,209	16%	4	27%	26%	−1%
Fruits	717	...	...	17%	19%	1%
Cotton	507	5%	4	91%	88%	−2%
Powder milk	225	1%	14	47%	44%	−2%
Others	7.061	...	...	...	...	...
Total 47,078		4%	3	8%	13%	−4%

Sources: Alice Database from Ministério do Desenvolvimento, Indústria e Comércio; FAOSTAT Database from Food and Agriculture Organization and Instituto de Estudos do Comércio e Negociações Internacionais.

cattle), coupled with discriminatory policies by the government against agriculture, undermine the country's potential.

In the case of meat, Brazilian production performance has a growth rate second only to China's. Contrary to Brazil, China is an importing country, and therefore its production growth is oriented toward the domestic market. Canadian meat production is also evolving well, but grain production, which is the raw material for animal feed, is not following the performance of meat production. In the sample of countries presented in figure 3-3, only Brazil combines strong growth of both grains and meats.

Cost comparisons between Brazil and the United States show that soybean and corn competitiveness are equivalent, as shown in table 3-2. As a general rule, operating costs per acre in the United States are lower than in Brazil, but Brazilian total costs are lower. Land and labor costs are lower in Brazil than in the United States, whereas costs per bushel are very similar in both countries, with a small advantage for Brazil in soybeans and for the United States in corn. The difference is explained by higher soybean productivity in Brazil and higher corn productivity in the United States.

FIGURE 3-4. Cereals, Oilseeds and Meat Production Index

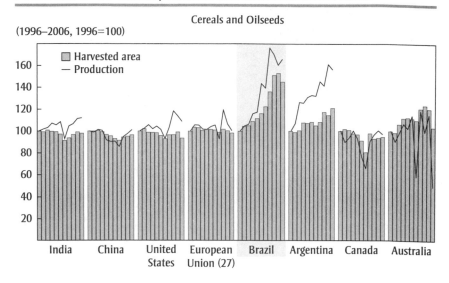

Cereals and Oilseeds
(1996–2006, 1996=100)

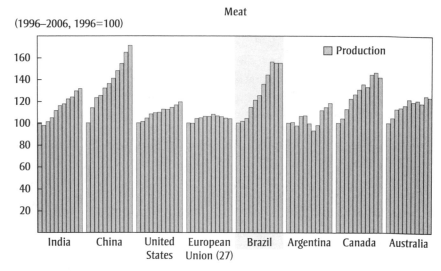

Meat
(1996–2006, 1996=100)

Source: Food and Agriculture Organization; Instituto de Estudos do Comércio e Negociações Internacionais.

TABLE 3-2. Comparison of Production Costs for Brazil and the United States, 2006

Soybeans

	United States				Brazil			
	Northern Great Plains		Heartland		Center-West		South	
	Per acre	Per bushel	Per acre	Per bushel	Per acre	Per bushel	Per acre	Per bushel
Operating costs	87.5	2.5	90.9	1.9	171.8	3.9	146.4	3.3
Total costs	214.6	6.1	280.7	5.7	268.0	6.0	242.7	5.4
Productivity (bushel/acre)	35.4		49.0		44.6		44.6	

Corn

	United States				Brazil			
	Northern Great Plains		Heartland		Center-West		South	
	Per acre	Per bushel	Per acre	Per bushel	Per acre	Per bushel	Per acre	Per bushel
Operating costs	170.5	1.4	194.7	1.3	180.5	1.9	177.3	1.9
Total costs	341.2	2.8	393.8	2.7	286.0	3.0	333.0	3.5
Productivity (bushel/acre)	122.0		147.0		95.6		95.6	

Sources: U.S. Department of Agriculture and Companhia Nacional de Abastecimento.
Note: The exchange rate used was R$2.20 to $1.00.

With respect to energy crops, the competitiveness of Brazilian sugar-cane as a raw material for ethanol is undeniable, not only because sugar-cane is, by its very nature, more efficient than corn in ethanol production per hectare and in energy balance, but also because the productivity of Brazilian sugarcane is higher than that of other large producers' sugar-cane (see figures 3-5 and 3-6). Countries like Australia, Colombia, and Guatemala have higher productivity of sugarcane per hectare—the first due to the use of irrigation and the second and third due to weather conditions—but they do not have land available to increase production, as Brazil does. Although sugarcane productivity is higher, the difference between Brazil and other countries in productivity in terms of energy content (or total recoverable sugar) in cane is much lower.

Weather and soil conditions in Brazil are extremely favorable for sug-arcane production. Taking into account only the Atlantic Forest and Savanna regions, Brazil has, hypothetically, 270 million hectares of land with very high, good, and medium conditions for sugarcane production. Including irrigation, this hypothetical area increases to 303 million hectares.[4] Although there are a few examples of sugarcane production in the Amazon biome, it is not expected that the crop will grow in that region. The most important limitation on an increase in sugarcane pro-duction in the Amazon biome is the fact that sugarcane needs a well-defined dry season to allow for the concentration of sugars in the stalk. In regions with high levels of precipitation year-round, sugarcane is able to grow but with very low sugar content in the stalk.

A comparison of ethanol production costs is made in figure 3-7, and it confirms the competitiveness of Brazilian production. It is important to note that costs have increased since 2005. According to market sources, current costs in Brazil are around 30 U.S. cents per liter. Costs are higher in Brazil mainly due to the real's overvaluation against the dollar and due to the higher prices of fertilizers. Costs are higher everywhere, because the factors that are pushing up costs are affecting all agricultural pro-ducers (oil prices and dollar devaluation). In the case of the United States, although the country is becoming more competitive as the dollar loses value, costly corn is making ethanol even more expensive.

---

4. State University of Campinas, "Estudo sobre as possibilidades e impactos da produção de grandes quantidades de etanol visando à substituição parcial de gasolina no mundo: Relatório final," December 2005.

FIGURE 3-5. **Comparison of Biofuel Indicators[a]**

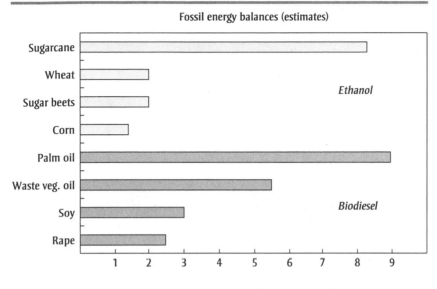

Fossil energy balances (estimates)

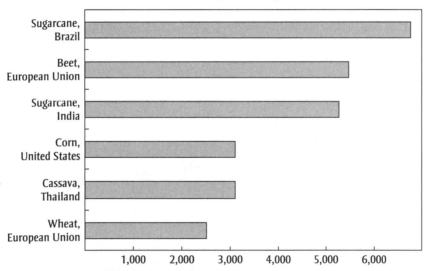

Ethanol yields (liters per hectare)

Source: Various sources, compiled by Worldwatch Institute (2008); International Energy Agency, 2005 data; National Metal and Materials Technology Center, Bangkok.

a. The data shown represent the amount of energy contained in the listed fuel (ethanol or biodiesel) per unit of fossil fuel input. That is, this is a ratio of two equal units of measure—of the amount of energy contained in the product to the amount of energy in the fossil fuel used in the production process.

FIGURE 3-6. Ethanol Feedstock, Average Yields and Production for Selected Countries, 2004–05

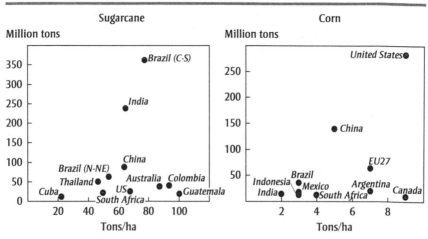

Source: Food and Agriculture Organization; Instituto Brasileiro de Geografia e Estatística.
Note: Brazil (C-S) = Center-South region; Brazil (N-NE) = North and Northeast regions.

FIGURE 3-7. Ethanol: Production Costs, 2005

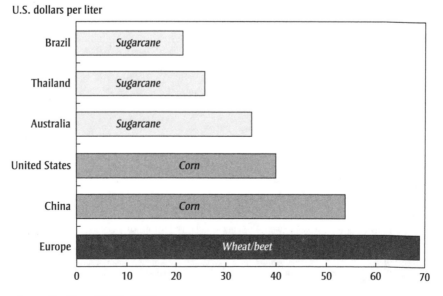

Source: Henniges and Zeddies (2005).

As a medium-term trend, Brazilian costs tend to decrease over time due to the increasing importance of electricity cogeneration in the industry income. As a simple figure, we would say that the income created from the sale of bagasse-derived electricity is equivalent to the income from distillers dried grains for corn ethanol producers. Sugarcane ethanol, for instance, has at least two competitive advantages over corn ethanol: there are zero energy costs in the industry, due to the cogeneration, and sugarcane ethanol is more efficient in terms of productivity (ethanol per hectare).

In the case of Brazil, the priority in the utilization of the sugarcane biomass is to improve the productivity of electricity generation. Using the biomass more efficiently is a strategy to reduce costs. The reason why power generation is so important for millers in Brazil is because electricity prices are going up there, reflecting the perspective of the short supply of hydropower electricity. Two actions have been adopted by the industry: (1) to invest in more efficient boilers (the majority of producers burn the bagasse in boilers to produce energy, which is then further used to run the plant;[5] and (2) to collect sugarcane straw and leaves that are left in the field to be burned together with the bagasse to increase the power generation (producers that are moving to mechanical harvesting and abandoning the sugarcane burning are taking the lead).

The increasing international insertion of Brazil as an exporter of agricultural commodities and, more recently, as a global player with companies that are becoming multinationals has implications for Brazilian trade policy. The dynamism of the agricultural sector does not seem to be accompanied by the country's trade policy. The Mercosur agreement no longer has any relevance for intra-agricultural trade. As a matter of fact, rice has been a contentious issue given that Brazil had been the principal destination of Uruguayan and Argentinean exports. This situation, however, has changed from 2007, when Brazil started to export rice. The Mercosur bloc was not able to prove that it is prepared to engage in bilateral agreements. The unsuccessful outcome of the negotiations between Mercosur and the European Union is just one example.

Without any relevant bilateral agreement on the agenda or in implementation by Brazil, the agricultural sector sees the Doha Round as the priority for reducing trade distortions and increasing trade liberalization. The elimination of export subsidies, reduction of trade-distorting domestic supports, and lowering of trade barriers are top priorities for

5. UNICA (2007).

Brazil. The reason why is easy to understand: Brazil will be one of the greatest beneficiaries of the liberalization of world agricultural markets.

Brazilian agriculture is also concerned about what one may call the "new generation of trade barriers." These are becoming increasingly complex with the incorporation of rules and regulations on market access issues. Some examples of pertinent issues are sustainability, traceability, labeling, and private standards. These new issues, which are not covered in the Doha Round's development agenda, are challenging Brazilian agricultural exporters.

Brazilian Agriculture: Key Figures

With 77 million hectares of planted area (permanent and annual crops), 172 million hectares of pastures, and 100 million hectares of forests (area of forests declared by landowners as part of a farm), Brazil is in a fortunate position in terms of land and water availability.[6] With few exceptions, grain, oilseed, and sugarcane production is rain fed. In the case of grains, only high-technology rice production—which is located in the South and makes up more than 60 percent of Brazilian production—is irrigated. Sugarcane production is also irrigated in the Northeast region, but the vast majority of production is in the South-Center. The Guarani aquifer, the most important source of underground water in South America, is better situated than the U.S. Ogallala aquifer.

Regardless of the feedlot termination system, which represents less than 5 percent of the beef cattle herd, cattle in Brazil are grass fed.[7] Even specialized milk production is a combination of stabled and grass-fed cows. Brazilian relief and soil structure is also very favorable for agriculture. Mechanized sugarcane harvesting, which requires a declivity below 13 percent, is becoming the practice on the more than 6 million hectares of sugarcane cropland. Grain and oilseed production is also totally mechanized.

6. These are figures from the preliminary results of the 2006 Agricultural Census. There is reason to believe that the land used for pastures will be corrected upward in the final census version. I estimate that pastureland will be, at a minimum, 185 million hectares. See Instituto Brasileiro de Geografia e Estatística, "Banco de Dados SIDRA," available at www.sidra.ibge.gov.br (June 2008); Instituto Brasileiro de Geografia e Estatística, "Censo Agropecuário 2006," available at www.sidra.ibge.gov.br (May 2008); and Instituto Brasileiro de Geografia e Estatística, "Pesquisa Agrícola Municipal," available at www.sidra.ibge.gov.br (June 2008).

7. These data are from the FNP, *Agrianual 2008*, www.fnp.com.br (June 2008).

Brazilian agriculture is not exempt from environmental responsibilities. The Brazilian Environmental Preservation Law requires farmers to keep a share of their plots of land in their natural state—20 percent in the Atlantic rainforest and *cerrado* regions, 35 percent in the *cerrado* of the legal Amazonian region, and 80 percent in the Amazon rainforest. Few countries have such stringent environmental regulations affecting the agricultural sector.

It is worth stressing the importance of investment in technology. Studies by the Instituto de Pesquisa Econômica Aplicada have shown that in Brazil, an increase of 1 percent in research expenditures induces an increase of 0.17 percent in total factor productivity—labor, capital, and land.[8] According to the same study, research expenditures play a greater role than rural credit in explaining the increased productivity levels of the three factors of production. Indeed, between 1990 and 1999, land productivity increased by 6.5 percent, while labor grew by 3.2 percent and capital by 3.1 percent. In the following period, 2000 to 2002, in view of the expansion of the agricultural frontier, land productivity fell while the productivity of labor and capital doubled. When comparing the importance of investment in research in Brazil during the 1990s internationally, it suffices to mention that total factor productivity increased 1.5 percent in the United States in that period, while in Brazil it soared to 4.9 percent; and in a more recent period, this indicator has reached a growth rate of 6 percent.[9]

As of 2000, sustained growth became a permanent fixture in the Brazilian agricultural sector. Grain production jumped from 80 million tons to 120 million tons.[10] The domestic market boomed, and China started to buy huge quantities of foodstuff and feedstuff. Chinese imports continue to make it the largest single importer of Brazilian soybeans, although the EU, as a bloc, continues to be Brazil's largest client.

Nevertheless, and in spite of its many positive circumstances, the period since 2000 has had its own downside, which has become increasingly apparent since 2005: (1) The national currency's appreciation against the dollar; (2) increased production costs derived from the higher cost of controlling diseases; (3) soaring transportation and logistics costs; and (4) new cases of foot-and-mouth disease in areas that had been previously

8. Gasques and others 2004.
9. Gasques and others 2004.
10. These data are from the Central de Informações Agropecuárias, www.conab.gov.br/conabweb/index.php?PAG=101 (June 2008).

FIGURE 3-8. Brazil's Production Performance for Cereals, Oilseeds, and Meat

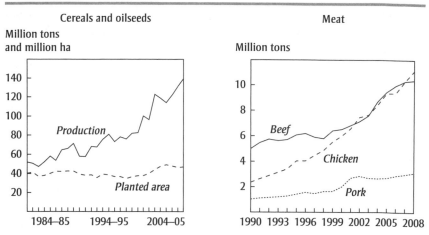

Cereals and oilseeds   Meat

Source: Companhia Nacional de Abastecimento; U.S. Department of Agriculture; Associação Brasileira das Indústrias Exportadoras de Carne; Associação Brasileira da Indústia Produtora e Exportadora de Carne Suína; Associação Brasileira dos Produtores e Exportadores de Frangos; Instituto de Estudos do Comércio e Negociações Internacionais.

certified by the World Organization for Animal Health (International Organization of Epizootics) as "free from foot-and-mouth disease with vaccination."

From the 1990s onward, Brazilian agricultural expansion was based on efficiency gains—productivity and scale—competitiveness, and strong demand. This scenario resulted from the elimination of subsidies and price controls, the opening of trade, a greater integration within Mercosur, and greater macroeconomic stabilization. Government action in that period was targeted at renegotiating rural debts and setting up income support programs through commercialization schemes. During this period, Brazil was able to consolidate its position as a global agricultural player and to further enhance this position with new opportunities for ethanol and bio-fuels. The increase in Brazilian agricultural exports can also be seen by going back to table 3-1.

With respect to the evolution of Brazilian agriculture, some observations should be made based on the analysis of figures 3-8, 3-9, and 3-10:

—Since the 1980s, and until the beginning of the 2000s, grain production in Brazil was based only on productivity gains, as can be seen in figure 3-8. Planted areas stayed stable at 40 million hectares for almost twenty

FIGURE 3-9. Brazil's Sugarcane, Sugar, and Ethanol Production

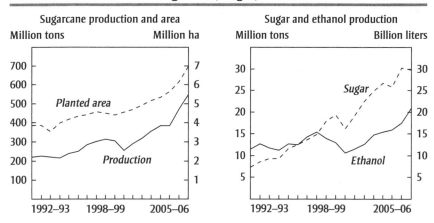

Source: Companhia Nacional de Abastecimento; Instituto Brasileiro de Geografia e Estatística; União da Indústria de Cana-de-açúcar; Instituto de Estudos do Comércio e Negociações Internacionais.

FIGURE 3-10. Productivity Index for Brazil

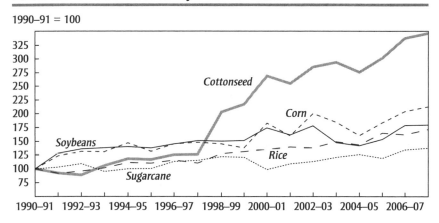

Source: Companhia Nacional de Abastecimento; Instituto Brasileiro de Geografia e Estatística; União da Indústria de Cana-de-açúcar; Instituto de Estudos do Comércio e Negociações Internacionais.

years. From the 2001–2 crop season onward, the planted areas started to grow, peaking in 2004–5, at 49 million hectares. Estimates for the 2007–8 crop season indicates 46.7 million hectares of grain planted area.

—Although planted areas were reduced from 2004–5 to 2007–8, production growth has not been interrupted. In the same period, production grew from 114.7 to 139.3 million tons (figure 3-8).

—Meat production responded to the increasing availability of feed, increasing even faster than grain production, as shown in figure 3-8. Chicken, beef, and pork productions are growing, and their growth has been accelerating since 2000.

—Sugarcane is not lagging behind grain production, as figure 3-9 demonstrates. Production and planted areas are also increasing. In contrast to grains, a sector in which Brazil still has productivity below its potential, sugarcane has already reached the crop's top yield. The way to increase productivity in sugarcane is not to produce more cane per hectare but to produce more energy per hectare. Second-generation ethanol and genetically modified sugarcane varieties will contribute to increasing energy content productivity.

—Sugar production shows a constant pattern of increases, but its growth rate will slow down in the coming years. Ethanol production, conversely, is growing faster than sugar production (figure 3-9).

—In terms of land use, sugarcane is much smaller than grains; 6.9 million hectares are devoted to sugarcane and 46.7 to grains.

—In terms of productivity gains, there is a generalized upward trend (figure 3-10).

Brazilian Agriculture's Potential and Challenges

With the high agricultural commodity prices and the increasing demand for biofuels, Brazilian agriculture is faced with two new challenges: What is the real agricultural production potential of the country? Will production potential be undermined by the concern about carbon emissions and the continuing crisis of Amazon deforestation? The answers to both questions are related to these topics: improvements in infrastructure, the development of agriculture-based new technologies, and land use and land availability in Brazil.

It is commonly said in Brazil that the fast evolution of the agribusiness sector has not been accompanied by public sector efforts related to infrastructure, regulations, institutions, and policies. Although Brazil is the fourth-largest world agricultural exporter, its transportation structure is not comparable with that of the United States. Though grain production in the U.S. Midwest is fully transported to the world market via the Mississippi River, Brazilian soybean production from the Center-West Savanna is still traveling on truck-wagons, at very high cost.[11] In a large country like Brazil, it is clear that the transportation matrix is badly distributed, given that road transportation represents 61 percent of the total freight in Brazil, whereas railroads and waterways account only for 23 and 13.6 percent, respectively.[12] Brazil's bad experience recently with the SISBOV, the system created to attend to the traceability requirements of the European Union for bovine animals, is also incontestable evidence that several areas of the public sector are lagging behind the agricultural sector.

The lack of investment in transportation logistics in Brazil is not only the result of capital constraints from the federal government but is also due to an unclear regulatory and institutional framework. Foreign observers, after hearing about all the infrastructure problems in Brazil, often ask why the private sector is not making the investments that are needed. Actually, many investments have been made by the private sector, especially since the government privatized part of the railway system. However, these new investments are not taking place in the Center-West region, where the lack of transportation infrastructure is a significant bottleneck for the development of grain production. Although there are two railways under expansion (Ferrovia Norte-Sul, connecting the state of Goiás to the state of Maranhão; and Ferronorte, connecting Rondônia and Mato Grosso to the Southeast region), it will be a while before both railways begin to operate. A third railway that would be very important, but is not even in the government's plans, is the connection between Cuiaba (Mato Grosso State) and Santarém (Pará State). Rather than paving the BR-163 Road, which is a controversial investment that is opposed by environmental groups, the construction of the railway would be a more feasible alternative.

The Programa de Aceleração do Crescimento (PAC) is planning the construction of 2,500 kilometers of railroads, for which less than 10 percent is coming from public investment. Although PAC is an indication that the federal government is concerned about the transportation bottleneck,

---

11. Damico and Nassar (2007, chap. II-4).
12. These data are from the Agência Nacional dos Transportes Terrestres, www.antt.gov.br (April 2008).

the program by itself will not solve the problems of the high logistical costs of Center-West agriculture.

Although the energy sector is also a bottleneck for Brazil in keeping fast rates of growth, it is also a window of opportunity for the ethanol sector, as was mentioned above. The main challenge for the ethanol sector in becoming a stronger supplier of power generation is the regulatory framework. In the current situation, ethanol producers are making the investments to connect the mills to the grid, but they claim that the price paid by the government in the energy auctions is not enough to cover these investments. A second challenge for the sector is to reduce the transportation costs of ethanol by investing in pipelines. According to market sources, there are three planned projects for ethanol pipelines in Brazil. The main challenge is not constructing a pipeline but making it financially viable. The key variable is the international market for ethanol. Pipelines have been planned to carry ethanol from the producing regions to ports for exports. To make the projects viable, exports must be higher than the volumes currently shipped out.

With regard to the unclear legal framework and the uncertainties associated with a long-term strategy that is not well defined, the best example is the permission to plant genetically modified organisms (GMOs). Companies interested in investing in research or producers interested in growing GMO crops are having a hard time in Brazil. Although the legal and institutional framework, defined by the Brazilian Biosafety Commission, has become clearer in recent years, uncertainties associated with obtaining authorization are high and the process is very long. The authorizations for the corn and soybean GMO varieties that are commercially available in Brazil took more than one year to be issued. GMOs are important not only for grains but also for sugarcane. The productivity of sugarcane has been growing at slow rates in recent years, and GMO sugarcane will speed up the yield growth.

In a world with a short supply of agricultural commodities and high prices for food and fuel, Brazil's potential is undeniable. Once the challenges are overcome, certainly the country will establish itself as an agricultural superpower. Though it is going to take a while to overcome all the problems that are undermining the agricultural sector's potential, the country meets all the necessary conditions for increasing food and biofuel production to meet future demand.

To increase agricultural production, Brazilian agriculture will have to deal with increasing pressure for sustainable production. In the past, the country's authorities used to say that it has around 100 million hectares of land available to be converted to agriculture. Although a precise number is not yet available, experts are now asserting that the amount of land available is much lower. Many reasons explain this perception, but it is important to note that the last few governments have created many indigenous reserves and conservation parks, reducing the amount of agricultural land, and that the legal reserve and the permanent preservation area, although acceptable from an environmental perspective, have also withdrawn land from production.

My preliminary estimates indicate that there are around 15 to 18 million hectares of land available in the Savanna biome that can be converted to agriculture (agriculture and cattle production now account for 60 million hectares). The incorporation of new land for agricultural production that is under natural landscapes has implications for sustainability, especially with regard to changes in land uses. As one of the few countries with excess land available for agriculture, and under pressure to pursue more sustainable agriculture, Brazil must take the lead in the debate on sustainability and land use changes.

Conclusion

If Brazil wants to be an agricultural and agroenergy superpower, it must be able to improve its institutions. It is a giant producer without a clear policy of insurance against unfavorable weather conditions and diseases. The agricultural sector has been dragging a debt-rescheduling program since 1995, and 2008 is the beginning of the third phase of the program; after two renegotiations, all new and old agricultural debts have been renegotiated and rescheduled for a longer payment period. Without judging if the rescheduling program is needed or not, the reality is that Brazilian agriculture has been facing strong cycles of expansion and retraction. The country has no policies to mitigate this instability, and therefore reactive policies must be implemented to manage the retraction phases.

Very little has been done in policies evaluation and long-term planning. The year 2007 was the first time in the last twenty years that the government released a study with long-term projections of supply of and demand for agricultural products.[13] Brazilian institutions still believe that

13. See Ministério da Agricultura, Pecuária e Abastecimento, "Projeções do Agronegócio," www.agricultura.gov.br/portal/page?_pageid=33,1299841&_dad=portal&_schema=PORTAL (June 2008).

commercial and family farmers are different groups and that agrarian reform is the solution for the country's unemployment problem. Although they are part of the same sector, the Ministry of Agriculture and the Ministry of Rural Development divide responsibilities, compete with each other for scarce resources, and put their constituencies on different sides.

Brazilian institutions find it very difficult to learn from past experiences. Federal and state governments were not able to create a credible, trustable traceability system after five years of operations. Outdated policies associated with anticompetitiveness and anti–market integration are still in place in Brazil or are still discussed within its public institutions. Some institutions in the federal government and legislative bodies do not hide their admiration for discriminatory policies against the agricultural sector, as Argentina has been doing.

Brazil's institutions and policies are, no doubt, the main bottleneck for the country in reaching the status of agricultural and agroenergy superpower. Although institutions change over time, this is a slow process. Yet the world is in a hurry, and the Brazilian agricultural sector must find ways to remove the obstacles that are undermining its capacity to respond to the world's desire for more food and biofuels.

References

Damico, F. S., and A. M. Nassar. 2007. "The Expansion of Agriculture in Brazil and Its Agricultural Policies." In *U.S. Agricultural Policy and the 2007 Farm Bill: Promoting the Economic Resilience and Conserving the Ecological Integrity of American Farmlands,* ed. Kaush Arha, Tim Josling, Daniel A. Sumner, and Barton H. Thompson. Stanford, Calif.: Woods Institute for the Environment.

Gasques, J. G., E. T. Bastos, M. P. R. Bachi, and J. C. P. R. Conceição. 2004. *Condicionantes da Produtividade Agropecuária Brasileira.* Textos para Discussão 1017. Brasília: Instituto de Pesquisa Econômica Aplicada.

Henniges, O., and J. Zeddies. 2005. "Economics of Bioethanol in the Asia-Pacific: Australia-Thailand-China." In *F. O. Licht's World Ethanol and Biofuels Report.* Tunbridge Wells, U.K.: F. O. Licht.

UNICA (União da Indústria de Cana-de-açúcar, Sugarcane Industry Union). 2007. "Ethanol, Production and Use in Brazil" (in Portuguese). São Paulo.

Worldwatch Institute. 2008. *Biofuels for Transport: Global Potential and Implications for Sustainable Agriculture and Energy in the 21st Century.* Washington. www.worldwatch.org/taxonomy/term/445.

CHAPTER FOUR

Brazil: The Challenges in Becoming an Agricultural Superpower

GERALDO BARROS

The impressive performance of Brazil's agribusiness (agriculture and agroindustry) during the twentieth century resulted from an ambitious national economic development strategy, conceived in the early 1930s, whose implementation took six or seven decades. This project promoting industrialization and urbanization demanded overcoming restrictions on the food supply and on foreign reserves, with a key role played by agriculture. The project also entailed territorial occupation based on infrastructure expansion, research and technology, and human capital investments (including substantial immigration), plus a set of sectoral policies that were intermittently but consistently carried out throughout several different political regimes and government administrations.

The major test of the success of this strategy took place in the mid-1980s, when government support had to be severely curtailed and the economy was opened to foreign competition. Despite that initiative, the value of agricultural production kept its post–World War II pace, doubling about every twenty years. Nonetheless, today agriculture accounts for only 5 percent of Brazil's GDP (one-fifth of its 1947 share), meaning that relative agricultural income has been shrinking. In the meantime, after the war, an increasingly sophisticated agribusiness sector developed, which currently represents some 30 percent of Brazil's GDP, with strong participation from multinational companies.

The social returns on investments in agriculture began to be perceptible starting in the mid-1970s, when real food prices began a continuous thirty-year fall of almost 80 percent at the retail level, and of 60 percent at the farm gate. It is remarkable that the agroindustry and retail margins have also declined at a time of strong market concentration and fierce competition. It took such a deep fall in food prices to make a historical improvement in Brazil's income distribution possible during the 1990s. On the external front, the agribusiness sector provided $10 billion to $15 billion in annual trade surpluses that were strategically important to securing the country's solvency in the turbulent 1990s. These surpluses helped keep Brazil from being forced into a period of growth slower than the then-present 2.5 percent annual rate.

How could farmers bear such a reduction in prices and still expand production? The major explanation lies in farming's total factor productivity, which doubled in the thirty years to 2005 and explains around 70 percent of the growth in farm output. In addition, artificially high labor costs, low interest rates, and growing land supplies all favored mechanization and large-scale farming. That meant that many farmers who could not keep pace with new technology had to abandon agriculture. Huge rural labor migrations and worrying environmental depletion were the main costs of the agribusiness success.

The structure of this chapter is as follows. The next section starts with a discussion of the Vargas project of industrialization that started in the 1930s; the third section introduces the role of agriculture in the Vargas project; the fourth section presents data on agribusiness's performance over the last decades; the fifth section discusses the growth challenges faced by the country, in light of economic integration, science and technology, human capital, environmental concerns, and investments; and the sixth and seventh sections present future perspectives for Brazil, taking into account the world scenario, as well as offering concluding remarks.

The Vargas Project of Industrialization

In 1994, President-elect Fernando Henrique Cardoso announced the end of the Getulio Vargas era in his farewell speech in the Senate. However, the death of the Vargas project of industrialization had been announced at least three times before: first in 1945, when the dictator Vargas was overthrown; again in 1954, when Vargas died; and last in 1964, when a military coup overthrew the constitutionally elected president João Goulart—a Vargas man.[1]

Since the beginning of the twentieth century, Brazil has firmly wished to move from an agrarian to an urban, industrialized society, implementing a national project aimed at that goal. At the time the Vargas project began, Brazil—like the rest of the world—was in the midst of the international financial crisis of 1929. Agriculture was the foundation upon which Brazil's economic system functioned up to the beginning of the twentieth century. Seventy percent of its foreign currency revenues came from coffee exports, which dried up when the external funds that helped to support the huge stocks of that commodity evaporated. No wonder a xenophobic mood focusing on import substitution tended to predominate in Brazil's political circles. In fact, a political revolution in 1930, led by Vargas, substituted an ancient agrarian-dominated political system with an industry-oriented one. The authoritarian Vargas government would last for fifteen years, during which many of the modern institutions (e.g., labor unions, social security, public funding for state companies) were created.

Investment capital was raised through public funds (fiscal and inflationary taxation) and foreign investment, which was heavily applied to transportation infrastructure. Human capital was available because of the in-migration of European and Asian people to southern and southeastern Brazil, which began in earnest following the ban on Africa-based slavery at the end of the nineteenth century. Nascent industry was assured a captive domestic market thanks to a package of protectionist tools, particularly an overvalued currency, import tariffs, and quotas. The strategy was to produce domestically those goods that had previously been imported, beginning with consumer goods, and followed by intermediary and capital goods. After Vargas, the strategy was maintained and even intensified by President Juscelino Kubitscheck (who brought the automobile industry to Brazil in 1956). In 1960, the national capital was moved from Rio de Janeiro to Brasília in the Center-West region to (among other reasons) stimulate the occupation of frontier areas and the development of agriculture in the savanna lands.

It is clear that during the Vargas period and beyond, Brazil showed outstanding performance as far as growth is concerned. From 1945 to 1980,

---

1. The source for this is "A Era Vargas: 1° tempo—dos anos 20 a 1945," Centro de Pesquisa e Documentação de História Contemporânea do Brasil, Fundação Getulio Vargas, www.cpdoc.fgv.br/nav_historia/htm/ev_saibamais.htm (July 2008).

FIGURE 4-1. Brazil's Inflation Rate and GDP Growth, 1945–2005

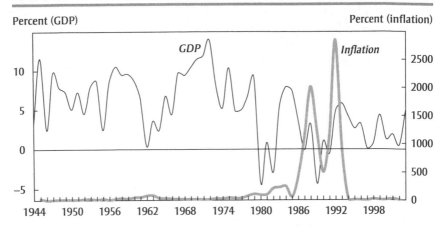

Sources: Data from Fundação Getulio Vargas, 2008; DADOS, Fundação Getulio Vargas (www.fgvdados.fgv.br/index.asp [May 2008]); data from Instituto Brasileiro de Geografia e Estatística, 2008.

the growth rate of its GDP was 7.5 percent per year, on average. Since then, that rate has fallen to a meager 2.5 percent. During this time, inflation surged and was only brought under control after a half dozen different economic plans were implemented. As can be seen in figure 4-1, in 1994, the Real Plan was able to bring inflation down; however, economic growth remained low. Brazil is still looking for a new project capable of bringing growth back, but only of that special type that keeps inflation down.

The Role of Agriculture

How did agriculture enter the Vargas development project? Agriculture was given a supporting role during Brazil's industrialization. As urbanization accelerated, the poor nutritional status of the population became a strong political issue. Josué de Castro, a medical doctor and geographer, led important studies concerning hunger in Brazil in the 1930s. In 1946, he published the book *Geografia da Fome* (The Geography of Hunger), which blamed hunger on two basic causes: a lack of production and a lack of income (purchasing power)—in other words, the forces of supply and demand. Vargas's reaction was twofold. The first, shortsighted but long lasting, focused on market intervention to make food accessible to the poor; a sequence of public institutions was created to control food production and prices, which were restructured in the 1960s and all but extinct by the 1990s. The second front was to open the "Marcha para o Oeste" (Westward March) designed to occupy the savanna areas of Brazil's frontier lands.

In addition to providing food, agriculture was supposed to continue generating foreign currency to fund the imports demanded by industrialization. Coffee exports, on one hand, provided much-needed foreign currency, but when revenues from coffee exports rose, the exchange rate appreciated, making life harder on the nascent industrial sector. To help the industrialization process, right in the beginning of his mandate (1930), Vargas instituted a multiple exchange rate regime. In practice, this was nothing more than a coffee export tax (*confisco*), through which exporters were taxed with an overvalued exchange rate. This heavy reliance on coffee exports served as a reminder that the country was in need of other exportable commodities.

The occupation of the so-called *cerrado* (savannas) was not a peaceful process; it was unfair and violent, with heavy costs for native populations and migrants from the Northeast. At some point, the occupation process got out of the control of the authorities, and as a result one of their stated objectives—establishing a reasonably equitable agrarian system—was not attained. Landownership concentration also resulted from a combination of technological and production factor prices; cheap land, low subsidized capital, and artificially high labor costs all led to large-scale farming.

Academic discussion tended to oppose, on the one side, the land reform solution—how to deal with the so-called agrarian problem (i.e., landownership concentration and too many landless people)—and, on the other, the farm modernization strategy—to solve the "traditional-agriculture problem," allegedly "efficient but poor." Although most analysts would say that the first option was rejected, the truth is that Brazil has since been involved with an intense and never-ending land reform and colonization program. The fact is that the political options fell upon a mixed strategy. A complex of agricultural modernization policies was put in place in the 1960s encompassing price supports and subsidized credit. Growth in the agrobusiness sector also had environmental costs, such as soil degradation, water misuse and contamination, air pollution, fauna and flora sacrifices, and deforestation. Only recently have concrete steps been taken to address these problems, and only more recently have the very first concrete results become visible.

By the mid-1980s, the federal government's financing capacity collapsed, so that even the agricultural credit and commercialization instruments had to be severely curtailed. The private sector took most regional development into its own hands, including the investment of hundreds of billions of dollars in farm capital, warehouses, and processing facilities. Fortunately, new technology was kept flowing in, and the agribusiness sector was able to employ it efficiently by exporting part of the increased output, thereby avoiding a weak domestic market that would have inhibited the growth of strong agroenergy, fiber, grain, and meat agribusinesses. Plenty of foreign reserves were generated to help Brazil keep its financial solvency during the severe financial crises of the 1990s.

The Performance of Agribusiness

Six decades after the initial official programs, and twenty years after the direct policy (credit, price support, and storage) instruments began to be curtailed, a long-term evaluation of Brazil's agribusiness experience is finally possible. Figures 4-2 and 4-3 show that farm prices—for both crops and livestock—fell about 60 percent in real terms from 1975 to 2006, while output more than tripled. These results are measurable by total increase in farms' productivity, which doubled over the same time period.

FIGURE 4-2. Farm Crops and Livestock Real Price Indexes, 1975–2006

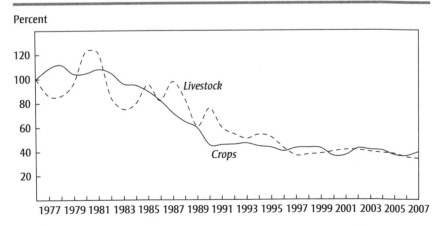

Sources: Data from Fundação Getulio Vargas, 2008; DADOS, Fundação Getulio Vargas (www.fgvdados.fgv.br/index.asp [May 2008]), with author's elaborations.

FIGURE 4-3. Farm Output, Inputs, and Total Factor Productivity, 1975–2006

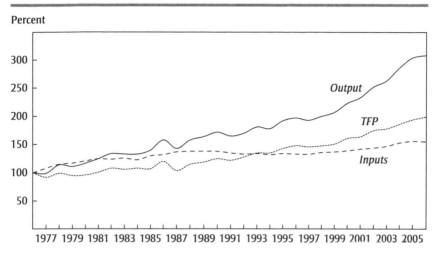

Sources: Gasques, Bastos, and Bacchi (2006).

Productivity growth permitted Brazil's agribusiness to expand impressively in international markets. As indicated in figure 4-4, the agribusiness sector contributed between $10 billion and $15 billion in trade surpluses per year during the 1990s, when the economy as a whole suffered chronic deficits. Thanks to the performance of the agribusiness sector, Brazil avoided insolvency until 1998, when the substantial capital flight demanded deep changes in the exchange rate regime (fluctuation and devaluation).

Also thanks to this productivity effect, since the mid-1990s Brazil has been able to reduce income concentration. As can be seen in figure 4-5, in the 1990s, minimum wage increases took place at a time of decreasing real food prices, thus leading to higher real wages; poor families were able to spend more, not only on food but on other consumer goods as well. That made possible, for instance, the redistribution of income through several sequential government programs, which culminated with the so-called Bolsa Família (Family Grant), which transferred cash to more than 11 million poor families. Figure 4-6 shows that the Gini index of income concentration has been decreasing since 2001, so that for the first time such money transfers have turned into real purchasing power increases for poor families. Increased consumption, which began with food, soon extended to other items, such as housing improvements, home stoves, refrigerators, and

FIGURE 4-4. Brazil's Total and Agribusiness Trade Surpluses, 1994–2007

U.S. dollars (millions)

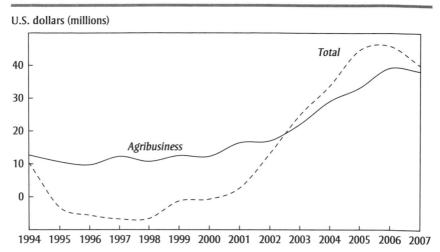

Sources: Ministério do Desenvolvimento, Indústria e Comércio Exterior, 2008 data; Centro de Estudos Avançados em Economia Aplicada, Universidade de São Paulo, 2008 data.

FIGURE 4-5. Nominal Minimum Wage Changes, Real Food Costs to Consumers, and Real Minimum Wages, 1975–2007

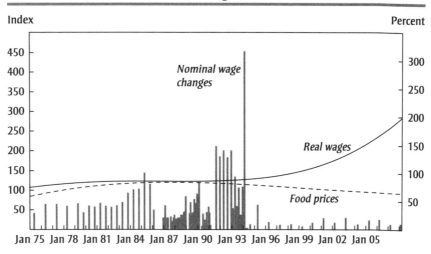

Sources: Fundação Instituto de Pesquisas Econômicas; "Salário Mínimo" (www.portalbrasil.net/salariominimo.htm [July 2008]), with elaborations by the author.

FIGURE 4-6. Gini Income Distribution Coefficient, Brazil, 1977–2005

Gini index coefficient

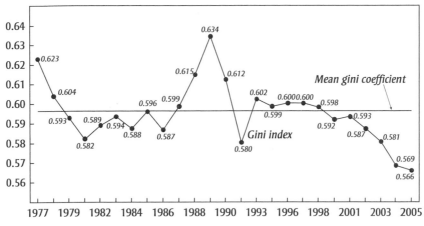

Sources: Paes de Barros (2006).

furniture. Recent data (shown in figure 4-7) indicate that the poorest 10 percent of Brazil's population had an 8 percent annual growth in per capita income from 2001 to 2005, while average (for the whole population) annual growth was 0.9 percent.

Brazil has relied, since the 1990s, on significant trade surpluses on agricultural products and on income redistribution measures that are no longer simple short-term solutions but are able to offer long-term benefits to the poor. Today Brazil appears to be on the verge of a long cycle of more domestically oriented economic growth; the country can count on a strong and competitive agribusiness sector as one of its leading sectors.

The story of this historical success would not be entirely told if the economic and social conditions of farmers—the main actors of the story—were not examined. Two points deserve to be stressed. The first is the extreme insecurity under which farmers conduct their business. The second is the sacrifices many farmers had to make during the changing process.

Among the many different ways of analyzing farmers' economic progress, it suffices to examine the evolution of the value of their main asset, land, as can be seen in figure 4-8. Over the last seventeen years, the real price of land at first decreased 50 percent compared with 1989 and then increased back 70 percent by 2007. Because land alone stands for 70 percent or more

FIGURE 4-7. Per Capita Income Growth According to the Poorest Accumulated Classes, Brazil, 2001–05

Percent growth

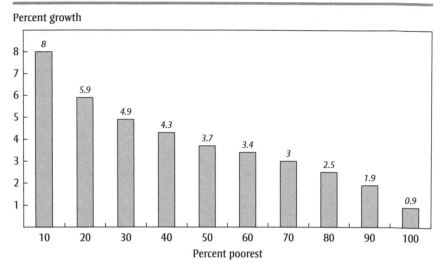

Percent poorest

Sources: Paes de Barros (2006).

FIGURE 4-8. Yields versus Price, Income, and Use of Land, 1989–2007

Percent

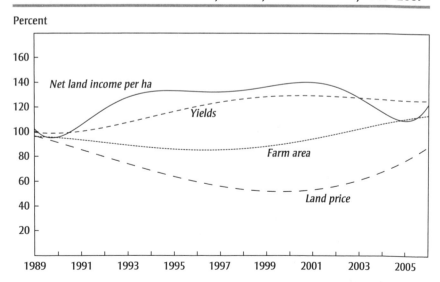

Sources: Data from Fundação Getulio Vargas, 2008; data from Instituto Brasilero de Geografia e Estatística, 2008; author's calculations.

of a farm's total assets, one concludes that farming is very risky in Brazil. Why did this rapid fluctuation in land value happen? In figure 4-8, one sees that the average return per hectare jumped more than 35 percent in the four years from 1989 to 1993 and fell 40 percent from 2002 to 2006.[2] That fluctuation is attributable not to prices but to increasing yields and the fall in chemical input prices, stimulating output expansion, which up to 1999 demanded no additional expansion of land. Indeed, as yields increased, the "effective" (yield-corrected) land supply was growing and its price was falling. When yields stopped increasing, more land was needed, but the "effective" supply of land stagnated and prices began to rise again. Farm asset value varies widely and helps explain why farmers have had hard times meeting financial obligations, despite yield gains and growing output.

The second point to complete the farmers' story may seem paradoxical: Though large numbers of farmers left the agricultural business, the government insisted on settling more people in the farming sector. Brazil's share of the rural population fell from 64 percent of the total in 1950 to 44 percent in 1970 and to 19 percent in 2000.[3] That has meant that since World War II, every decade has seen about 10 to 15 million people in Brazil leave rural areas and move to urban centers.[4] In 1998, the mean per capita income in rural areas was still only half that in urban areas.[5] Despite this income discrepancy, the official agrarian reform programs have been settling (or promising to settle) around 70,000 to 80,000 families per year over the last ten years.[6] In addition, the land reform program is proceeding without a visible conclusion and under practically continuous conflicts over landownership, thus deepening the environment of uncertainty in farming activities.

Brazil's Growth Challenges

Sustainable economic growth must be a consequence of productivity increases, as pointed out by Helpman and Krugman.[7] Brazil and the Latin American countries in general have lagged behind as far as economic

---

2. Land net return is an index dividing terms of trade (the price received by farmers over the price paid, multiplied by yield per hectare).
3. Censos Demográficos, 1950, 1970, 2000, Instituto Brasileiro de Geografia e Estatística.
4. Camarano and Abramovay (1999).
5. Kassouf (2005).
6. Gomes (2006).
7. Helpman and Krugman (1993).

development is concerned in the four decades since World War II.[8] Labor productivity in these countries has remained at about 30 percent of labor productivity in the United States during this period, according to Van Ark and McGuckin.[9] One hypothesis is that closing their economies to trade— a strategy to reach industrialization—was one major factor explaining the observed stagnation in productivity in the Latin American countries. Other factors were underinvestments in human capital, in science and technology, and in infrastructure.

Pires and Garcia show a decomposition of total factor productivity among countries in terms of technical progress, technical efficiency, scale effect, and allocative efficiency.[10] Brazil's total factor productivity was hit by allocative factors but not by a lack of technical progress, as were other Latin American countries. Allocative efficiency has been directly associated with the degrees of openness and inversely associated with the importance of the public sector in the economy. Brazil has a 40 percent share of its GDP spent by the government and still is a rather closed economy, with a ratio of imports plus exports to GDP of 21.5 percent.[11]

As can be seen from figure 4-9, growth policies can be targeted at the production function (science and technology and economic integration) and/or at the factors of production. For labor, human capital policies can be designed; for capital, economic (capital market) integration and savings policies can be developed; and for natural resources, environment policies can be devised.

Economic Integration

Brazil has partially opened its economy. As imports were taxed, by the mid-1980s, the ratio of imports to GDP had fallen to only 6.6 percent (during which time the mean tariff rate was 45 percent). In 1996, this mean rate had fallen to 13.6 percent (while the highest one was still kept at 35 percent). From 2000 to 2006, the imports ratio was close to 9 percent.[12]

---

8. Summers and Heston (1991).
9. Van Ark and McGuckin (1999).
10. Pires and Garcia (2004).
11. These data are from the Penn World Table 6.1 (http://datacentre2.chass.utoronto. ca/pwt61 [July 2008]) and the Ministério do Desenvolvimento, Indústria e Comércio Exterior (www.desenvolvimento.gov.br).
12. The external trade data are from the Ministério do Desenvolvimento, Indústria e Comércio Exterior (www.desenvolvimento.gov.br/sitio/interna/interna.php?area=5&menu= 1486&refr=608 [May 2008]).

FIGURE 4-9. Policies for Enhancing the Factors of Production and the Production Function

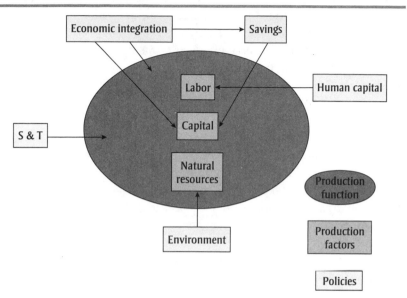

Sources: Author's conception.

For Brazilian agribusiness, the remaining barriers to industrial trade and services have been obstacles at the trade negotiation tables.

The negotiations over the Free Trade Area of the Americas (FTAA) failed to progress because either Brazil's demands for market access or the United States' requirements for intellectual property rights, trade in services, and government procurement and investment protection were not met at the depth desired by each party.[13] Anderson, Martin, and Valenzuela argue that market access is more important than domestic subsidies because of the amounts of support involved and because of its higher potential for distortion.[14] Not only should tariffs be reduced, but technical and sanitary barriers should be properly reconsidered and better disciplined.

As a matter of fact, Brazil has concentrated its trade efforts on Mercosur, within which the performance of each member has been dictated mostly by macroeconomic factors, particularly the cyclical exchange rate and GDP growth. This trade agreement, as should be expected in cases

13. U.S. Government Accountability Office (2005).
14. Anderson, Martin, and Valenzuela (2006).

involving similarly endowed countries, has led predominantly to intra-industry trade, although Brazil was favored on manufactured goods and Argentina on agricultural commodities, fuel, and other nontraditional goods, thanks to gains of scale. Thanks to growth in productivity, Brazil has been able to expand as a global trader faster than Argentina, and it has also done better in trading within Mercosur.

Although Brazil's trade strategy has been condemned for lacking focus, Harrison and colleagues argued that Brazil can benefit from the strategy of simultaneously negotiating trade agreements such as the FTAA and the Mercosur–European Union agreement while supporting the Doha Round liberalization agenda.[15] Because Brazil's tariff structure favors capital-intensive industry, liberalization would strengthen labor-intensive sectors, thus increasing the demand for, and wages of, unskilled labor. Therefore, Brazil could gain if both the United States and the EU offered tariff-free access to agricultural markets in exchange for liberalized industrial markets. If the most protected markets of each were not opened, the FTAA would be preferred as a trade partner (because of the other FTAA partners). The FTAA and EU-Mercosur are trade-creating agreements for the countries involved, but multilateral negotiations with only 50 percent tariff liberalization would bring gains to the world as a whole four times greater than just the FTAA or Mercosur-EU agreements.[16]

Anderson, Martin, and Mensbrughhe showed that full liberalization in the Doha Round would lead to a 0.67 percent gain in the world's real income ($287 billion a year), 70 percent of which would accrue to high-income countries.[17] Interestingly enough, two-thirds of the gains would be derived just from agricultural liberalization. Half the benefits would come from South-South liberalizations because of the observed recent increase in trade within emerging market countries at slightly higher than average tariffs. Ninety-three percent of the gains from liberalization would come from tariff removal versus export and domestic subsidies.

Most analyses of economic integration—static as they are from a technological perspective, and subject to several methodological constraints—point to very small gains for liberalizing countries. The results for the United States prompted Krugman to conclude that "yet there is a dirty little secret in international trade. The measurable costs of protectionist policies—the reductions in real income that can be attributed to tariffs and

15. Harrison and others (2003).
16. Harrison and others (2003).
17. Anderson, Martin, and Mensbrughhe (2005).

import quotas—are not all that large. . . . For example, most estimates of the cost of protection in the United States put it well under 1 percent of GDP."[18] Similar results were found by Ferreira Filho and Horridge,[19] who showed that Brazil's GDP would rise by 0.31 percent under a full worldwide liberalization scenario.[20]

Most Latin American countries implemented the import-substitution strategy, thus ignoring factors such as the minimum size of plants, increasing returns to scale, and indivisibilities in the production process, which explain the observed relationship between exports and economic growth. In addition to these sources of inefficiency, Bacha and Bonelli estimate that the relative price of investment goods in Brazil doubled between the 1950s and the 1980s—most of which is attributable to an import-substitution development strategy that protected the domestic industrial sector. In other words, closing the economy brings about underinvestment in capital goods because it makes these goods more expensive.[21]

Increasing returns to scale is a key factor in explaining major puzzles of recent integration experiences, such as the predominance of trade between similar countries (in terms of factor endowments) and the strength of intraindustry trade. Scale economies may arise from the expansion of exports and imports of intermediate goods (or parts). Consumers benefit from cheaper imports of large-scale production, both nationally and abroad.

The role of trade as an important factor affecting the availability and distribution of knowledge is discussed by Grossman and Helpman, who show that trade can distribute knowledge directly and indirectly (through the transference of intermediate goods, which embody research and development, R&D).[22] In their analysis, Targetti and Forti use the Kaldorian "cumulative causation" and the "technology gap" approaches to describe how a country lagging behind the technological frontier can benefit from technology spillover, if it has the potential to do so.[23] Baumol and Wolf identify some convergence clubs (groups within which convergence takes

18. Krugman (1995, 31).

19. Ferreira Filho and Horridge (2006).

20. This study, for instance, uses a computable general equilibrium static interregional model of Brazil based on the ORANIG model of Australia (Horridge 2000), with the technological input/output data given for 1996. Other relevant assumptions are that national levels of labor employment and capital are fixed, that land is fixed in each sector, and that the trade balance is a fixed share of GDP.

21. Bacha and Bonelli (2004).

22. Grossman and Helpman (1995).

23. Targetti and Forti (1997).

place) as being industrialized countries, centrally planned economies, and middle-income economies.[24] Convergence was not observed in the low-income-country group.

In the case of agriculture, it has long been shown that trade is a crucial condition for sustainable technical innovation and growth. Cochrane argued that because of what he called the "technological treadmill," innovation is profitable for the first adopters, but the incentives soon wane.[25] As more and more farmers adopt the new technology, prices decline and profits are reduced because of the inelasticity of domestic demand. Economic integration, however, has the fortunate effect of expanding the market and increasing demand elasticity, thereby taking farmers—at least partially—off the treadmill trap, making it possible for scale economies to be exploited for the benefit of producers and consumers alike. The growing efficiency of modern agriculture in Brazil could be attributed in great part to the international integration the country engaged in during the 1990s.

It is worth mentioning that protectionism, by depressing agricultural prices, leads to the gradual loss of that providential role attributed to external markets. It is as if the security net is gradually moved down, so that farmers will need to reduce costs as protectionism advances. This may be related to continuous increases in farm size—to explore economies of scale—with probable negative social effects, or even to the need to look for new, cheaper lands, with probable negative environmental effects.

Science and Technology

Brazil has a structured science and technology (S&T) system that is increasingly integrating governmental and private business sectors. For Krieger, however, Brazil still lags behind other emerging market countries like China, India, and South Korea, with a total expenditure in S&T representing 4 percent of GDP.[26] Two aspects of the evidence for Brazil's performance in S&T, presented by Krieger, are that its scientific production is increasing around 8 percent a year; and doctor graduation rates are increasing 14 percent a year, with a current flow of around 7,500 doctors a year (but the number of researchers graduating annually, 126,000, is still very low, at less than 0.5 per 1,000 people). The major challenge is to expand S&T production and capacity building while at the same time

24. Baumol and Wolf (1988).
25. Cochrane (1953).
26. Krieger (2005).

accelerating the transfer of technology to the business sector. Private and foreign companies have a small but increasing contribution; American companies spend 0.5 percent of sales revenue on R&D in Brazil,[27] which ranks fifth in terms of countries receiving American R&D money over the next three years—behind China, the United States, India, the United Kingdom, and Germany—according to the Economist Intelligence Unit.[28]

Investments in agricultural technology have not been disregarded. In the early 1970s, Embrapa—Empresa Brasileira de Pesquisa Agropecuária, the Brazilian Agricultural Research Company—was created by the military regime as the core agricultural institution and the coordinator of a structured agricultural research system. The funding of the system has not been maintained at desirable trends, but minimum levels have been assured, so the flow and standard of research have been preserved by different administrations since the system was implemented. Recent figures presented by Alves and Oliveira indicate that Embrapa's yearly budget is close to $300 million, or 0.6 percent of agricultural GDP.[29] It is important to emphasize that Embrapa is the leading public institution generating technology for the agricultural sector; however, most universities also conduct research and develop agricultural technology. For instance, the University of São Paulo's share of overall scientific publications is 24 percent of Brazil's total, according to Leta and Pereira.[30]

One major challenge faced by the agricultural research system was to make the occupation of the *cerrado* viable, particularly with the adaptation of soybeans, but also with beef, pork, poultry, milk, and vegetables.[31] Among the notable techniques produced or adapted by Embrapa was the no-till system, which simplified operations and reduced the costs associated with the diversification, rotation, and succession of (multiple) crops. Additionally, Embrapa devised cattle-crop association and its optimistic perspectives regarding the *cerrado*'s sustainability. *Cerrado* soils have favorable physical conditions but are highly acid and low in phosphorus, calcium, magnesium, and potassium. New techniques were also developed to detect and correct the acidity and fertility problems adapted to different production systems. Agricultural gypsum—a by-product of phosphatic

27. Hiratuca (2005).

28. Economist Intelligence Unit, *Scattering the Seeds of Invention: The Globalisation of Research and Development,* www.eiu.com/GlobalisationOfRandD (July 2008).

29. Alves and Oliveira (2005).

30. Leta and Pereira (2005).

31. See www.cpac.embrapa.be/tecnologias for information on Embrapa's contribution to *cerrado* agriculture.

fertilizers—is used to correct calcium deficiencies in the deepest soil layers, reducing aluminum saturation and providing for the soil's sulfur needs.

Maize (corn), soybeans, and coffee are the crops that benefited the most from the use of gypsum. Soybeans, beans, and peas, meanwhile, have expressly benefited from the nitrogen-fixing bacteria inoculation practice. Besides saving large amounts of urea, inoculation also provides environmental gains because it avoids water source contamination.

Embrapa's current priorities encompass (1) precision in agriculture; (2) environmental services in agriculture; (3) health-promoting (functional) foods; (4) aquaculture technologies; (5) biosafety for genetically modified crops; (6) high-quality beef; (7) organic agriculture; (8) the conservation of national genetic resources; (9) tools for plant sanitary protection; (10) forests for energy production; (11) the environmental, social, and economic effects of the beef industry; (12) nanotechnology; (13) the sustainable production of sugarcane for energy purposes; (14) genomics technologies for the development of water-use-efficient plants; (15) technologies for biodiesel production; (16) genomics for the advancement of animal breeding and production; and (17) climatic risks zoning for small farming agriculture, bioenergy, and pastures.[32]

Still regarding the technological side of the agribusiness in Brazil, the case of ethanol is worth mentioning. Interestingly enough, a significant part of research efforts have been made by the private sector. In the agricultural field, technology results have been observed for new varieties, thanks to the Genoma Project, biological pest control, and soil management. At the industry level, improvements have been made in fermentation, through DNA analysis; in energy cogeneration, through the use of bagasse; and in the destination of residuals for soil fertilization. Over the last thirty years, the national average yield has increased around 30 percent; in the Center-West (*cerrado*) region, the increase has reached as much as 75 percent. During the same period, the cane sugar content was raised from 9.5 to 14 percent, and the cane sugar extraction rate grew from 88 to 98 percent. As a result, ethanol production per hectare has grown 56 percent since 1980. Currently, besides continuous efforts in these areas leading ultimately to higher productivity and lower costs, frontier research is being carried out on such matters as the production of ethanol from the cellulose of, for instance, cane bagasse.[33]

32. Lima (2007).
33. Bon and Ferrara (2007).

Human Capital

With respect to human capital, Brazil has positive educational results to show for the last thirty years, but there remains a long way to go.[34] For instance, illiteracy (for those age fifteen years or older) was reduced from 33.6 percent of the population in 1970 to 11.1 percent in 2005, which is still a large rate and only lower than Bolivia's in Latin America. In addition, in 2006, 22 percent of the Brazilian population age fifteen years and older was functionally illiterate (with illiteracy defined as having fewer than four years of schooling).

The rural population over 15 years old has a mean 4.3 years of schooling, while the urban mean is 7.7 years, so farm activity is mostly hit by the lack of formal education. The rural sector has an illiteracy rate of 30 percent for people over 15 years of age, and functional rural illiteracy is 44 percent. Only 27 percent of rural youth 15 to 17 years of age are attending school. Conversely, World bank data show that most of the progress in basic schooling took place within the poor part of the population; from 1992 to 2001, enrollment in primary education increased from 97 to 99 percent for the richest 20 percent of the population and from 75 to 94 percent for the poorest 20 percent.[35] The same data indicate that because illiteracy ranges from 2.7 percent for the population age 15 to 19 years to 30 percent for those between 65 and 69 years, the dynamics of the population indicate a strong trend toward reducing the problem over time.

Brazil has a long way to go to improve the educational level of the majority of its population not only for competitive edge but also as the essential way to seriously and permanently fight poverty. Quantitative results at the elementary level from efforts of the 1990s and 2000s are good; however, overall student proficiency is very low. Human capital investments take a long time to mature, so the sooner they begin, the better for the country.

The Environment

Brazil's environmental problems must be examined within a social and economic cost/benefit analysis, provided that costs are duly internalized to firms. For instance, it is usual to observe that expanding agriculture anchored in green revolution practices and stimulated by fiscal incentives

34. The data for education are from Instituto Brasileiro de Geografia e Estatística, *Síntese dos Indicadores Sociais*, 2007.

35. See http://siteresources.worldbank.org/EDUCATION/Resources/Education-Notes/EdNotesBrazil.pdf (July 2008).

and cheap credit provokes a series of negative environmental effects. But most of these effects are reported to have no grounding in hard evidence. It is an unproven matter that deforestation is caused by crop or beef cattle activities. There is, conversely, evidence that both may be carried out in economically sound ways.[36] Beef cattle ranching has been shown to be a profitable activity, apart from deforestation revenues. Yet it is true that beef cattle are associated with the emission of methane, for it corresponds to 60 percent of carbon dioxide emissions from the farm sector.[37]

Technology alone does not help much. About 17 percent of the open area in the *cerrado,* for instance, is currently abandoned;[38] land (a major asset for many farmers) is used up to exhaustion, which does not take a long time, despite the availability of technology to circumvent degradation through no-tillage systems and pasture-crop integration or rotation. Going after new land is still privately cheaper than preserving the older, more degraded land currently in use.

Among the environmental risks, one can mention illegal deforestation, intentional and unintentional burning, river sedimentary deposits, provoking water scarcity and a reduction of water quality, and air pollution (nitrogen oxide, carbon monoxide, hydrocarbons, and particulate matter, in addition to other highly toxic substances). Again, there is not enough hard evidence on the extent and effects of these events.

As has been the case for food security (and quality), the world market—and ultimately consumers in general—will learn to play a fundamental role in the interaction between the production of food and natural resources that is required for that production. This will come through price incentives as far as consumers are willing to pay a higher price for the output of environmentally friendly production processes. Also, punishment through tariff and nontariff barriers may induce farmers and agroindustries toward desirable production processes. Then, technology will be able to play a key role in enhancing production efficiency, intensifying land use, and improving grass and feed quality.

Environmentally recommended practices, when privately profitable, have been adopted at fast rates by farmers. Soybeans and corn in successive (multiple) croppings have permitted the use of the same land tract twice.

36. Margulis (2003).
37. Ministério de Ciência e Tecnologia, "Influência do Manejo da Produção Animal sobre a Emissão de Metano em Bovinos de Corte, Brasília-DF," www.mct.gov.br/upd_blob/0012/12921.pdf. (July 2008).
38. This finding was reported by Shiki (1997).

That is a highly intensive use of land with possible harmful environmental consequences, but high-intensity land use is also a substitute for deforestation. On the positive side, the accelerated expansion of the no-tillage system is a strong example of an environmentally friendly practice.

Savings and Investment

The Brazilian farm sector has shown enough capacity to grow expansively over the past thirty years, while prices decreased thanks to substantial productivity growth. A significant part of the investment necessary to achieve this was facilitated by cheap government credit from the 1960s to the 1980s.[39] Cheap credit also played the role of partially offsetting policy discrimination against agriculture through, for instance, overvalued currency and price controls.[40]

During the sequence of inflation-fighting economic reforms in the 1980s—marked by deep market intervention and price controls—credit supply was curtailed, and the outstanding debt was adjusted at monetary correction rates. These rates were considered too high by many farmers, who since that time have been involved in cyclically renegotiating repayments. Additionally, as the flow of official credit was curtailed and/or access to it was denied because of overdue debt, farmers adopted the only strategy left: investing when savings or suppliers' credit was available, that is, during periods of high profitability. This creates a cyclical pattern that leads to the majority of farmers investing simultaneously when the prices of capital goods and inputs are high. As a result, during years of low profitability, farmers are unable to fully repay their debts. This, then, leads to a new wave of renegotiations. Usually, as a palliative measure, the government agrees to facilitate current repayments related to both official and suppliers' debt. Of course, within a couple of years, the problem will show up again. The current 2008 agricultural debt is estimated to be $50 billion,[41] a value very close to half the farm sector's GDP.[42]

The agricultural debt ended up being transferred to the National Treasury as part of the program that restructured the banking system in the 1990s, known as PROER. So the definitive solution to the problem will come if and when the government takes time to formulate a long-term

---

39. Rahal estimates that the highest rural credit subsidy was reached in 1979–80 and that since 1991 its average has been near zero (Rahal 2003).

40. Barros (1992).

41. This is according to Central Bank data, elaborated by Rezende and Kreter (2007).

42. For Brazilian agribusiness GDP estimates, see www.cepea.esalq.usp.br/pib/ (July 2008).

repayment scheme compatible with the real cash or savings flow from farming. The next step will then be to reestablish normal loans to farmers and, more important, to promote the creation of a savings and loans system, by and for farmers, to avoid the present vicious cyclical investment pattern.

As farmers reenter the financial market, it is essential to make sure that the nonfarm investments needed for agribusiness's expected growth are forthcoming. On the one hand, there are those general, nonspecific infrastructure investments like energy and transportation facilities, which are general preconditions for private investment. On the other hand, there are those agribusiness-specific investments, like farm and nonfarm processing and storage facilities. Barros and colleagues estimate that capital/output ratio in Brazil's agribusiness sector is close to 2.6,[43] a number very close to the national (whole economy) average.[44] According to Barros and colleagues, the agribusiness sector has been investing around 9 percent of its GDP. In general, land stands for half the typical supply chain's capital stock. Considering a constant capital/output ratio of 2.6, then, if the agribusiness output grows at 3.1 percent a year to meet a 2.6 percent yearly growth in domestic demand and 9.4 percent growth in exports, capital stock will have to expand 30 percent in the coming ten years. The amount of new capital is $38 billion (9 percent of the agribusiness GDP) on average per year for the next ten years.[45]

Farmers will be responsible for 9 percent ($3.4 billion a year) of the overall amount—excluding land—of farm investment per year. Official rural investment credit,[46] which has been financing just half that amount, has to be expanded proportionally (i.e., doubled). That points to the importance of solving the agricultural debt problem to open the possibility of farm investment intensification.

The two major challenges to agribusiness expansion are related to capital restriction. First, there is the issue of available land, which is widely estimated to be around 90 million hectares, not counting current native forestland.[47] Second, there is the additional capital needed to put that land

43. Barros and others (2007). See also Feu (2001) and Silva Filho (2001).
44. Feu (2001).
45. See the appendix for detailed calculations of investment needs.
46. Most of the credit for farm investment proceeds from nonmonetary sources, mainly from the Worker Support Fund (known as the FAT). Working capital credit, conversely, is funded by demand deposits; see Rezende and Kreter (2007).
47. Sampaio (2004).

to work, which this naive estimate ignores. Many analysts are optimistic about the potential for alternative ways of increasing production based on the lowest possible land use expansion, by increasing the adoption of multiple croppings in the same land tract, together with crop-cattle-forest cycles in degraded pasturelands.

Among the major obstacles facing the expanding agribusiness sector in Brazil, it is important to remember the amount of available capital investment and the lack of previous infrastructure investments in transportation and energy, which also inhibit private investments in agribusiness-related capital. With respect to this latter aspect, there have been efforts to set up a regulatory system to attract private partners to invest in infrastructure. There is currently an investment plan, the Programa de Aceleração do Crescimento (PAC, Growth Accelerating Plan) to be executed with $35 billion in public and private capital from 2007 to 2010, which includes reforming and building new roads (45,000 kilometers), railways (2,300 kilometers), water transportation systems (sixty-seven ports, one canal lock) and airports (twenty). The feasibility of the plan's implementation is still in question, due to the generally observed bureaucratic inefficiency of the public sector.

Because PAC involves both public and private funds, its execution is subject to many jurisdictional questions, as demonstrated by similar previous initiatives, which faced many controversies related to illegalities and corruption. In addition, the major political party supporting the federal government is somewhat ideologically divided insofar as private capital entering public investment is concerned. Finally, many PAC initiatives will take place in native forest and Indian regions and must be approved by their national government institutions (IBAMA and FUNAI, respectively).

Still another investment-inhibiting factor is the lack of economic security related to institutional uncertainty, which affects landownership. For example, several farms and technology companies have been subject to unaccountable property-invasion events, most of which have gone unpunished. Despite the growing number of people settled in rural areas, the completion of the land reform process is still beyond the horizon.

The World Scenario

The new century brought a worrying scenario with respect to the performance of Brazil's agribusiness sector on the global stage. Brazil will play an important role as the world finds its way out of a dangerous crisis, in which the prices of agricultural commodities and production inputs have exhibited an unprecedented upward trend. The World Bank predicts that to meet growth in demand, cereal supply would have to increase by 50 percent and that of meat by 85 percent from 2000 to 2030. The problem emerges if these changes occur too rapidly. According to the International Monetary Fund,[48] commodity dollar prices for food increased by 57.3 percent and those for beverages by 47.6 percent from 2005 to March 2008. Starting in 2002, the rise was 65.5 and 58.5 percent, respectively, during the period in which the Food and Agriculture Policy Research Institute (FAPRI) estimates that fertilizer prices more than doubled.[49] This evidence suggests that both output and input prices have moved markedly upward, leading to the conclusion that output may increase in response to an expansion of demand and to the rise in commodity prices—but so too will costs.

The price surge is the result of a worldwide expressive growth in emerging market and other developing countries where the income elasticity of demand for food—cereals and meat—is higher than the world average. At the same time, there is an expectation that world agribusiness will help produce energy from new, cleaner sources like ethanol and biodiesel. The fast-growing demand in the natural resources sector—for things such as food, fibers, clean energy, oil, and minerals—means that at least in the short and medium terms such commodities will see their relative prices rise when compared with industrial goods and services.

Unfortunately, an offsetting new wave of productivity increases is not in sight. In the United States, for example, agricultural multifactor productivity, which grew at an annual rate of 2.01 percent from 1950 to 1989, has been increasing at half that rate since 1990.[50] In Brazil, the last couple of years have seen yields practically stagnate. Nevertheless, the productivity gap between developed and African countries is widening rather than closing.[51] At this time, therefore, it is hard to see that prices will end up declining in response to increasing output.

48. International Monetary Fund, "Indices of Primary Commodity Prices," www.imf.org/external/np/res/commod/table1b.pdf (July 2008).

49. See www.fapri.missouri.edu/outreach/publications/2008/FAPRI_MU_Report_03_08.pdf (July 2008).

50. See www.farmfoundation.org/projects/documents/2007PardeyAlstonHandout.pdf (July 2008).

51. World Bank (2007).

At the current rate of world economic growth—particularly in China, African oil-producing countries, and other emerging economies—it is expected that demand for agribusiness commodities, such as grains, meat, fibers and energy, will continue to grow firmly, and that the prices of both output and inputs will remain higher than their 2005–6 level. Agribusiness price increases, coupled with high and increasing oil prices, indicate that accelerated economic growth will continue in tandem with inflation. If inflation is to be restrained, economic growth must be sacrificed. Ironically, the need to grow at a slower rate comes when a leading developed country looks for measures to avoid a recession, and when emerging market countries appear to have, at least in part, decoupled themselves from the United States. It is probable at this point to say that while economic independence is not very useful, a reduction in growth is inevitable.

If the demand for agribusiness output is not contained, the world risks not only high inflation but also a renewed attack on natural resources. Brazil in particular already faces the challenge of finding ways to effectively preserve its natural resources, especially its rainforest, but also its soil and water supply. A surge in agribusiness production in response to skyrocketing prices and costs will not help to circumvent these difficulties.

Conclusion

What challenges does Brazil face in becoming an agricultural superpower? First, it is necessary to restore the investment pattern in infrastructure, science and technology, and human capital of previous decades—with the difference that this time the role of the private sector will necessarily be much more important, financially speaking. The role of the public sector will be very important as well because, to begin with, the private sector depends on proper regulation and institutions developed by the public sector. Fortunately, the federal government has recently launched several infrastructure projects to be developed by the private sector, and important progress has been made in the use of biotechnology in agriculture. However, many farmers still feel insecure with respect to land-related ownership conflicts involving so-called social movements. In addition, the public sector is supposed to efficiently deal with new twenty-first-century issues such as environmental matters (i.e., air and water pollution, deforestation), sanitary and food quality/security conditions, and trade negotiations related to various types of protectionism. Meanwhile, the public sector has yet to deal with centuries-old issues such as rural labor relations, agrarian reform, and indigenous peoples' issues.

Within ten years, according to FAPRI, Brazil's agribusiness is expected to reach a share of 50 percent of world coarse grain production, one-third of soybean production, and one-fourth of sugar production; 50 percent of the exports of broiler fowl and beef will come from Brazil.[52] At the same time, Brazil will double its ethanol production. Along with the investments in basic infrastructure (transportation, energy, etc.), substantial direct agribusiness (farm and agroindustry) investment will be needed, much of which is expected to come from the nonpublic sector, as well as from abroad.

Appendix

According to the Centro de Estudos Avançados em Economia Aplicada of the University of São Paulo,[53] the constant-price output (Y) of Brazilian agribusiness had an average of R\$523 billion from 1994 to 2007; domestic demand has taken 92 percent of that output and external demand, thus, 8 percent. Agribusiness output has been increasing at the average annual rate of 2.5 percent over that period, while agribusiness net exports' yearly rate of growth is estimated to be 9.4 percent.

The following identity may be considered:

$$DOM_t + EXT_t = Y_t, \tag{1}$$

where DOM is domestic demand, EXT is net exports, and Y is the constant-price GDP. The growth rates for these variables are related as follows:

$$\alpha r_{DOM} + (1 - \alpha) r_{EXT} = r_Y, \tag{2}$$

where r is the rate of growth and α is the share of domestic demand (DOM) in GDP. If, as FAPRI assumes, $r_{YB} = 4$ percent—that is, Brazil's real GDP increases at 4 percent per year—then, because domestic agribusiness demand elasticity $\eta_{DOM,Y} = 0.65$,

$$r_{DOM} = \eta_{DOM,Y} r_Y = 0.65(0.04) = 0.026, \text{or } 2.6 \text{ percent.} \tag{3}$$

---

52. FAPRI (2008).
53. See the center's website, http://cepea.esalq.usp.br.

Then, using equation 2, the agribusiness constant-price GDP has to grow at the annual rate of

$$\hat{r}_Y = (0.92)(0.026) + (0.08)(0.094) = 0.031, \text{ or } 3.1 \text{ percent.} \quad (4)$$

This is very close to its recent historical rate. Because agribusiness output was evaluated at R\$628 billion (\$393 billion) in 2007, it is predicted to be R\$812 billion by 2017. Considering a capital/output ratio of 2.6, annual investment will present an average of R\$61.5 billion (\$38.5 billion), so that agribusiness capital stock will increase from R\$1.6 trillion (\$1 trillion) to R\$2.3 trillion.

References

Alves, E., and A. J. Oliveira. 2005. "O Orçamento da Embrapa." *Revista de Política Agrícola* 14, no. 4: 73–85.

Anderson, K., W. Martin, and D. Mensbrughhe. 2005. "Doha Polices: Where Are the Pay-Offs?" In *Trade, Doha, and Development: Window into the Issues,* ed. Richard Newfarmer. Washington: World Bank (http://web.worldbank.org/ WBSITE/EXTERNAL/TOPICS/TRADE/0,,contentMDK:20732399~pagePK: 148956~piPK:216618~theSitePK:239071,00.html [July 2008]).

Anderson, K., W. Martin, E. Valenzuela. 2006. "The Relative Importance of Global Agricultural Subsidies and Market Access." World Bank Research Working Paper 3900. Washington: World Bank.

Bacha, E. L., and R. Bonelli. 2004. *Accounting for Brazil's Growth Experience. 1940–2002.* Texto para Discussão 1018. Brasília: Instituto de Pesquisa Econômica Aplicada.

Barros, G. S. C. 1992. "Effects of International Shocks and Domestic Macroeconomic Policies upon Brazilian Agriculture." *Agricultural Economics* 7, no. 1: 317–29.

Barros, G. S. C., et al. 2007. "Análise dos Impactos Econômicos e Sociais do Programa do Biodiesel no Brasil." Centro de Estudos Avançados em Economia Aplicada, Universidade de São Paulo; Escola Superior de Agricultura Luiz de Queiroz, Universidade de São Paulo; and World Bank.

Baumol, W., and E. Wolf. 1988. "Productivity Growth, Convergence and Welfare: Reply." *American Economic Review* 78: 1155–59.

Bon, E. P. S., and M. A. Ferrara. 2007. "Bioethanol Production via Enzymatic Hydrolisis of Cellulosic Biomass." Food and Agriculture Organization (www.fao.org/bitech/seminaroct2007.htm [May 2008]).

Camarano, A. A., and R. Abramovay. 1999. *Êxodo Rural, Envelhecimento e Masculinização no Brasil: Panorama dos últimos 50 anos.* Texto para Discussão 621. Brasília: Instituto de Pesquisa Econômica Aplicada (www.econ. fea.usp.br/abramovay/artigos_cientificos/1999/Exodo_rural.pdf [May 2008]).

Cochrane, W. W. 1953. "A Theoretical Scaffolding for Considering Governmental Pricing Policy in Agriculture." *Journal of Farm Economics* 35, no. 1: 1–14.

FAPRI (Food and Agricultural Policy Research Institute). 2008. *FAPRI 2008 World Agricultural Outlook.* Ames: Center for Agricultural and Rural Development, Iowa State University.

Ferreira Filho, J. B. S., and M. Horridge. 2006. "Economic Integration, Poverty and Regional Inequality in Brazil." *Revista Brasileira de Economia* 60, no. 4: 363–87.

Feu, A. 2001. "Evolução da Razão Capital/Produto no Brasil e nos Países da OCDE." *Economia & Energia* 28 (http://ecen.com/eee28/ocde.htm [July 2008]).

Gasques, J. G., E. T. Bastos, and M. R. P. Bacchi. 2006. "Produtividade e Fontes de Crescimento da Agricultura Brasileira." Instituto de Pesquisa Econômica Aplicada, Brasília.

Gomes, M. 2006. "Reforma agrária: ONG diz que reforma agrária de Lula é 'residual.'" *Reporter Brasil* (www.reporterbrasil.org.br/exibe.php?id=510 [July 2008]).

Grossman, G., and E. Helpman. 1995. "The Politics of Free Trade Agreements." *American Economic Review* 85, no. 4: 667–90.

Harrison, G. W., J. F. Rutherford, D. G. Tarr, and A. Gurgel. 2003. "Regional, Multilateral, and Unilateral Trade Policies of Mercosur for Growth and Poverty Reduction in Brazil." Development Research Group, World Bank, Washington.

Helpman, E., and P. R. Krugman. 1993. *Market Structure and Foreign Trade.* MIT Press.

Hiratuca, C. 2005. "Internacionalização de atividades de presquisa e desenvolvimento das empresas transnacionais: análise da inserção das filiais brasileiras." *São Paulo em Perspectiva* 19, no. 1: 105–14.

Horridge, J. M. 2000. "ORANIG: A General Equilibrium Model of the Australian Economy." Working Paper OP-93. Melbourne: Centre of Policy Studies, Monash University.

Kassouf, A. L. 2005. "Acesso aos serviços de saúde nas áreas urbanas e rurais do Brasil." *RER* 43, no. 1 (www.scielo.br/pdf/resr/v43n1/25834.pdf [May 2008]).

Krieger, E. M. 2005. "Perspectivas da Ciência e Tecnologia no Brasil." Slide presentation, www.iea.usp.br/iea/online/midiateca/perspectivas.ct.krieger.ppt (June 2005).

Krugman, P. 1995. "Dutch Tulips and Emerging Markets: Another Bubble Bursts." *Foreign Affairs,* July–August, 28–44.

Leta, J. C. R. J., and H. Pereira. 2005. "The Life Sciences: The Relative Contribution of the University of São Paulo to the Highest Impact Factor Journals and to Those with the Largest Number of Articles, 1980 to 1999." *Scientometrics* 63, no. 3: 599–616.

Lima, S. M. V. 2007. "R&D Priorities and Portfolio." Research and Development Department, Empresa Brasileira de Pesquisa Agropecuária, www.anodaciencia.com.br/multimidia/multimidia_20080318163314.pdf (May 2008).

Margulis, S. 2003. "Causes of Deforestation of the Brazilian Amazon" (www.diesel-ebooks.com/cgi-bin/item/5551407977/Causes-of-Deforestation-of-the-Brazilian-Amazon-eBook.html [May 2003]).

Paes de Barros, R. 2006. "A Recente Queda na Desigualdade no Brasil: Magnitude, determinantes e conseqüências." Slide presentation, Instituto de Pesquisa Econômica Aplicada, Brasília.

Pires, J. O., and F. Garcia. 2004. *Productivity of Nations, a Stochastic Frontier Approach to TFP Decomposition.* Texto para Discussão 143. São Paulo: Escola de Economia de São Paulo, Fundação Getulio Vargas.

Rahal, C. S. 2003. "A Evolução dos Preços da Terra no Estado de São Paulo: Análise de seus determinantes." Dissertação de mestrado, Escola Superior de Agricultura Luiz de Queiroz, Universidade de São Paulo.

Rezende, G. C., and A. C. Kreter. 2007. "A Recorrência de Crises de Endividamento Agrícola no Brasil e a Conseqüente Necessidade de reforma da Política de Crédito Agrícola." *Revista de Política Agrícola* 16, no. 4: 4–20.

Sampaio, E. 2004. "O Estado da Arte da Agricultura Brasileira. Ministério da Agricultura, Pecuária e Abastecimento," www.bndes.gov.br/conhecimento/seminario/EduardoSampaio.pdf (May 2004).

Shiki, S. 1997. "Sistema Agroalimentar nos cerrados brasileiros: caminhando para o caos?" In *Agricultura, meio ambiente e sustentabilidade do cerrado brasileiro,* ed. S. Shiki, J. G. Silva, and A. C. Ortega. Uberlândia: Universidade Federal de Uberlândia.

Silva Filho, T. N. T. 2001. *Estimando o Produto Potencial Brasileiro: Uma abordagem de função de produção.* Texto para Discussão 17. Brasília: Banco Central do Brasil.

Summers, R., and A. Heston. 1991. "The Penn World Trade Table (Mark 5): An Expanded Set of International Comparisons, 1950–88." *Quarterly Journal of Economics,* May, http://pwt.econ.upenn.edu/papers/SummersHestonMark5_1991.pdf (July 2008).

Targetti, F., and A. Forti. 1997. "Growth and Productivity: A Model of Cumulative Growth and Catching Up." *Cambridge Journal of Economics* 21: 27–43.

U.S. Government Accountability Office. 2005. "Free Trade Area of the Americas: Missed Deadline Prompts Efforts to Restart Stalled Hemispheric Trade Negotiations," www.gao.gov/new.items/d05166.pdf (July 2008).

Van Ark, B. R., and H. McGuckin. 1999. "International Comparisons of Labor Productivity and per Capita Income." *Monthly Labor Review,* July, www.bls.gov/opub/mlr/1999/07/art3full.pdf (July 2008).

World Bank. 2007. *World Development Report 2007: Development and the Next Generation.* Oxford University Press for World Bank.

PART II

Opening Markets:
Brazil's Trade Policy

CHAPTER FIVE

Brazil's Trade Policy
Moving Away from Old Paradigms?

PEDRO DA MOTTA VEIGA

This chapter analyzes the political economy of trade policies in Brazil since the unilateral liberalization undertaken in the early 1990s, as well as the emergence of structural trends whose consolidation could challenge the dominant policy paradigms and shift the balance of power in the trade policy arena. After an episode of intense trade liberalization in the early 1990s, import policies in Brazil remained virtually unchanged, while activist export and investment policies were reintroduced during the second half of the decade. The level of tariff and nontariff protection that resulted from liberalization was much lower than the one prevailing in the preliberalization period, but industrial and trade policies in the postliberalization era have not changed a major feature of the long-lasting protectionist policies: the high degree of intersectoral discrimination in favor of import-competing industries.

At the same time, Brazil's foreign policy paradigm, dating back to the 1960s, was only marginally affected by the liberalization trends of the 1990s. Trade strategies continued to be designed in accordance with the broad political framework defined by the basic assumptions of the foreign policy put in place during the long period of protectionist industrialization. Hence, it is not by chance that despite the fact that Brazil entered into many trade negotiations during the late 1990s and the beginning of the 2000s, these have generated few economic results.

Despite the continuity observed in foreign and trade policies, the Brazilian economy is going through a set of structural changes that are pushing it toward deeper integration with the world economy. Under a fairly plausible scenario for the next several years, these trends will gain strength, and the current policy preferences in the fields of trade policy and foreign policy will become less functional for the "real" dynamics of the relationships between Brazil and the world. The legitimacy of these policies will be increasingly challenged, and this fact will surely have important effects on the support they receive from a large segment of Brazil's public opinion.

This chapter proceeds in six sections. The following section focuses on the role of domestic factors in explaining the continuity in trade policies during the 1990s, despite the liberalization episode of the early years of that decade. The subsequent two sections describe the main features of the unilateral and negotiated trade policies adopted by Brazil after its unilateral liberalization, under Fernando Henrique Cardoso and Luiz Inácio Lula da Silva, and the fifth section summarizes the domestic debate on Lula's trade policies. Finally, the sixth section analyzes the effects of the emergence of offensive interests in the trade policy arena in Brazil and proposes a policy agenda geared toward promoting the deepening integration of Brazil with the world economy.

The Political Economy of Trade Policy in Brazil: The Role of Domestic Factors

Although the unilateral trade liberalization undertaken at the beginning of the 1990s was a moment of important change in the history of Brazilian industrial and trade policies, a major feature of the trade policy implemented since this liberalization episode—as compared with the preliberalization period—has been continuity. In the field of unilateral trade policies, continuity has been manifested through the "activation" of newly designed mechanisms to finance and promote exports, and especially through the permanence of a protectionist structure that discriminates strongly among sectors and that applies nontariff barriers (especially antidumping duties) to imports. In the sphere of negotiated trade policies, the participation of Brazil in the wide array of trade negotiations opened during the 1990s was characterized by defensive positions.

Two domestic factors seem especially important in explaining continuity in Brazil's trade policies and negotiations. The first involves the political economy of the country's liberalizing reforms. The relevant point here is the primacy that import-competing sectors managed to maintain in the area of trade policy compared with the exporting sectors and interests, despite the unilateral trade liberalization launched at the beginning of the 1990s. After liberalization, manufacturing sectors that benefited from the import-substitution regime were able to maintain high levels of nominal and effective protection, and some of them received new tailor-made incentives to invest (autos, informatics, etc.).

On the basis of sectoral indicators of trade flows, tariff protection, and access to public mechanisms in the field of financing and import special regimes, Markwald reaches similar conclusions and sheds light on the existence of a set of import-competing sectors that benefit from high levels of protection and make intense use of the mechanisms of public policy.[1] Automobiles, electrical and electronic equipment, rubber and plastics, textiles, and clothing are among these sectors. These sectors concentrate a large share of the stock of foreign direct investment in Brazil, and their trade agenda combines with the defense of public policies to foster exports and a resistance to negotiating tariff reductions in multilateral and preferential forums. They played the protagonist role in the political economy of trade policy before the unilateral liberalization of the early 1990s and were able to keep this central position afterward.

The second factor refers to the fact that the paradigm of foreign policy consolidated during the period of import-substitution industrialization remained dominant despite the liberalization trend of the 1990s. This model was strongly associated with the protectionist industrialization strategy and gathered large support from the elites during the period of import substitution. This paradigm of foreign policy was historically driven by the objective of "neutralizing" external factors that might have jeopardized national economic development and the consolidation of domestic industrial capacity—conditions perceived as indispensable for the country to act autonomously in the international system. In this area, continuity prevailed quite unambiguously during the liberalization period; the dominant paradigm in Brazil's foreign policy since the 1960s remained firmly in place and framed the political logic of its participation in Mercosur, as well as in its other initiatives of preferential liberalization and multilateral negotiations.

1. Markwald (2006).

The weight of the foreign-policy paradigm in defining trade policy objectives and instruments could not be minimized in the case of Brazil. In Brazil's history, the definition of foreign threats and the perception of external risks by its elites relates essentially to economic vulnerabilities rather than to security concerns. This led to a perception—widespread among these elites—that the main function of foreign policy is to reduce this type of vulnerability and to "open up space" for national development policies.

Trade policy (and, more broadly, international economic policy) has traditionally been strictly subordinated to foreign policy objectives, as defined by the "autonomist" paradigm. In the field of trade policy, this led to a view where the North-South cleavage played a central role, not only in explaining the difficulties faced by Brazil in the international economic arena but also in setting the parameters for the alliances and coalitions that it sought in trade negotiations and, more broadly, in the international economic arena.

During the 1990s, the liberalization trend that affected economic policies of Latin American countries only partially challenged the Brazilian policy framework inherited from the import-substitution period. In trade negotiations, the protectionist paradigm (the "Brasília consensus") was shared by a large coalition of bureaucrats and business associations from the manufacturing sectors, which played a central role in setting the national negotiating positions during the Cardoso and Lula governments. The main consequence of this coalition's hegemony is that Brazil participated in many trade negotiations but adopted systematically defensive stances.

Brazil's Unilateral Trade Policies since 1990

Since the second half of the 1960s, Brazil has adopted an active policy of fostering and diversifying its exports. This policy has taken advantage of various fiscal and credit instruments, and most of the time the exchange rate policy has been favorable to foreign sales. However, incentives to export were gradually withdrawn throughout the 1980s as the macroeconomic situation deteriorated and pressures from trade partners intensified.

In the early 1990s, the priority for Brazil's trade policy shifted to import liberalization, and the almost exclusive target of economic policy was the enormous rate of inflation. Export policies were relegated to second place and had to wait until 1995 to regain some priority. That year, under the combined effect of the growth of domestic demand and the appreciation of the exchange rate, trade deficits reappeared, bringing in their wake concerns as to the sustainability of the stabilization plan. (The main components of this second cycle of export-boosting policies were, first, efforts to improve the intragovernmental coordination of the export policies, resulting in the setting of the Chamber of Foreign Trade, known as CAMEX; second, partial tax waivers for exports; third, reestablishing public export-financing mechanisms and providing guarantees for the credits granted; fourth, setting up an export-promoting agency; and fifth, adapting institutional organization in the area of trade negotiations.)

The result of the set of initiatives adopted in 1995 is not obvious, but in general, its net impact on the propensity of Brazil-based companies to export has proved positive. In particular, the steps made to provide tax exemptions for exports and the consolidation of financing mechanisms created during the decade received a positive evaluation for their effects on the profitability of Brazilian exports.

Although the export policy grew more "horizontal" and less discriminatory in intersectoral terms than the policy followed before the 1990s, the postliberalization policy of protection inherited a strong bias toward industrial sectors from the phase of import substitution. Up to the start of the process of trade liberalization, the tariff structure applied in Brazil was practically the same one implanted thirty years before, in 1957, at the onset of the import-substitution period. In the late 1980s, the import coefficient hardly went beyond 3 percent in manufacturing, and liberalization got off to a timid start in 1988, eliminating tariff redundancy, suppressing certain surcharges on imports, and simplifying the countless special tax regimes in place. These measures led the average nominal tariff to fall from 57.5 percent in 1987 to 32 percent in 1990.[2]

Unilateral trade liberalization intensified in 1990 and concluded at the end of 1993, eliminating a wide range of nontariff barriers and bringing the average tariff from 32 percent in early 1990 down to around 13 percent in late 1993.[3] Trade liberalization—implemented amid the aggravation of the macroeconomic crisis, with domestic demand retracted and the real exchange rate quite high—had little impact on import flows and

2. Markwald (2006).
3. Motta Veiga (2007).

practically no effect on domestic supply until 1994. Only when the Real Plan came into play, with the consequent appreciation of the nation's currency and expansion of domestic demand, were the effects of trade liberalization felt widely in the internal market, making an impact on companies and sectors according to their competitiveness and capacity to adapt to a more competitive environment.

At the aggregate level, this evolution produced successive trade deficits, and in the circumstances where the Mexican crisis raised fears of a rapid worsening of Brazil's external accounts, two complementary forces converged in the Brazilian scenario. First, there was an increase in protectionist pressures from sectors threatened by the surge of imports; and second, there were macroeconomic concerns from policymakers. These forces led to a moderate inversion of the trade-opening process. In 1997, the average nominal tariff was 4.5 percentage points above the tariff registered in 1994. Only in 1999, following the adoption of the floating exchange rate regime, did the average levels of tariff protection return to those applied in the mid-1990s. As imports were increasing strongly, trade policymakers resorted increasingly to instruments of contingent protection, especially antidumping. During this period, there was a significant increase in the number of investigations leading to positive determinations of dumping, and it is worth noting the high percentage of cases of revision that ended up with new duties being applied.[4]

The Brazilian experience in this field took to an extreme a characteristic already identified in many countries, as far as the use of antidumping measures by trade policymakers is concerned; that is, these measures protected industries with a high level of concentration of domestic supply: "In Brazil, more than half of the 247 cases opened in this period were to protect domestic monopolists; in 26 percent of the cases, the petitioning industry was a duopoly; and in a mere 9 percent of the petitions was the number of participating firms higher than six."[5]

At the same time that measures were being reintroduced to protect domestic producers, new mechanisms were being implemented to foster exports and investment: automotive and information technology regimes, lines of favored credit to support sectors affected by the combination of opening with exchange rate appreciation (as textiles and footwear), and subnational incentive programs to attract productive investments.

4. Markwald (2006).
5. Tavares de Araújo and Miranda (2008).

The convergence of these processes generated the structural protection of industrial aggregate value. This protection was highly heterogeneous in intersectoral terms and largely benefited the same sectors favored by the industrial and export policies of previous decades, that is, automobiles, electric and electronic appliances, textiles, clothing, and footwear. Throughout the 1990s, these sectors benefited from levels of nominal and effective protection well above averages for the manufacturing industries.[6] Although the import policy of the 1990s introduced a significant rupture with the protectionist tradition of Brazil's trade policy, in doing so, and by interacting with other policies—such as industrial policy—it did not abandon the option for protection (and incentive) structures that were highly discriminatory in intersectoral terms—a major feature of the import-substitution industrialization period.

Despite its limits, several studies underscore the role of trade opening as a factor that induced the growth of industrial productivity as a whole, produced a remarkable increase in the import coefficients of the various sectors, and reduced the margins and costs of industrial companies. On the basis of a comprehensive review of the works on this topic, Markwald concluded that opening up trade clearly had positive effects on the Brazilian economy's productivity levels and on its various industrial sectors, as well as the investments made by industry and the technological performance of corporations.[7]

As far as the effects of trade liberalization on income distribution are concerned, they seem to have been quite limited when considered in aggregate terms; positive and negative effects were registered in some studies, but these effects are always very small.[8] It is worth pointing out that concerns with the distributive implications of trade liberalization clearly played a secondary role in formulating and implementing policies in the trade and industrial areas in the postliberalization period.

The Strategy of Trade Negotiations: From Cardoso to Lula

Although there was no major rupture with the framework of domestic factors conditioning the setting of trade policies in Brazil, as described above, the strategy of trade negotiations in the Cardoso government was not a

6. Markwald (2006).
7. Markwald (2001).
8. Paes de Barros and Corseuil (2005).

mere continuation of the trends inherited from the protectionist period. The distinctive feature of the strategy adopted under Cardoso was the place accorded to ambitious preferential negotiations with the European Union and the United States, Brazil's main economic partners in the developed world. Especially during Cardoso's second term, the negotiations over the Free Trade Area of the Americas (FTAA) and the European Union were Brazil's top priorities on the trade front. Those initiatives "tested" the limits of the policy framework inherited from the protectionist period and, if successful, would challenge these limits not only with respect to the trade strategy but, more important, also in the foreign policy field.

Upon deciding to negotiate free trade agreements with its two main partners in the developed world, Brazil faced two "ghosts" of the protectionist paradigm: the prospect of an extensive opening of its economy to competition from imported goods; and the adoption of rules and disciplines beyond trade areas, as in investments and government procurement. It is true that in these negotiations Brazil adopted an essentially defensive posture, but this was never translated into refusing to negotiate any of the issues included in the agendas, whether they were sensitive for Brazil or not.

The Lula government has clearly abandoned the "ambiguity" of the preceding administration with regard to preferential negotiations with developed countries, which lost the priority granted under Cardoso. In these negotiations, the Lula government has adopted more conservative guidelines as the initiatives became increasingly assessed as "risky" for the objectives of national development. The strategic shift of the Lula government in the field of trade negotiations has had three characteristics: the downgrading of negotiations with the United States and the EU, resistance to negotiating disciplines from the World Trade Organization (WTO), and a new priority given to South-South negotiations.

The first change introduced by the Lula government in the policy inherited from Cardoso was to downgrade the preferential negotiations with the United States and the EU within the ranking of priorities for Brazil's trade strategy. The main impact of this strategic shift was surprisingly not felt with great intensity during negotiations with the United States on the FTAA. The explanation is simple—within the dominant foreign policy framework, the FTAA was perceived as the less desirable strategic option, for it is viewed as a project pushed by the United States and one that potentially threatens the unity of Mercosur, the subregional initiative backed by Brazil. As preferential negotiations with the Northern countries lost weight within the strategy of the new government, Brazilian demands from developed countries—essentially in the area of agriculture—tended to concentrate in the multilateral sphere.

The second element of the strategic shift of the Lula government in the field of trade negotiations was resistance to negotiate WTO-plus disciplines. Especially in preferential talks with developed countries, Brazil came to adopt a "minimalist" approach in the "beyond-trade" issues: services, investment, and government procurement. A "radicalization" of the defensive stance inherited from previous governments is noticeable on these issues, which are held to be sensitive for their potential implications on the margins of freedom to formulate industrial policies.

The third strategic shift made by the Lula government in its trade negotiation strategy concerns the new priority accorded to South-South relationships. From 2003 on, negotiations with other developing countries became increasingly relevant to Brazil's strategy. Two elements are present in the revival of the South-South dimension of Brazilian negotiating policy: approaching other regional economic blocs and enhancing the Mercosur project.

On the one hand, setting a wide agenda of economic cooperation is sought with other large developing countries outside South America. The India–Brazil–South Africa initiative is an illustration of this kind of proposal, in which the trade component of bilateral relations may not even play the central role, although the initiative itself is expected to produce positive externalities for Brazil in multilateral (trade) forums.

At the bilateral level, these understandings have generated two limited trade agreements so far: one between Mercosur and India, and one between Mercosur and the Southern Africa Customs Union (SACU). Both agreements are based on the reciprocal concession of fixed tariff preferences for a limited number of products—958 for Mercosur–SACU, and 450 for Mercosur–India.[9]

On the other hand, priority is explicitly given to deepening and enhancing Mercosur, the subregional project, while intensifying economic relations with the rest of South America. This second component of the South-South strategy intends to put the region at the center of the Brazilian strategy. In South American negotiations, the trade component is seen by policymakers as only one of the elements in the strategy to strengthen

9. CNI (2005).

Brazil's regional links. With respect to Mercosur, for example, it is claimed that there is a need to include issues related to industrial policy and the treatment of asymmetries between member countries on the agenda, whereas in the case of relations with the rest of South America, infrastructure became a priority matter for Brazil.

However, not everything in the trade strategy of the Lula government is a break with the strategy of Cardoso. One of the main lines of continuity in trade strategy relates to the growing weight accorded to the agribusiness sector in setting the Brazilian trade agenda, which reflects a structural change in the country's economy. The emergence of an export-oriented and very competitive agribusiness sector translated, in the negotiating agenda, into intensifying demands for market liberalization and the elimination of trade-distorting subsidies, both in preferential negotiations and in the WTO.

Another line of continuity from Cardoso to Lula is the zero-tolerance position concerning the link between the trade-environment and trade-labor issues in multilateral or preferential negotiations. Brazil has traditionally rejected this link as a protectionist device, a position that has not changed under Lula. This set of developments combining both inflections and lines of continuity defines the Lula government's strategy for trade negotiations. Under Lula, the trade negotiations strategy was driven back to the rails of the "national-developmentalist" tradition of Brazilian foreign policy. This movement was accomplished in two steps.

The first step was made in the field of foreign policy, which rehabilitated two key concepts of the "national-developmentalist" tradition that had lost some of its prestige during the 1990s. The North-South divide is the first of these concepts. This opposition has played—in foreign policy hegemony during the protectionist period—a major role in explaining not only the problems of development faced by countries such as Brazil but also the logic of the prevailing international economic order. On the basis of this cleavage, Brazil formulated its foreign policy's political and economic priorities along with its strategies for its international alliances and coalitions. This second concept attributes to foreign policy the key function of "insulating" the design and implementation of industrial policies from the restrictions and threats represented by external agreements, external commitments, and the interests of the developed countries.

The second step directly subordinated the strategy of trade negotiations to the revamped "autonomist" foreign policy. Under Cardoso, a movement was made to "autonomize," or separate, the strategy of trade negotiations from the more general objectives of foreign policy, based on the general idea (subject to some specific qualifications) that such negotiations and their results would not be capable of jeopardizing those objectives and might even make some positive contribution to their accomplishment. In the present government, this trend has been reverted; negotiations are again in large measure assessed according to political criteria, prominent among these being the North-South cleavage and the preservation of "national autonomy."

There is, nonetheless, one major element in the current strategy that was not present in the earlier versions of the "national-developmentalist" vision: For the first time, the strategy includes significant offensive interests. These, of course, are the interests of the competing Brazilian agribusiness sectors. The process of including an offensive element in a defensive strategy was traditionally devised to "mitigate risks" and to help keep distance between the national and the international. This process is not immune to difficulties. How have these two components— the offensive and the defensive—interacted in the strategy put into practice by Brazil?

In the Lula government, the offensive component of the trade strategy was integrated in a policy framework largely determined by the priorities accorded to the North-South cleavage through the setting of the Group of Twenty (G-20) in the WTO agricultural negotiations. As a matter of fact, the constitution of the G-20 is fully compatible with Brazil's current strategy, because it raises the country to a leading position among the *demandeurs* of agricultural liberalization. Simultaneously, the country was sanctioning the North-South cleavage in areas where up until now developed and developing countries had shared a common position. Domestically, it received approval from export-oriented sectors as well as from "developmentalist" constituencies.

But the offensive and defensive components of the strategy cannot always be accommodated in an instrument of negotiation such as the G-20. In fact, whereas a negotiating strategy based on the logic of North-South opposition and the preservation of national autonomy discourages trade agreements with the developed countries, agribusiness sectors perceive these agreements as unique opportunities to access the large markets of the North. Hence, the gradual insertion of an offensive component into the negotiating strategy is leading some (relevant) domestic players to challenge the limits of the framework inherited from the Brazilian protectionist tradition in trade negotiations.

The Recent Debate on Trade Policy

Unilateral and negotiated trade policies in Brazil have evolved during the postliberalization period (i.e., from 1994 on), within the limits defined by the "developmentalist" paradigm for foreign policy and by the interests of the import-competing sectors. The initiatives with some potential to challenge these limits have been aborted (e.g., the FTAA) or have been managed by the government and the private sector through defensive strategies.

However, when assessed from an economic point of view, even those initiatives that have gained the priority for Brazil's trade strategy under Lula have produced very limited results. The trade agreements with the SACU and with India refer exclusively to trade in goods and cover only a small fraction of the tariff nomenclature. Beyond that, the products included in the agreements are given fixed preferences, which seldom reach 100 percent. In South America, Mercosur is going through a large period of difficulties, and the so-called agenda of consolidation and deepening for the bloc has been left aside. Brazil has adopted a strategy of "risk mitigation," accepting that it needs to deal with the "asymmetries" issue as a way to contain the dissatisfaction of the small countries in Mercosur (e.g., Uruguay and Paraguay). After a decade of ultraliberalism, Argentina became the most protectionist country in the bloc, and this is having a strong impact on negotiations within Mercosur and with third countries (whether they are preferential or multilateral). For many analysts and business representatives in Brazil, the country is paying a high price for its decision to negotiate together with the currently protectionist Argentina in preferential (EU-Mercosur) and multilateral (WTO) forums.

These meager results, together with the option of reducing the priority of the North-South preferential negotiations, have generated an intense debate on trade policies and negotiation strategy in Brazil over the last few years. This debate has also been fed by Brazil's strong export performance from 2002 onward, and by the significant growth of its inward and outward foreign direct investment (FDI) in the last several years. Is it possible to infer from this performance that trade agreements are irrelevant as a mechanism for fostering exports and investments, at least in the case of Brazil?

As a matter of fact, two debates have overlapped in the arena of trade policies. The first one refers specifically to the relevance of trade agreements as mechanisms to foster trade and investment. The second one targets the foreign policy options that define the priorities and preferences of the trade negotiation strategy. In this case, the critics of the government's strategy put less emphasis on the need to sign trade agreements and instead target the negative effects of the strategy—and of the political view that is behind it—on the capacity of Brazil to play a relevant role on the international scene, especially referring to its relationship with developed countries.

As for the first debate, at the end of the Lula government, the balance sheet of its trade strategy will almost certainly register the irrelevance of the net results (in economic terms) of the initiatives of negotiations in the preferential sphere, whether these were inherited from previous governments or initiated by the current government. These limited results stand in sharp contrast to the performance of foreign trade—exports in particular—during the Lula government. As a matter of fact, after a decade of poor performance on the foreign trade front, over the last few years Brazil's foreign trade has enjoyed impressive growth. A good deal of this positive performance can be attributed to exports, which more than doubled between 2000 and 2005, reaching 118 billion U.S. dollars.[10]

The growth of exports is the main factor behind the increase in the Brazilian economy's trade coefficient (i.e., foreign trade / GNP). In the early 1990s, this coefficient was slightly above 10 percent, and by the end of the decade it had surpassed 16 percent. After 2000, it grew strongly, in 2004 reaching 24 percent (with exports being responsible for 15 percent). In many manufacturing sectors, the growth of the export coefficient between the end of the 1990s and recent years has been impressive; electronic equipment, automobiles, auto parts, wood and furniture, and footwear are among these sectors.[11] Also during this period, the export markets diversified and the number of Brazilian products sold overseas grew substantially.

Within this context of an export boom, the performance of the agribusiness sector has been outstanding; exports in this sector grew at an annual rate of 16 percent between 2001 and 2005. The diversification of exported products and the geographical destinations of exports has been a major feature in the recent performance of the agribusiness sector. Between 2000 and 2005, agribusiness exports to developing countries

10. These data are from the Ministério do Desenvolvimento, Indústria e Comércio Exterior do Brasil (www.desenvolvimento.gov.br/sitio/).
11. Markwald (2006).

showed an average annual growth rate of 26 percent, while exports to developed countries grew at an annual rate of 13 percent. Currently, Brazil ranks first among world exporters of sugar, ethanol, beef, chicken, pork, and coffee. Brazil is also one of the top four exporters of soy, orange juice, and cotton.[12]

Analysts usually mention the growth of the world economy, the emergence of China as the "vacuum cleaner" of the world production of primary goods, the effects of these two factors on the prices of commodities, and the integration of exports with the growth strategies of leading Brazilian companies as among the main factors driving Brazil's export boom. More recently, Brazilian companies have substantially increased investments abroad, in sharp contrast to their historical record of a low degree of operational internationalization. South America has been the destination of an important share of this flow, but Brazil's FDI has also targeted the markets of developed countries in North America and Europe, as well as China. In 2004, "outward investment flows scored an exceptional growth, putting Brazil among the top five foreign investors in the developing world."[13] In 2006, outward FDI flows surpassed inward flows for the first time in Brazil's history. A still-limited but rapidly growing set of Brazilian companies is today referred to as an example of "multi-Latinas" with a diversified portfolio of investments in both developing and developed regions of the world.

Just as the unilateral trade policy seems to have made little contribution to the current export and outward FDI booms, it is worth noting that these dynamics took place without Brazil signing any relevant preferential trade agreement. So are preferential agreements even necessary for Brazil?

The question then, in this first debate, is to know whether, in an international environment less favorable to Brazilian exports, the absence of trade agreements would have any impact. After all, preferential trade agreements have grown quickly in the last few years, especially in the Americas and Asia, a region that previously seemed immune to a regionalization process. Though other countries negotiate and exchange preferential access to their markets, Brazil will go on seeing its exports treated by most-favored-nation tariffs—and this will be the case more frequently as its exports gradually lose the benefits of unilateral schemes for the Generalized System of Preferences. Although the results of foreign trade and

12. Jank (2007).
13. CNI (2008).

the boom in commodity prices over the last few years have reduced domestic pressure to push preferential negotiations forward (especially those with developed countries), this issue is bound to gain relevance as the Doha Round of multilateral trade negotiations is concluded (with probably limited results), bilateral agreements continue to proliferate, and domestic and/or external factors decrease the growth rate of exports.

In the second debate, critics of the current trade strategy attack the subordination of trade and economic objectives to an "autonomist" foreign policy, a criticism that essentially reflects the emerging presence of offensive interests in the trade policy arena. As a matter of fact, the key position of mitigating the risks and threats arising from trade agreements with developed countries explains why the net result of Brazil's current strategy, when evaluated in terms of trade, is so limited. Conversely, although strengthening economic relationships with other Southern countries is assessed positively by those defending a more offensive strategy, critics target the fact that the potential of these relationships is not reached, because trade policy has been directly subordinated to foreign policy. As a result, South-South agreements tend to be negotiated politically, without any major concerns for creating or taking advantage of export opportunities. Furthermore, the multiplication of South-South agreements becomes a political objective in itself, leading to a complete loss of focus and priorities in the negotiations agenda when analyzed from the point of view of the country's trade and investment interests.

In 2006, the Confederação Nacional da Indústria (CNI, National Confederation of Industry), in a document addressed to the presidential candidates, proposed a strategy of trade negotiations whose priorities were based on explicit economic criteria: the dynamism and size of the markets, and the level of barriers to Brazil's exports. Recently, the CNI presented the government with a proposal to negotiate a free trade agreement with Mexico. It is the first time that the Brazilian manufacturing sector has formally adopted an offensive stance in trade negotiations and pushed for a comprehensive and ambitious agreement.

At the end of the day, the main target of this kind of criticism lies in the political rationale behind Brazil's strategy for trade negotiations, with a favorite target being the use of the North-South cleavage as the main criterion for analyzing the international economic order and certain negotiating positions. According to this view, this criterion is no longer suitable for guiding Brazil's international behavior in a world where the differences in interests between developing countries are accentuated and these countries increasingly attempt to establish or maintain preferential relations with developed countries. This raises pertinent questions: Can South-South relations produce an increase in Brazil's political capital in the international arena? Is it possible to make South-South strategies operational beyond specific initiatives like the G-20, when the cleavages between developing countries are made increasingly more manifest in multilateral and preferential negotiations?

The debate on Lula's trade strategy makes it explicit that no consensus has been reached among Brazilian elites concerning the "ideal" degree of international integration for the Brazilian economy. This lack of consensus appears clearly in the debate on the relevance of preferential agreements with developed countries and, more broadly, on the assessment of the costs and benefits of trade liberalization aiming to foster competition and productivity in the domestic market. Notwithstanding this situation, from now on the trade policy arena in Brazil will include the competitive sectors mainly concentrated in agribusiness as relevant players, and this represents a huge change in the political landscape where this policy is designed and implemented.

Looking Ahead: The Challenges of Deeper Integration

Decades of trade protectionism and of a foreign policy vision whereby economic relations with the world were perceived as a threat to national development left deep marks on the hearts and minds of the leading public and private actors who influence the course of trade policy in Brazil. Nevertheless, from the 1990s onward, Brazil's economic evolution has enabled the emergence, in both the private and public sectors, of less defensive interests and visions from the perspective of the country's international insertion. The determining factor behind this change was the consolidation of a highly competitive exporting sector with geographically diversified offensive interests. To a considerable extent, the agribusiness and mining sectors are the core of this "competitive bloc," but it increasingly also tends to include the manufacturing sectors.

In this sense, it is interesting to notice that the driving force behind this evolution was not a policy option with a strong dose of willfulness, such as the one that pushed forward the unilateral liberalization of the early 1990s, but rather the fact that the Brazilian economy underwent a structural change related to the consolidation of competitive exporting sectors. Only lately have the effects of this structural change been felt in the trade policy arena. As long as Brazil had only defensive interests, trade policy was assessed basically for its ability to "prevent damages" and to "mitigate external threats and risks" for the strategy of "autonomous" industrial development. However, when powerful offensive-interest sectors are part of the game, a new concept emerges of what the positive results and policy and trade negotiations should be. Accordingly, the expected results of trade policy can no longer be restricted to minimizing risks and threats but rather ought to include the "capture" of the opportunities opened in the international markets for exporting sectors and the Brazilian economy as a whole. It is in light of this concept of "positive results" that the trade strategy of the Lula administration is criticized by Brazil's exporting sectors.

The internal legitimacy of Brazil's foreign policy came from the perception that its effects and implications for economic development were positive. The structural evolution of the economy and the emergence of offensive interests reduce the usefulness of an overwhelmingly defensive trade policy. Hence, under the pressure of structural factors (rather than because of a policy option), fine-tuning—historically consolidated between the orientation of foreign policy, on the one hand, and the model of international insertion of the Brazilian economy, on the other—is broken.

So, at the start of the twenty-first century, the "maturing" of the changes introduced in the 1990s—the consolidation of a competitive agribusiness, the integration of exports into the growth strategies of large companies, the dynamism of the world economy, and China's hunger for commodities—converged to produce an export boom that substantially increased the trade coefficient of the Brazilian economy. More recently, outward FDI from Brazil has also shown an impressive dynamism, being directed not only to neighboring countries in South America but also to the United States, China, and the European Union. Brazil's economy has been undergoing a series of structural evolutions whose net result is the gradual change in the environment where trade policies are defined. But the forces behind this ongoing change in the model of international insertion have not exclusively originated domestically. They have also been the result of the evolution of both the global economic and political system and the region where Brazil is located, South America.

At the global level, there is a growing perception that Brazil will be one of the most important players in the twenty-first century's world economy, together with the other BRIC countries (Brazil, Russia, India, and China—the four very large rapidly emerging economies). This perception is nurtured by the country's growing weight as a great global supplier of food, the key role it plays in multilateral trade negotiations, and the realization that it will be called to play a relevant role in addressing energy and environmental issues being assigned priority status on the international agenda. In different fields of international relations, Brazil has been frequently invited to participate in an agenda-setting process that brings a limited group of emerging market countries together with the leading developed countries. Last year, Brazil received positive feedback from various sources; its new international dimension has been perceived and evaluated positively outside the country. The president of the United States proposed a special relationship with Brazil in the area of biofuels, and the European Union extended its proposal for a strategic partnership formulated earlier to other BRICs. At the same time, the Organization for Economic Cooperation and Development (OECD) expressed its interest in opening negotiations to bring Brazil into the organization. Though such progress has been slow, Brazil is taking part in a dialogue known as the Heiligendamm Process, where the OECD plays a pivotal role on policies, with the G-8 group of developed countries and the G-5 group of five emerging market countries.

On the regional level, "demands" for a revision of Brazil's South American policy have arisen among analysts in the country,[14] and they are originating from three different perceptions. The first is that South American countries have a common broad economic agenda that includes trade, investments—flows of intraregional FDI are increasing—infrastructure, and energy. Hence, privately driven flows, intergovernmental initiatives (e.g., the South American Initiative on Infrastructure Integration), and conjunctural phenomena have combined to bring to light a common economic agenda with great potential for creating positive-sum games in all these areas.

The second perception refers to the fact that in a scenario where the options for economic policy within the region have diverged and the political conflicts between countries are producing very tense situations, the risk of missing the opportunity arising from a diversified intraregional economic agenda is large. Fragmentation would get the better of integration, and the economic and energy assets of the different countries would be used to pressure their neighbors, thereby jeopardizing the possibility of any cooperation.

14. CINDES (2007).

The third perception refers to the role of Brazil in such a context. It outlines the fact that it is up to Brazil, given its economic and political clout, to play a key role in the strategy of seizing the opportunities for economic cooperation and integration and in mitigating the political risks associated with bilateral friction among the various South American countries. Therefore, updating Brazil's foreign strategy will call for the country to simultaneously reposition itself in both the global/multilateral and regional spheres. Neither of these two challenges can be ignored. The strength of Brazil in the global arenas of policies will depend partly on its capacity to play the protagonist role throughout the region and contribute to maintaining peace, economic growth, and democracy in South America.

Today, the hypothesis of this Brazilian repositioning comes up against the weight that the paradigms inherited from the period of protectionist industrialization exert on the design of foreign and trade policies. This weight and its consequences are clearly considered in the way that the present Brazilian government reacts to initiatives and proposals coming from developed countries. For instance, the prospect of being invited to join the OECD provoked considerable discomfort among Brazilian diplomats and policymakers; after all, how can Brazil keep the developing world's "seal of approval" while participating in an organization identified in the *tiermondiste* rhetoric as "the rich countries' club"?

In the regional field, too, Brazil's current strategy does not favor taking on a role compatible with the opportunities and threats prevalent in South America. On one hand, the priority granted to Mercosur in Brazil's regional strategy lost consistency at the economic level with the leaking of the bloc's agenda and the practical abandonment of the proposals to consolidate and deepen the Customs Union. For Brazilian diplomacy, the usefulness of Mercosur has become essentially political, and that explains why, in the bloc's negotiations with third-party countries, Brazil accepts that Argentina's "hyperprotectionism" imposes its limits on the agenda and concessions of the bloc. Brazil's interest in Venezuela's adhesion to Mercosur follows the same political logic of strengthening the bloc, although this specific stance could be questioned in light of the same criterion.

On the other hand, Brazil's efforts to "push forward" South American integration face an adverse scenario of tension and conflict among its neighbors. But they are also hindered by the political priority Brazil assigns to its relationships with Argentina and Venezuela. This priority, especially the one with Venezuela, drastically lowers the chance of Brazil acting as a mediator between divergent stances and as a promoter of positive agendas in the region.

Therefore, the repositioning of Brazil on the international scene in terms compatible with the structural changes under way in the country and in the world will require it to revise the paradigm for its foreign policy—which sees North-South relations essentially as a source of threats—as well as making more flexible the priority assigned today to Mercosur in its South American strategies.

There is nothing to guarantee that this repositioning will come about, at least in the short run. Although strong economic trends "push" Brazil toward such a scenario, its emergence may be substantially delayed or complicated by political options. This consideration is particularly relevant when one takes into account the importance of the current "leftist" foreign policy as a mechanism to legitimate Lula's government among certain segments of the Workers' Party and broader public opinion.

The convergence of internal and external conditions can also delay the process; the simultaneity of the financial crisis in the United States and the vigorous growth of domestic demand in Brazil tends to strengthen—at least in the short term—the position of those Brazilians who see the "external world" as a source of danger and who oppose deepening the international integration of the economy due to a domestic-market-led model of growth. Furthermore, it is very likely that, even if the scenario resulting from this policy shift materializes, it will take place gradually and pragmatically, without any radical break with the previous trajectory of the policies in question. In this context, prointegration views and interests are likely to gain influence over policy setting in years to come. But this process will not be a linear one, for it will most likely be negotiated with public and private actors favorable to autonomist policies. It is more likely that this evolution will occur through a set of inflections similar to that introduced by the Fernando Collor de Mello and Cardoso governments, in which trade policy and negotiations were inherited from the period of protectionist industrialization.

If this evolution is to occur in the next few years, an important question arises about the factors that could facilitate the change. One obvious candidate is a slowing of the commodity prices boom that has benefited Brazilian exports in the last years—and, as a consequence, has reduced the pressure exerted by offensive business interests for the negotiation of preferential free trade agreements. Though this factor could help push Brazil toward a change of paradigm in the trade policy field, it is far from clear that it will be strong enough to provoke such a huge change.

This leads us to another important question: Which coalition of actors (in the public as well as in the private sectors) would be strong enough to provoke this change in the trade policy arena in Brazil? Nowadays, offensive interests are concentrated in the agribusiness and mining sectors (and their sectoral associations) as well as in the Ministry of Agriculture. Defensive interests largely dominate among manufacturing sectors (multinational companies being, in general, among the most protectionist actors on the trade policy stage), their associations, and the Ministry of Development and Industry. The Ministry of Foreign Affairs mainly backs the protectionist interests whose defensive positions converge with the "threat-minimizing" logic behind the dominant paradigm for foreign policy.

A shift in the current balance of power is required to gradually open the way to a new paradigm for trade policy. This shift must be at least twofold. On one hand, at least some competitive manufacturing sectors would have to voice offensive interests, breaking the current divide between agriculture (competitive) and manufacturing (protectionist) and strengthening the pro-offensive coalition. On the other hand, a "cultural" shift in the dominant views prevailing in the highest ranks of the public sector is also required. Unless import competition is perceived by policymakers as positive for their impact on the productivity and the competitiveness of Brazilian firms, it is hard to envision a scenario of significant changes in the positions expressed by bureaucrats of different public agencies.

The policy agenda to push forward a strategy of deeper integration should include both trade and nontrade policy issues. In fact, this agenda should be aimed at fostering competition in the domestic market and, more broadly, favoring the diffusion of a "culture of competition" among public and private actors. This would translate not only into a revision of the current import tariff structure (substantially reducing tariff peaks) but also into a closer scrutiny of protectionist policies by the competition regulatory board to avoid the abuse of antidumping actions designed to protect concentrated industries.

If competition is positively valued and procompetition policies are to be implemented, ambitious preferential trade negotiations with Northern and large Southern countries should be seen more favorably than they currently deserve to be. Although the contribution of such agreements to fostering trade and investment flows between Brazil and its main partners should not be overestimated, under a new and procompetition scenario, the resistance to engaging in such negotiations will not be as strong as it is today.

By the same token, Brazil should adopt a less defensive stance in services negotiations and, even before doing that, unilaterally promote procompetition policies in the service sectors. Competition in services, like transportation, whose provision is costs for the goods-exporting sectors, can have a very positive effect not only on the competitiveness of these sectors but also on their stances toward trade policies and negotiations.

In the regional sphere, the policy shift compatible with a new trade strategy includes (1) a new priority given the efforts of establishing a free trade area in South America; (2) the inclusion of energy, environmental, and infrastructure issues on the agenda for regional cooperation and integration; and (3) less emphasis on the Custom Union dimension of Mercosur, freeing its members to negotiate trade agreements with third countries and, afterward, recovering intrabloc negotiations on the likelihood of setting a new Common External Tariff.

Furthermore, any policy agenda aimed at promoting the deeper integration of Brazil with the world economy needs to include measures addressing the systemic impediments to competitiveness, the improvement of domestic infrastructure, and the reduction of the tax burden that currently hinders investments and production as essential to enhancing the competitiveness of domestic producers. The lack of improvements in these domestic policy areas feeds protectionist resistance to deeper integration. By the same token, if Brazil is to strengthen the procompetitiveness dimension of its public policies to meet the challenges of deeper integration, it will need to address issues that, if not appropriately managed, could undermine the legitimacy of this policy shift. The distributional dimension of trade policies is one of the most important of these issues. This is particularly relevant in a country like Brazil, where the groups that oppose trade integration are economically and politically powerful. Therefore, a strategy to revise trade policy must address the concerns of the potential losers in the economic opening process. This can prove fundamental for reducing resistance to liberalization and increasing the degree of domestic legitimacy of this type of process.

The Brazilian experience since the liberalization of the early 1990s suggests that worrying about the losers tends to translate into measures that revert, if only partially, to the opening process, thereby reducing the beneficial effects of liberalization. "Finer" evaluations—with a view toward identifying potential losers, focusing on these social groups' or economic sectors' compensatory and restructuring actions—have not been part of Brazil's policy menu. The agenda of industrial policy and of measures to manage the structural and distributive effects of trade liberalization are disconnected in Brazil, perhaps because the country has seen only one— albeit limited—movement of opening trade.

The task of connecting both agendas is particularly complex but absolutely necessary in a scenario of deepening the integration of Brazil with the international economy. The challenge facing Brazil is not just to administer change in trade policy but also to find new measures and instruments to manage the permanent pressures of globalization on its economy and social structures. These pressures come not only from changes in national policies—whether unilateral or negotiated—but also from structural processes and business strategies that have a permanent effect on the map of comparative advantages between sectors and countries, generating significant potential effects on trade policy.

References

CINDES (Centro de Estudos de Integração e Desenvolvimento). 2007. "O Brasil na América do Sul." Relatório final da força-tarefa CINDES/CEBRI. Rio de Janeiro.

CNI (Confederação Nacional da Indústria). 2005. "As relações comerciais do Brasil com a Índia e a África do Sul." *Comércio Exterior em Perspectiva* 14, nos. 8–9: 1–10.

———. 2008. "O investimento direto no exterior e os interesses empresariais brasileiros na América do Sul." Brasília.

Jank, M. S. 2007. "A importância do agronegócio da soja e o desafio da sustentabilidade." Slide presentation for a course on sustainability and the soybean agribusiness, São Paulo, March 30.

Markwald, R. 2001. "Abertura comercial e indústria: Balanço de uma década." *Revista Brasileira de Comércio Exterior* 68: 4–25.

———. 2006. "The Political Economy of Foreign Trade Policy: The Brazilian Case." In *Domestic Determinants of National Trade Strategies: A Comparative Analysis of Mercosur Countries, Mexico and Chile*, ed. R. Bouzas. Paris: Chaire Mercosur de Sciences Po.

Motta Veiga, P. 2007. "Política comercial do Brasil: Características, condicionantes domésticos e policy-making." In *Políticas comerciais comparadas: Desempenho e modelos organizacionais*, ed. M. S. Jank and S. D. Silber. São Paulo: Editora Singular.

Paes de Barros, R., and C. H. Corseuil. 2005. "Brazil: Economic Opening and Income Distribution." In *Liberalización, desigualdad y pobreza: América Latina y el Caribe en los 90*, ed. E. Ganuza, R. Paes de Barros, L. Taylor, and

R. Vos. Brasília: Programa de las Naciones Unidas para el Desarrollo/ Comisión Económica para América Latina.

Tavares de Araújo, J., and P. Miranda. 2008. *Antidumping e Antitruste: Peculiaridades do Caso Brasileiro.* Série Breves CINDES 7. Rio de Janeiro: Centro de Estudos de Integração e Desenvolvimento.

CHAPTER SIX

Brazil's Trade Policy
Old and New Issues

MAURICIO MESQUITA MOREIRA

After a half century of overtly inward-oriented policies, Brazil finally moved to open its trade regime in the early 1990s. Being one of the last countries to make this move in a region that notoriously lagged behind East Asia, Brazil was quick to implement a comprehensive trade liberalization program that had strong unilateral and regional components. In roughly five years, tariffs were slashed, nontariff barriers (NTBs) were removed, and Mercosur became a reality. Later on, even the possibility of a free trade zone for the hemisphere was entertained.

Yet this initial momentum lost steam in the mid-1990s, undermined by inhospitable macroeconomic and international environments. Brazil's failure to adopt sound fiscal and monetary policies led to a substantial loss of the growth and allocational benefits of opening up, with the economy alternating periods of runaway inflation with those of severe exchange rate appreciation, while enduring strong external shocks ranging from Mexico in 1994 to Asia in 1999. However, not all the benefits were lost to volatility.

There is plenty of evidence that Brazil's greater exposure to import competition boosted productivity growth in manufacturing, the most protected sector of its economy, whose stagnation was behind the country's dismal growth performance. Likewise, the evidence is unequivocal in pointing to a drastic reduction in the cost of investment—that is, cheaper equipment—one of the key drivers of growth.[1]

When, at the turn of the century, the right mix of macroeconomic policies was finally put in place—a combination of fiscal austerity, inflation targeting, and a floating exchange rate—and Brazil began to enjoy the benefits of a more benign external environment—for example, a China-led commodity boom—the political support for deepening the trade reforms had waned and a new government took over that clearly had a skeptical view of trade.

Fortunately for Brazil's growth prospects, the political transition, despite concern, did not bring a significant policy reversal. Yet trade policy reform never regained its momentum, despite its unfinished agenda. This chapter looks at this agenda and argues that if Brazil really wants to fully enjoy the growth and welfare benefits of trade, it needs to further lower and rationalize its structure of protection; adopt a more aggressive, World Trade Organization (WTO)–plus, policy to open markets abroad; redesign, in light of the two previous measures, Mercosur to advance both the country's interest and that of its smaller partners; and, finally, bring trade facilitation, particularly transport costs, to the core of its trade agenda.

The chapter is organized in six sections, including this introduction and a section that summarizes the conclusions. The four core sections take each of the topics of the "unfinished agenda" in turn. The first section makes a case for further tariff reform; the second section questions the rationale of a de facto South-South market access strategy; the third section argues that the reforms and strategy discussed in the first and second sections would help turn Mercosur into a more sustainable and mutually beneficial initiative; and the fourth section seeks to draw attention to a type of trade costs that is usually not seen on the agenda of trade negotiators but has turned into one of the more important, if not the most important, obstacle to the country's trade.

Making Sense of Protection

There is little doubt that Brazil has come a long way toward reducing and rationalizing its tariffs. As can be seen in figure 6-1, in 1987, before the

---

1. See, e.g., López-Córdova and Moreira (2004), Moreira (2004), and Muendler (2004). For a recent discussion on Brazil's growth constraints, see Blyde and others (2007).

FIGURE 6-1. Brazil's Most-Favored-Nation Tariff, 1987–99

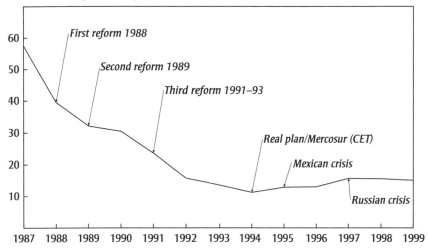

Value-added weighted-average tariff, in percent

Sources: Kume, Piani, and Souza (2000).

first tariff reform, the value-added weighted-average tariff was as high as 57 percent. The first two tariff reforms brought this average down to 32 percent but left in place an elaborate system of NTBs, which made sure that the tariff reduction had little effect on trade.[2] Trade liberalization in earnest had to wait until 1991, when, after removing all the relevant NTBs, the government began to implement a four-year tariff reduction schedule and to phase in its regional integration agreement with the other members of Mercosur.[3] This schedule, alongside measures taken in 1994 to facilitate the implementation of a stabilization plan (the Real Plan), brought the weighted-average tariff to its lowest point in more than half a century.

This promising first half of the 1990s, however, soon gave away to paralysis and even to a small but significant reversal of the tariff reforms, as Brazil entered a period of increasing current account deficits driven by a severe exchange rate appreciation and negative external shocks.

2. See Kume, Piani, and Souza (2000) for details of the tariff reforms.
3. Mercosur was launched by the Treaty of Asunción, signed in 1991 by Argentina, Brazil, Paraguay, and Uruguay. The treaty asked for the implementation of a common market by 1995, which would include 90 percent of the tariff lines.

The change of government in 2001—which took place amid increasing "fatigue" in public opinion with market-oriented reforms—did not, as expected, push the reversal to greater lengths (although it did raise the tariffs of some products such as apparel and shoes to as much as 35 percent in 2007), but it effectively ruled out any possibility of further reducing and rationalizing tariffs, unless as a part of an (increasingly elusive) agreement in the Doha Round of multilateral trade negotiations. The prospects for further opening through comprehensive regional trade agreements such as the Free Trade Area of the Americas and the European Union–Mercosur agreement also faded away as negotiations were stalled by the intransigent negotiating positions of all the parties involved.

Without the perspective of change any time soon, Brazil remains stuck with a level and structure of protection that is not as costly as that of the late 1980s but whose reform can still bring substantial welfare and growth gains. As shown in figure 6-2, the median most-favored-nation tariff places Brazil solidly in the top quartile among a large sample of countries around world. The median tariff is used because it minimizes the problems that affect simple (outliers) or weighted (bias toward low-tariff, high-volume items) averages, but the picture does not change significantly when these measures are used. Moreover, the use of most-favored-nation tariffs tends to underestimate the relative level of Brazil's protection vis-à-vis other large developing countries such as Mexico and China, which have, respectively, massive preferential trade agreements (the North American Free Trade Agreement, NAFTA, and the European Union–Mexico agreements) and special trade regimes.

Having this still relatively high level of protection means that Brazil is forgoing, apart from the traditional welfare gains, the opportunity, for instance, to boost its productivity, whose level and growth are known to lag well behind those of East Asia. According to one estimate based on firm-level data, a 10 percent reduction in tariffs increases total factor productivity by 1 percent, which would have a far from negligible impact—given that in the second half of the 1990s manufacturing total factor productivity grew at an annual rate of 2.8 percent.[4] Relatively high protection is also a cause for concern in a world where production is increasingly fragmented and the high growth benefits of joining global value chains hinge on low trade costs, among other competitiveness factors. Lacking large-scale North-South agreements or special trade regimes,

4. López-Córdova and Moreira (2004).

FIGURE 6-2. Median Nominal (Most-Favored-Nation) Tariff for Selected Economies, 2006

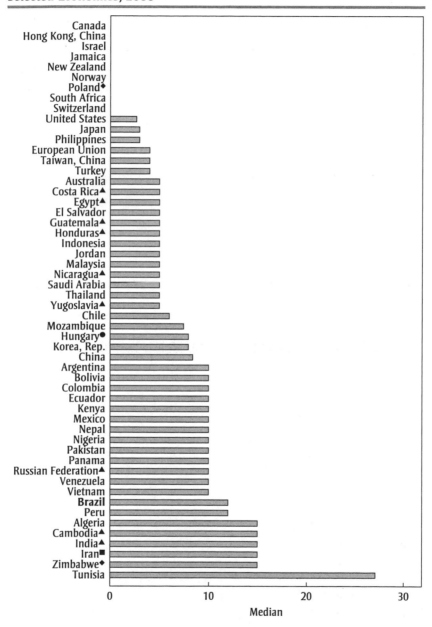

Median

Sources: United Nations Conference on Trade and Development, Trade Analysis and Information System (TRAINS) database.

Note: ● = 2002; ◆ = 2003; ■ = 2004; ▲ = 2005. For the first nine economies listed, the median is zero or close to zero.

Brazil is far less equipped than countries such as Mexico and China to take advantage of this trend, and, indeed, the available evidence suggests that the country's participation in global chains is still incipient.[5]

But the problem is not only the level of protection but also its variance. Figure 6-3 shows nominal and effective tariffs for 2007 at the three-digit level of Brazil's National Accounts System Classification. Nominal tariffs vary from 0 to 35 percent, an interval high enough to fuel rent seeking and impose severe costs on resource allocation. Yet the picture is even worse from the point of view of Corden effective tariffs, which take into account protection for both final products and inputs. Rates vary from −4 to 133 percent. Such figures beg the question: What is the rationale, if any, behind such disparate rates?[6] The answers, though, are difficult to find. A promising explanation might be found in the power of lobbies and special interest groups in shaping protection along the lines of the "protection for sale" argument developed by Grossman and Helpman.[7]

The prevailing structure of protection is particularly damaging for Brazil's growth. Most economists would agree that high investment rates in equipment and machinery play a key role in sustaining high rates of growth. De Long and Summers, for instance, show that there is a strong and negative correlation between growth and the relative price of capital goods, and a strong and positive correlation between growth and investment in capital goods.[8] Such types of evidence suggest that there is a link between trade and growth other than productivity. Because machinery and equipment are tradable goods, trade liberalization would lower their relative prices, reducing the cost of investment and boosting growth.

There is suggestive evidence that the trade liberalization of the first half of the 1990s made a substantial contribution to lowering the prices of capital goods in Brazil. Their relative prices, measured by the wholesale price index (IPA) and general price index (IGP), fell by 47 percent

5. Calfat and Flôres (2002).
6. The effective rates of protection were calculated using the Corden method (Corden 1971), with free trade technical coefficients. The coefficients were estimated using 2005 data on the use of 110 intermediate goods by 55 activities of the National Accounts System Classification–SCN (IBGE 2007, table 2, "Uso de Bens e Serviços"). The data for tariffs came from the Common External Tariff 2007 (www.desenvolvimento.gov.br/sitio/interna/interna.php?area=5&menu=1848 [May 2008]). An IBGE correspondence between SCN and the NCM (Nomenclatura Comun do Mercosur) was used to combine tariff and production data.
7. See Grossman and Helpman (1994). There is some evidence that this is the case. See, e.g., Calfat and Flôres (2002).
8. De Long and Summers (1991).

FIGURE 6-3. Brazil's Nominal and Effective Tariffs, 2007

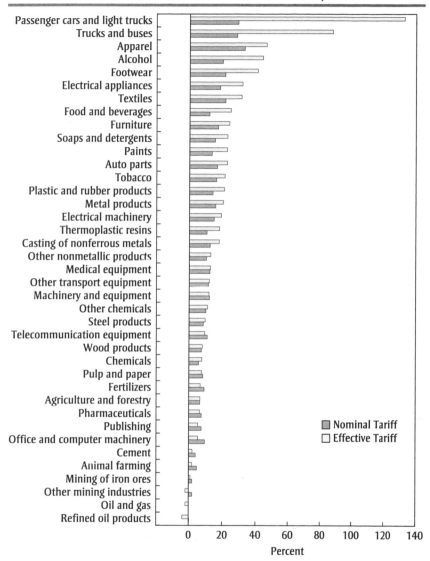

Sources: Author's calculations based data from Brazil's National Accounts Classification and from the Ministry of Development, Trade, and Industry.
Note: Data are at the three-digit level from Brazil's National Accounts Classification.

FIGURE 6-4. Capital Goods Tariffs for Selected Countries, 2006

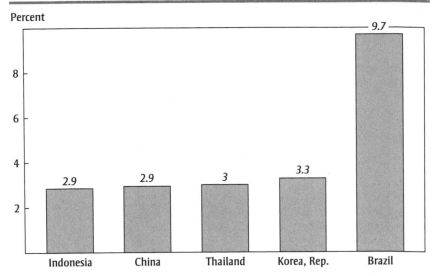

Sources: United Nations Conference on Trade and Development, Trade Analysis and Information System (TRAINS), database.
Note: These tariffs are for the UN broad economic categories, weighted by imports.

in 1990–2001, a drop that appears to be strongly correlated with the rise in import penetration.[9] As figure 6-4 shows, there appears to be considerable room for further reducing these prices. The tariffs on these goods (9.7 percent in 2006) are still well above those in force for the fast-growing economies of Asia, and are clearly punishing investment.

It is true, when measured by actual (tariff revenue divided by imports) rather than nominal tariffs, that protection in Brazil now seems to be lower (7.2 percent in 2007).[10] Yet this is still considerably higher than the nominal tariffs seen in Asia, and this figure alone tends to underestimate the costs of importing capital goods. The lower actual tariff is mostly the result of special import regimes, which target capital goods not produced locally. The discretionary nature of these programs is a fertile ground for red tape and corruption. In other words, they carry hidden costs that are not captured by tariff revenue.

9. Moreira (2004).
10. These data are from the Secreteria da Receita Federal (www.receita.fazenda.gov.br/ Historico/Aduana/Importacao/2007/dezembro/RenunciaFiscal.htm [May 2008]).

Overall, there seems to be no clear economic justification for Brazil to continue to pay the costs of this chaotic and counterproductive structure of protection. One can argue that maybe this is not the right time for tariff reform because of the WTO negotiations or because Brazil is yet again facing the consequences of a steep exchange rate appreciation driven by the recent commodity boom.[11]

Though legitimate, these arguments do not undermine the case for urgent reform. First, Brazil was a latecomer to trade reform, and it has already been more than a decade since the last measures was taken to cut and rationalize tariffs. The cumulative costs of these delays in terms of welfare and growth are hard to measure, but given the level of protection and the gap between the country's growth performance and those of countries that have adopted a more open trade regime, they are likely to be substantial and to continue to escalate, particularly as some of the initial gains are reversed.

The potential gains from waiting for the conclusion of a WTO negotiation have to be balanced against these welfare and growth costs. In fact, these costs call for Brazil to temper the "enlightened mercantilism" that has prevailed in its recent trade policy with a more careful assessment of the costs and benefits of further delaying tariff reform—the more so because the offers seen so far on the Doha negotiating table do not seem to translate into any significant change of the status quo.[12]

For instance, the last text produced by the chair of the Doha Round negotiations on nonagricultural market access (February 2008) called for "Swiss formula" coefficients of 19 or 23 for developing countries,[13] which would imply tariff cuts for Brazil of between 55 and 60 percent, with tariff ceilings equivalent to the coefficients. Given that there is a considerable difference between Brazil's bound and applied tariffs, a coefficient of 23, for instance, would only affect approximately 56 percent of the applied tariff lines, and to a considerably smaller extent than the bound tariffs.[14] In addition, these cuts are likely to be accompanied by

11. According to Brazil's Central Bank (www.bcb.gov.br/?INDECO), in the first quarter of 2008, the real exchange rate against the dollar was roughly at the same level it was in December 1998, before the real prompted mega devaluation.

12. The quotation here is from Krugman (1991).

13. See *Bridges Weekly Trade News Digest*, April 17, 2008 (www.ictsd.org/weekly/08-04-17/story1.htm [May 2008]).

14. This is the author's calculation, using data on published bound tariffs (www.wto.org/english/tratop_e/schedules_e/goods_schedules_table_e.htm [May 2008]) and applied tariffs (www.desenvolvimento.gov.br/sitio/interna/interna.php?area=5&menu=1848 [May 2008]).

"flexibilities," which would exempt 5 to 10 percent of the tariff lines from the full extent of the cuts, with a phase-in period of between eight and nine years.

Despite its modest impact, the press reported that Brazil and its partners in Mercosur see this proposal as a threat to their industries and are asking for a coefficient of 35.[15] Negotiating tactics aside, it seems reasonable to assume that is very unlikely that the Doha Round would do much to address the more blatant distortions of Brazil's current structure of protection. In other words, the "wait-for-Doha argument" would make sense if the government's negotiating position included a scenario where both the level and structure of the country's projection would be significantly overhauled. From what has been revealed so far, that does not seem to be the case.

It is also not clear that Brazil's bargaining power would be severely reduced if the country sat at the negotiating table with lower and more homogenous applied tariffs. The negotiations are about bound tariffs, and there are also other important trade-offs to put on the table, such as the expiration of the peace clause for agriculture, which, by the way, has allowed Brazil to challenge the U.S. subsidies for cotton. Open markets and the elimination of subsidies for agriculture are clearly welfare- and growth-enhancing outcomes for Brazil. What is not clear is that the country has to punish its economy with a dysfunctional tariff structure to achieve these results.

As to exchange rate appreciation, it is hard to dispute the fact that the recent steep appreciation of the exchange rate poses a challenge to the survival of manufacturing in Brazil, at a time when already-fierce competitive pressures from India and China will only increase. Yet tariffs are a very blunt instrument for dealing with this issue. This is a job for classical fiscal, monetary, and exchange rate policies. If every time the notorious volatile exchange rate moves, the government decides to change tariffs, the damage to price incentives and to resource allocation is likely to be severe—particularly because it is very likely that constant changes in tariffs are going to trigger special interest pressures that would inevitably shape an unexpected and undesired outcome. But even if we ignore these issues, the appreciation argument is a case for keeping tariff levels where they are right now. It does not give any justification for keeping the wide variation of tariffs across sectors seen earlier.

15. See, e.g., www.ictsd.org/weekly/08-04-17/story1.htm (September 2008).

Leaving aside those very circumstantial arguments about trade negotiations and the exchange rate, the road ahead for Brazil's tariff reform could not be clearer. The country should aim for a homogenous tariff across sectors, close to the average for countries belonging to the Organization for Economic Cooperation and Development (between 4 and 6 percent), which could only be changed by Congress.[16] This is important not only for enabling the country to enjoy the full benefits of trade but also for ensuring that its commercial policy is transparent and less vulnerable to lobbies and special interests—to put it simply, for ensuring that protection in Brazil "is not for sale."

Market Access and Regional Integration

There is both theoretical and empirical evidence suggesting that the gains from trade are maximized when a country not only opens up its own market but also has greater access to markets abroad.[17] This was not so much a concern for Brazil in the late 1980s, because protection was so high that the gains from bringing it down alone would dwarf any progress made in market access. At the current levels of protection, however, a strategy that combines lower tariffs at home with greater market access abroad is more likely to produce the best results. Unfortunately, Brazil's results in opening markets have been mixed.

Multilateral cum South-South Strategy

Brazil's market access strategy appears to be a combination of a multilateral thrust with an emphasis on South-South agreements. On the multilateral front, there were important advances in agriculture as Brazil, together with its partners in the Group of Twenty, successfully managed to push an agenda of substantial tariff cuts and greater discipline for subsidies and specific tariffs—issues that remained off limits during the last round of international negotiations. But these gains have yet to materialize, because the completion of the Doha Round remains uncertain and elusive. Brazil's reluctance in opening up its own market for manufacturing goods might not be the main obstacle to the agreement, but it clearly does not work in its favor.

16. Moreira (2004).
17. See, e.g., Harrison, Rutherford, and Tarr (2003).

It is the other strand of the strategy, however, that gives more cause for concern. Judging by Brazil's attitudes toward preferential agreements during the last decade, there appears to be an assumption that South-South agreements bring more net gains than their North-South equivalents. This is an assumption that may survive in the realm of politics, but it has a very short life when it comes to economics. This is not to deny that the trade gains of free trade agreements (FTAs) such as Mercosur are important and worth fighting for, but their limitations cannot be ignored.

The limited size of the market and the similarity of factor endowments impose severe constraints on scale and efficiency gains.[18] By contrast, the gains from North-South agreements are more promising for involving considerably larger markets and a longer array of comparative advantages. True, the risks of this type of initiative are higher, especially of dislocation of knowledge-intensive, growth-enhancing sectors. Yet Brazil's response to trade liberalization in the last decade plays down the likelihood of any catastrophic scenario.

Moreover, one cannot overlook the costs of nonparticipation, that is, the prospect of seeing Brazilian exporters paying higher tariffs than their competitors in the world's large markets and, therefore, being on the receiving end of trade diversion. Rather than a theoretical possibility, this is already the reality they are facing in the U.S. and EU markets where an increasing number of agreements are being signed (NAFTA, CAFTA-DR, Peru-U.S. FTA, U.S.-Australia, the EU enlargement, the EU-Mexico, and EU-Chile FTAs, to name but a few) and implemented.

The cost of nonparticipation acquires particularly dramatic contours in the context of the emergence of China and India, whose labor costs and size advantages leave Brazilian manufacturers in no position to forgo preferences in the markets of the North, particularly in the U.S. market.[19] As shown in figure 6-5, the tariffs levied on Brazilian goods entering the U.S. market are not that different from those levied on Chinese and Indian goods and are well above those paid by Mexico and Costa Rica. With the implementation of the new generation of agreements signed by the United States with Australia, with Central America, and with South America, Brazil's disadvantages are only going to increase.

To make things even more worrying, Brazil's preference for the South has only produced a very small number of very limited trade agreements,

18. Venables (2003).
19. See, e.g., Moreira (2007).

F I G U R E   6 - 5 . Tariffs Levied on Manufactured Goods Entering the U.S. Market, 2006

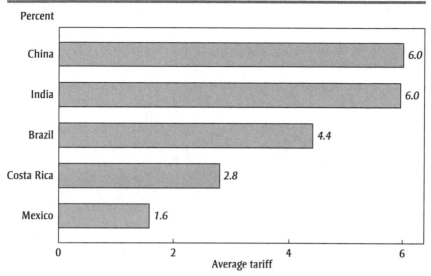

Sources: U.S. Census Bureau, data on U.S. imports of merchandise, 2000–06.

which, with the exception of Mercosur, either cover a very restricted number of tariff lines or have a long period of implementation (e.g., Brazil-Mexico, Mercosur–Andean Community, Mercosur-India, and Mercosur–Southern African Customs Union). This not only increases the costs of not having signed any major agreement with countries in the North but also leaves Brazil vulnerable to "negative preferences" or to having its preferences erode in the markets of the South, even in its own region.

Figure 6-6 illustrates this point, by comparing the "real" tariffs (tariff revenue divided by the value of imports) paid for similar Brazilian and U.S. goods when entering selected markets in Latin America. Whereas preferences are considerable in Mercosur and Colombia, that is not the case in Chile and Peru. In the case of the latter, U.S. preferences are even higher. With the full implementation of the U.S.-Chile and U.S-Peru FTAs, Brazil's position will deteriorate further, as will also be the case for Colombia if its FTA with the United States is eventually approved by the U.S. Congress. Data for Central America are not available, but given the depth and scope of the CAFTA-DR, it is very likely that Brazil will face a difficult situation there, too.

FIGURE 6-6. Tariffs Paid for Similar Brazilian and U.S. Goods When Entering Selected Markets in Latin America

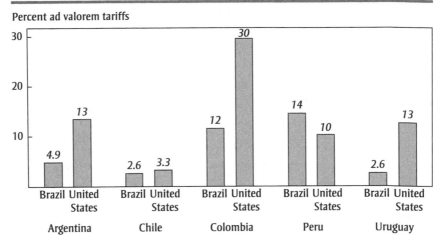

Percent ad valorem tariffs

Sources: Author's calculations based on data from the Latin American Association of Foreign Trade's Foreign Trade Statistics System.
Note: Products have the same 6-digit codes in the Harmonized Tariff System.

Mercosur

Brazil's South-South strategy faces steep challenges even in its more successful achievement: Mercosur. Despite repeated signs of discontent with the results of the agreement among its smaller partners, there is no evidence that Brazil is willing to tackle the fundamental flaws of the initiative.

The problems begin with misguided expectations. Mercosur was to a great extent sold on the idea it would help industrialize the smaller partners. Whereas it seems warranted to expect that an enlarged common market would deliver gains of scale and efficiency to all members of the bloc, there was nothing in the economic fundamentals of the countries involved that would indicate that this outcome was likely. Quite the contrary. Economic theory suggests that custom unions between partners that have similar factor endowments (and therefore similar factor prices, such as labor and capital) are more likely to promote the concentration of manufacturing activities in the largest partners, given the interplay of economies of scale and transport costs.[20]

20. See, e.g., Venables (2003).

The expectation of the industrialization of the smaller Mercosur members looks even more misguided when the mix of policies and incentives adopted by member countries is taken into account. For instance, Brazil, apart from being the bloc's largest and most industrialized economy, has by far the most generous industrial policy in the bloc.[21]

But the coup de grâce on these expectations comes from the available empirical evidence, which shows that the distribution of manufacturing activity among Mercosur's members has not changed significantly since 1991, with the bulk of industry still concentrated in Brazil.[22] To be sure, given the similarity of factor endowments and the asymmetries of size and policy, it is somewhat surprising that Brazil's share has not increased substantially. Yet Mercosur was just one of a large number of developments that have affected these economies during this period, ranging from unilateral liberalizations to different stabilization plans and different exchange rate policies, to name but a few.

The main problem with Mercosur, however, is not one of misguided expectations or asymmetric policies but one of policy design. The key pillar of the agreement, the Common External Tariff (CET), closely reflects Brazil's industrial interests and promotes an unfair distribution of costs and benefits. This is the bloc's most serious deficiency and the one that puts in doubt its long-term sustainability.

Because Brazil's applied tariffs follow closely the CET, the latter has exactly the same problems of level and variance as the former, but with the aggravating circumstance that it shifts part of the burden of protection to Mercosur's smaller partners. When the CET charges up to 16 percent on capital goods, it is shifting demand from producers outside the bloc to producers in Brazil (where regional production is concentrated) and is asking consumers in Uruguay and Paraguay to help pay the extra cost without getting any of the benefits.[23]

Fortunately, and precisely because of its shortcomings, the CET has not been fully implemented, which has helped to attenuate the costs. Yet without a functioning CET, countries cannot enjoy the full-scale benefits of a common market as they are forced to introduce costly regulations, such as rules of origin. Tariff reform for Brazil along the lines advocated above

21. For a thorough discussion of the policy and economic asymmetries within Mercosur, see Blyde, Giordano, and Fernández-Arias (2008).

22. Sanguinetti (2006); Blyde (2008).

23. On capital goods, see the Common External Tariff 2007 (www.desenvolvimento. gov.br/sitio/interna/interna.php?area=5&menu=1848).

would do more to consolidate the future of Mercosur than any amount of presidential declarations of commitment and support. With a more solid economic base and with down-to-earth expectations about what the bloc can deliver, it would be easier to advance in other problematic areas such as the harmonization of policies and incentives.

The "Other" Trade Costs

As in most of Latin America, trade policy in Brazil during the last two decades has been mostly about bringing down tariffs and NTBs and signing trade agreements. Whereas the focus on this single source of trade costs was justifiable in the earlier 1990s, given their sheer size, the country now faces a different reality.

For one thing, as shown above, unilateral trade liberalizations and preferential agreements have brought those barriers to a fraction of what they were in the past, and even though they are still unduly high for both imports and exports in some sectors and markets, they have clearly lost relevance vis-à-vis other less visible trade costs, such as transportation and regulatory costs.[24] Figure 6-7 illustrates this point vividly. As can be seen, the average freight expenditure for Brazil's exports to the United States stands well above what is paid for import tariffs and exports to Latin America.

For another thing, Brazil now faces a much-transformed world economy, which bears little resemblance to that of the 1980s and early 1990s. The combination of worldwide trade liberalization—which has brought vast and resourceful countries such as China and India into the world's markets—fast technological development, and falling communication and transport costs has reshaped countries' comparative advantages and has imposed a much higher penalty for economies that are complacent about nonpolicy trade costs.

This new reality calls for a more balanced trade agenda, whereby the government would strive not only to cut tariffs and NTBs at home and abroad (a job, as shown, that is far from over) but would also focus on what is generally referred to as trade facilitation. The pressing need for this new agenda is clear for both intraregional and extraregional trade. Without, for instance, improving a poor transport infrastructure—whose

24. For a thorough discussion of the impact of transport costs on trade in Latin America, including Brazil, see Moreira, Volpe, and Blyde (2008).

FIGURE 6-7. **Ad Valorem Freight and Tariffs Paid for Brazil's Exports to the United States and to Latin America, 2005–07[a]**

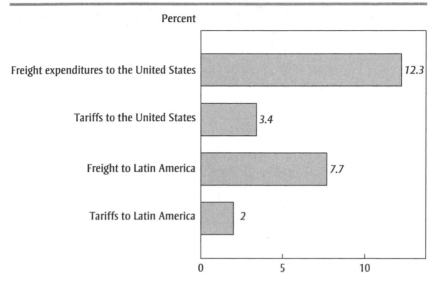

Percent

Sources: Latin American Association of Foreign Trade's Foreign Trade Statistics System; U.S. Census Bureau.
a. Tariffs and freight rates are simple averages. The data for Latin America are for 2005 exports to Argentina, Chile, Colombia, Eduador, Peru, and Uruguay; the data for exports to the United States are for 2007.

development was biased toward extraregional markets by centuries of colonial rule, and which has suffered badly from underinvestment in recent decades—it is unlikely that Brazil will maximize the gains of scale and specialization that can arise from preferential agreements such as Mercosur.[25]

Likewise, to expand and diversify its exports and take full advantage of the increasing fragmentation of production and the time-sensitiveness of international trade, Brazil can no longer rely solely on trade agreements, on relative proximity to large markets such as that of the United States, on low labor costs, and on an abundant supply of natural resources. Having much higher labor costs than Asia (and lower productivity growth),[26] and having seen its geographic advantage eroded

25. Brazil's investment in infrastructure has fallen abruptly in recent decades, dropping from 5 percent of GDP in the early 1980s to 2 percent during the 1990s. The decline in transport infrastructure has been even more drastic, falling from 1 to 0.2 percent over the same period (Calderón and Servén 2003).
26. Moreira (2007).

by rapidly falling air freight rates and by economies of scale and oligopolies in ocean transport, Brazil's role as a producer of manufacturing goods hinges crucially on improvements in its dilapidated transport infrastructure. Brazil's export transport costs to the key U.S. market do not reflect its proximity advantage. The ratio between Brazil's and China's export freight to the United States for similar goods is over 0.8, while the distance ratio is less than 0.6. Issues such as the volume of trade, the quality of infrastructure, and the degree of competition on shipping routes seem to be behind these figures.[27]

Transport costs also play a key role in Brazil's ability to extract the full benefits of its abundant natural resources. The deficiencies in its infrastructure have been depriving producers of a substantial part of their profits. This seems to be the case, for instance, for soy producers in western Brazil, which reportedly spend four times more to ship their product abroad than their counterparts in the U.S. Midwest. Along the same lines, worldwide ship shortages, driven mainly by growing Chinese demand for raw materials, have been pushing shipping rates to ever-growing heights. The Baltic Dry Index, which reflects freight rates for transporting raw materials, has increased by a factor of 6 since 2001 (as of January 2008), leading to odd situations such as that of iron ore, where ocean shipping from Brazil to Asia can be more expensive than the cargo itself.[28]

Summing Up

Brazil's trade agenda has both old and new issues, which are equally challenging. The old issues are related to a process of trade liberalization that clearly came to a halt in the 1990s. Whereas considerable progress was made until then, there is still an important job ahead to give Brazil the best chances of enjoying the welfare and growth benefits of trade. Protection is still relatively high and has a structure that is as dysfunctional and costly as it is incomprehensible. It distorts the allocation of resources and punishes growth with its high tariffs on capital goods, and it can only be understood as the product of lobbies and special inter-

---

27. See Moreira, Volpe, and Blyde (2008).
28. The Baltic Dry Index is published by the Baltic Exchange (www.balticexchange.com). See, e.g., *Wall Street Journal*, October 22, 2007.

ests. The way ahead is clear: a low, homogenous structure of protection that would remove once and for all these lingering trade costs from Brazil's trade agenda.

Unilateral liberalization alone, however, would not be enough to exploit the full benefits of trade. Market access remains high on the agenda, and Brazil's dual, multilateral South-South strategy has been producing mixed results. On the positive side is the progress made in putting agriculture at the center of the multilateral agenda. But concrete results have yet to come. On the negative side is a South-South agenda that has left Brazil without preferential access to the world's major markets, while failing to sign enough and significant South-South agreements to at least reduce the disadvantages of not making inroads in the North. Even Brazil's most significant achievement in the South, Mercosur, faces significant problems of misguided expectations and dysfunctional incentives, the latter due in great part to Brazil's unfinished job in opening its economy.

The new issues on Brazil's trade agenda have come from the increasing strategic importance of nonpolicy trade costs, which traditionally have been left out of the main thrust of trade policy. Costs such as transportation have gained importance in part because tariffs and NTBs are now much lower than they were a decade ago. But that is not the whole story. The transformation of the world economy—which, on the one hand, has increased the fragmentation of production and the timeliness of trade, and, on the other, has brought large and extremely competitive economies to the world's markets—is also behind the growing importance of trade facilitation. For a country like Brazil, which has traditionally underinvested in its infrastructure, the need to respond to these changes is gaining even more urgency, thus calling for a trade policy that can quickly and effectively reduce all the costs relevant to trade.

References

Blyde, J. 2008. "Convergence Dynamics in Mercosur." In *Deepening Integration in Mercosur: Dealing with Disparities,* ed. J. Blyde, P. Giordano, and E. Fernández-Arias. Washington: Inter-American Development Bank.

Blyde, J., P. Giordano, and E. Fernández-Arias, eds. 2008. *Deepening Integration in Mercosur: Dealing with Disparities.* Washington: Inter-American Development Bank.

Blyde, J., A. C. Pinheiro, C. Daude, and E. Fernández-Arias. 2007. "Competitiveness and Growth in Brazil." Inter-American Development Bank, Washington.

Calderón, C., and L. Servén. 2003. "The Output Cost of Latin America's Infrastructure Gap." In *The Limits of Stabilization: Infrastructure, Public Deficits and Growth in Latin America,* ed. W. Easterly and L. Servén. Stanford, Calif.: Stanford University Press for World Bank.

Calfat, G., and R. G. Flôres Jr. 2002. "Endogenous Protection in Mercosur: An Econometric Analysis." Paper presented at Regional Integration Network, Punta del Este.

Corden, W. M. 1971. *The Theory of Protection.* Oxford: Clarendon Press.

DeLong, J. B., and L. H. Summers. 1991. "Equipment Investment and Economic Growth." *Quarterly Journal of Economics* 106, no. 2: 445–502.

Grossman, G., and E. Helpman. 1994. "Protection for Sale." *American Economic Review* 84: 833–85.

Harrison, G. W., T. F. Rutherford, and D. G. Tarr. 2003. "Chile's Regional Arrangements: The Importance of Market Access and Lowering the Tariff to Six Percent." Working Paper 238. Banco Central de Chile.

IBGE (Instituto Brasileiro de Geografia e Estatística). 2007. *Sistema de Contas Nacionais Brasil 2000–2005.* Contas Nacionais 19. Rio de Janeiro.

Krugman, P. R. 1991. "The Move toward Free Trade Zones." Paper presented at Policy Implications of Trade and Currency Zones, symposium sponsored by Federal Reserve Bank of Kansas City, Jackson Hole, Wyoming, August 22–24.

Kume, H., G. Piani, and C. Bráz de Souza. 2000. "A política brasileira de importação no período 1987–1998: Descrição e avaliação." Instituto de Pesquisa Econômica Aplicada, Brasília.

López-Córdova, E., and M. Moreira. 2004. "Regional Integration and Productivity: The Experiences of Brazil and Mexico." In *FTAA and Beyond: Prospects for Integration in the Americas,* ed. A. Estevadeordal, D. Rodrik, A. Taylor, and A. Velasco. Cambridge, Mass.: David Rockefeller Center for Latin American Studies and Harvard University Press.

Moreira, M. M. 2004. "Brazil's Trade Liberalization and Growth: Has It Failed?" INTAL-ITD Working Paper 24. Washington: Inter-American Development Bank. Also in Portuguese: "Abertura e Crescimento: Passado e Futuro." In *Reformas no Brasil: Balanço e Agenda,* ed. F. Giambiagi, J. G. Reis, and A. Urani. Rio de Janeiro: Editora Nova Fronteira.

———. 2007. "Fear of China: Is There a Future for Manufacturing in Latin America?" *World Development* 35, no. 3: 355–76.

Moreira, M. M., C. Volpe, and J. Blyde. 2008. *Unclogging Arteries: A Report on the Impact of Transport Costs on the Region's Trade.* Cambridge, Mass.: Harvard University Press for Inter-American Development Bank.

Muendler, M. 2004. "Trade, Technology and Productivity: A Study of Brazilian Manufacturers, 1986–1998." CESIFO Working Paper 1148. Munich: Ifo Institute for Economic Research.

Sanguinetti, P. 2006. *Asimetrías en el Mercosur: ¿Son compatibles con el proceso de integración?* Estudio 005/06. Montevideo: Secretaria Técnica del Mercosur.

Venables, A. 2003. "Regionalism and Economic Development." In *Bridges for Development. Policies and Institutions for Trade and Integration,* ed. R. Devlin and A. Estevadeordal. Washington: Inter-American Development Bank.

PART **III**

Extending Brazilian
Multinationals' Global Reach

CHAPTER SEVEN

Big Business in Brazil
Leveraging Natural Endowments and State Support for International Expansion

BEN ROSS SCHNEIDER

> Name some Brazilian multinationals. Even harder than "famous Belgians," isn't it?
>
> —*The Economist,* September 23, 2000

By the late 2000s, *The Economist* was no longer poking fun at Brazilian multinational corporations (MNCs) and was instead running fairly breathless stories on emerging MNCs from developing countries, with Brazil prominent among them.[1] In the 1990s and early 2000s, neither the business press nor academics had much to say about Brazilian business. Most attention then was devoted to more macroeconomic issues of stabilization and market reform, and, as the reform process progressed, to reforming the reforms. There was little mention, in the evolving Washington Consensus, of the fate of big business in developing countries and the impact it might have on development prospects. This was a surprising lapse, given that the main agents of economic

The author is grateful to the Tinker Foundation for financial support, to Pedro Arieira for research assistance, and to Diego Finchelstein, Andrea Goldstein, Julia Guerreiro, and Leonardo Martinez-Diaz for comments on previous versions of this chapter.

1. E.g., *The Economist* ran several stories (March 1, 2008, January 10, 2008, and December 6, 2007) based largely on the report by the Boston Consulting Group (2007) on the largest 100 MNCs from developing countries.

activity, once the state withdraws, are large businesses, and the fact that earlier trajectories of successful development were closely associated with leading firms.[2]

Big Brazilian businesses are quite different from leading firms in earlier industrializing countries or in the high-growth countries of Asia, because they are largely concentrated in natural resources, semi-processed commodities, and some services, especially banking.[3] This chapter takes a historical and comparative perspective and seeks to answer several core questions about big businesses in Brazil:[4] Why these leading firms and not others? Out of which sectors did they emerge, and why? Why have they emerged as large global players in the 2000s (most are recent entrants into the global challengers category)? Why, in comparison with Asian countries, are there so few global giants, and why, in comparison with other countries of Latin America, are there so many?

Why these firms? To understand which firms grew to dominate the Brazilian economy and grow beyond it, we need to examine what Suzanne Berger calls "dynamic legacies."[5] In Brazil, these legacies almost always include a large contribution from the state. A number of the largest Brazilian MNCs—most prominently Vale and Embraer—were formerly state owned and continue to benefit from protection. Other firms also enjoyed protection (banking, steel, telecommunications, and transport) or received in the past sustained state assistance (construction and petrochemicals). This is not to deny the impressive entrepreneurial drive—the very dynamic part of "dynamic legacies"—of many of these firms after the reduction of state intervention in the 1990s, but it should also not be forgotten that few of these firms would have been in a position to expand as they did without prior state help.

The commodity bonanza of the 2000s had a profound impact on the growth of large firms in Brazil and the timing of their emergence as

2. Chandler, Amatori, and Hikino (1997).

3. Amsden (2001).

4. Note that my focus is exclusively on private firms that originated in Brazil and are still majority owned by domestic investors. This is only a partial view of big business in Brazil, because so many of the largest firms are either state owned (e.g., Petrobrás and Banco do Brasil) or foreign (the entire automobile sector). In addition, I exclude several firms that began as large private Brazilian firms but were subsequently acquired by or merged with foreign MNCs (e.g., Ambev). See table 7A-1 in the appendix for a recent ranking.

5. Berger (2005).

global players.[6] Brazil's commodity exports continued to boom through 2008 when they were expected to top $100 billion. Agriculture accounts for nearly three-quarters of commodity exports, and iron ore makes up most of nonagricultural commodity exports.[7] Among agricultural products, soybeans are the largest export, followed by meat, timber, and ethanol. Coffee, which accounted for half or more of total exports in the mid-twentieth century, is no longer even one of the main agricultural exports. However, outside the meat producers, other major agricultural exporters do not yet rank among the largest fifty or so firms in Brazil.

This chapter focuses primarily on the sectoral and more microlevel strategies of large firms, rather than on other important dimensions such as aggregate flows of investment, increasing corporate concentration, burgeoning equity markets, continuing family management, and other issues in corporate governance.[8] Suffice it to note here that large Brazilian firms manifest some distinctive traits on these dimensions, as well as some significant recent changes. For example, unlike large firms in developed economies like the United States, most large Brazilian firms are diversified business groups, as well as family owned and managed.[9] On the ownership side, the rapid expansion of the Brazilian stock market in the 2000s, and the large increase in the number of initial public offerings, introduced important shifts in financing options, especially for some of the new service firms. The conclusion to the chapter considers some implications of this expansion.

The following sections examine major Brazilian business groups and leading Brazilian MNCs by sector. The analysis begins with steel, meat, and other semiprocessed commodities (second section), then turns to manufacturing (third section), especially aircraft manufacturing by Embraer. The fourth section considers important firms in services like banking, engineering (and construction), transportation, and telecommunications. The fifth section provides a comparative overview of the evolution of big business in Brazil relative to other countries in Latin America as well as other developing regions, and it considers several aspects of the contribution of big business to Brazilian development.

6. See Ocampo (2008).
7. This was reported by *Folha de São Paulo,* March 16, 2008.
8. See Aldrighi and Postali (2007).
9. Schneider (2008).

Basic Commodities: Steel, Meat, and Other Semiprocessed Products

Most of Brazil's largest firms and earliest entries into global markets have succeeded by leveraging growth in commodities that grew in the 1990s and boomed through the late 2000s.[10] At first glance, steel, aluminum, cement, beef, frozen chicken, and cellulose would seem not to fit under the same heading. Though these sectors are clearly different in production technologies, labor intensity, and consumer markets, they do share a number of core features. First, these are commodity markets where firms compete more on price than quality (and brand). Second, the manufacturing component of operations is fairly limited to processing raw materials. For most firms, their outputs are basic inputs for other industries, so they deliver large quantities to a small number of customers and consequently have few costs in marketing, advertising, and distribution (and the white-collar jobs they generate). Put differently, value added per unit is low, especially by labor, either because there are few workers involved (e.g., mining and steel) or because they are unskilled (meat packing). Third, these are old industries that are not innovation intensive and whose research and development (R&D) expenditures are consequently relatively low.[11] Beyond these broad common features, the development paths of the major commodity sectors, and the large firms in them, follow very different trajectories.

Steel

Brazil's steel industry took off in the 1940s with Companhia Siderúrgica Nacional (CSN), a state-owned steel mill.[12] Over the next several decades, the government created additional firms (the largest, Usiminas and Açominas, in the state of Minas Gerais), and it ultimately combined them into a state holding company, Siderbrás. Over the course of this expansion, especially in the 1950s and 1960s, the Banco Nacional de Desenvolvimento Econômico e Social (BNDES, National Economic and Social Development Bank) was crucial both in financing and planning, so much so that

---

10. This is a common pattern throughout the region. For the 500 largest firms in Latin America as a whole (including state-owned firms), 50 percent of their sales came from energy, mining, and food, and another 10 percent from beer and cement; see *América Economia,* April 23, 2007.

11. Corrêa and Lima (2008, 255).

12. For more history, see Schneider (1991).

for some it came to be known informally as the "Steel Bank." Although output expanded steadily, it was not until the recession of the 1980s and privatization of the 1990s that steel firms became highly productive and competitive internationally.

When the Fernando Collor de Mello government announced an ambitious program for privatization in 1990, the government's steel firms were at the top of the "for sale" list, and, ironically, the BNDES was put in charge of fixing up the firms it had helped build and managing their transfer to private ownership. Between 1991 and 1993, the government sold off its eight main steel firms, all to Brazilian buyers, because the privatization program put a ceiling on foreign participation of 40 percent (though initially it was less than 5 percent in all firms sold).[13] By the mid-1990s, the privatized firms were profitable, much more productive, and exporting much of their output.[14] By the 2000s, Brazilian steelmakers had consolidated into four large groups (one of them foreign owned), employment had dropped by almost two-thirds, productivity had more than tripled, and Brazil was one of the lowest-cost steel producers in the world.[15] By 2003, Brazil was the world's eighth-largest producer and exported nearly a third of total production of 30 million tons per year.

Yet by the 2000s it was clear that the three main Brazilian firms had adopted different strategies and corporate governance.[16] Usiminas, the first to be privatized, remained largely a standalone producer of rolled steel, and it expanded domestically by acquiring another large public producer, Cosipa. CSN was purchased by the scion of an existing business group in textiles (Vicunha). CSN also participated in subsequent privatizations, notably in Vale and Light (electricity distribution), though it later sold off its stake in Vale. In the mid-2000s, CSN made an unsuccessful bid for a major international expansion (Corus in Britain), but otherwise neither Usiminas nor CSN had a major presence outside Brazil. Gerdau pursued a much different strategy. It was one of the few major private, pre-privatization steel producers. Gerdau had been in the steel business for nearly a century and capitalized on its expertise and

13. Amann, Ferraz, and Paula (2006, 157–60).
14. Montero (1998).
15. Siekman (2003).
16. The fourth large group, constituted by the flagship Companhia Siderúrgica de Tubarão and several smaller subsidiaries, was acquired by Arcelor in 2005, and, in turn, Mittal bought Arcelor in 2006. Arcelor-Mittal's total capacity in Brazil as of 2008 was 11 million tons (see http://cst.com.br).

the opportunities to buy up several smaller state-owned firms and leveraged its domestic expansion to acquire steel firms throughout the Americas and become one of Brazil's largest private firms. By the mid-2000s, Gerdau was the largest steel producer, with an annual output of around 15 million tons. In 2006, Gerdau had thirty plants (eleven in Brazil and nineteen spread over Latin America, Europe, and United States) and 27,500 employees.[17]

Although the state no longer produces steel, it still has had a profound effect on the evolution of the sector since privatization. As noted above, privatization statutes protected domestic investors by prohibiting foreign takeovers. In addition, major shareholders included other state-owned enterprises, the BNDES, and the pension funds of several state enterprises. Although the ownership structure has gone through numerous transformations, the indirect hand of the state has usually been visible. Last, the BNDES continued at least through the 1990s to finance a significant and increasing share of total sectoral investment.[18]

Cement, Pulp and Paper, Aluminum, and Other Commodities

Votorantim is active in all these sectors and represents the classic Brazilian business group. It is run by the visible and iconoclastic Antônio Ermírio de Moraes (grandson of the founder), and it has major subsidiaries in a range of processed bulk commodities, including cement, aluminum, electric energy (hydroelectric plants), paper and cellulose, other metals, chemicals, orange juice, the Internet, and finance (Banco Votorantim).[19] Although it is one of the best known, and most traditional, business groups, Votorantim stands apart for its independence and reluctance to accept government support and suggestions.[20] Among the firms covered in this chapter, Votorantim owes less to direct government support. However, it is also noteworthy that it probably needed that help less than other firms that were in less naturally protected sectors. That is, most of Votorantim's activities are in sectors tied to natural resources (juice, mining), tied to natural advantages (hydropower), or

---

17. These data are from *Dinheiro,* August 2, 2006.

18. Amann, Ferraz, and Paula (2006, 172).

19. Two other large business groups, Suzano and Klabin, are also major cellulose producers. Klabin is more specialized, but Suzano has major holdings in petrochemicals as well. See table 7A-1 in the appendix for more on these firms.

20. Evans (1979).

sheltered from international competition (cement), so it had less need for government help.[21]

Meat

After soybeans, meat is Brazil's second-largest agricultural export. Argentina dominated meat exports from Latin America in the twentieth century, but Brazilian exports expanded much more rapidly after 1990 and now dwarf Argentine exports. Three firms grew to be world leaders in this expansion. In one of the most rapid and spectacular expansions, JBS combined a string of aggressive international acquisitions to become the largest beef producer in the world in 2007.[22] With these acquisitions, revenue tripled from 2006 to 2007 to over $7 billion, and JBS came to have more employees abroad than in Brazil.[23] JBS is also a major pork producer and had the capacity by 2008 to slaughter nearly 100,000 cattle per day. The other two major meat producers, Sadia and Perdigão, both had revenues close to $5 billion by 2008.[24] In contrast to JBS, both firms were more concentrated in poultry, had most of their operations in Brazil, and exported a large share of total production. Each company also had significant operations and domestic sales in other food sectors—processed and frozen food in the case of Sadia, and dairy products in the case of Perdigão.

Vale

Vale—which was previously known as the Companhia do Vale do Rio Doce (CVRD), established in the 1940s—had some rocky moments in its early decades. But by the 1980s, it was a huge, well-run mining firm.[25] It grew up around the iron ore mines in the central state of Minas Gerais, and it established efficient transportation networks. It then replicated this experience in a series of new mining projects, for both iron ore and other

21. Another major cement producer in both Brazil and Argentina, Camargo Corrêa, is considered below because it grew out of engineering and construction.

22. JBS did not figure among the 200 largest business groups in 2003 (*Valor Econômico* 2004). It was not until its acquisitions of 2006 and 2007 that its total revenues would put it in the ranks of the top twenty business groups; see the appendix.

23. See the JBS website, www.jbs.com.br.

24. See *Gazeta Mercantil,* March 19, 2008.

25. Petrobrás is the other giant in natural resources, but is not covered here because it is state controlled. Vale and Petrobrás accounted for 30 percent of the stock market (*The Economist,* March 7, 2008).

minerals, in the Amazon, at the same time it entered into upstream joint ventures in steel and aluminum.[26] The other keys to its early success were more idiosyncratic, in that it enjoyed early political protection from the state government of Minas Gerais and later benefited from the long tenure of several effective managers. In addition, it did not face such tough challenges in being competitive in world markets, given the relatively low technology of production and the high quality of Brazilian ore deposits.

At the time of privatization in 1997, the Brazilian government retained a golden share in Vale that gave it veto power over major changes in corporate governance.[27] In the decade after privatization, Vale's growth was dramatic. It invested tens of billions of dollars in both greenfield operations and acquisitions, especially abroad. These investments, as well as very favorable mineral prices (especially for iron ore and nickel, which accounted for more than two-thirds of its revenues), generated remarkable revenue growth—from less than $5 billion in 1997 to more than $30 billion in 2007.[28] Vale's new private managers sold off many non-mining subsidiaries, but at the same time diversified out of iron ore into other minerals, especially nickel, copper, and bauxite, as well as logistics, energy, and upstream ventures in steel and aluminum. They also diversified geographically, moving from nearly all production in Brazil to about half. By 2008, Vale was the largest iron ore producer in the world and second in nickel, one of a handful of global mining behemoths, and one of the most remarkable corporate successes in the past decade in Latin America.

EBX

EBX differs in most respects from Vale. It is new (founded in 1980) and more diversified outside its core activities in gold and iron ore mining (with subsidiaries in petroleum, energy, real estate, and entertainment). Though EBX owes little to direct government promotion or protection, it has drawn a lot of executive expertise from state-owned enterprises or

---

26. Schneider (1991).

27. The golden shares give the government veto power over changes in name, location of head offices, liquidation of the company, and closing or sale of important mining or transportation operation. By 2008, the government still owned, in addition to the golden shares, 10 percent of Vale's stock (the BNDES held 7 percent and the Treasury 3 percent; these data are from http://vale.com [June 2008]). In addition, the BNDES and government-related pension funds held 60 percent of the shares in the controlling shareholder bloc, Valepar (which has 53 percent of Vale's voting shares) (Aldrighi and Postali 2007, 10).

28. See http://vale.com.

former state enterprises because many of its directors and engineers were hired away from firms like Vale, Petrobrás, and Electrobrás.[29] EBX is also much more dynamic in buying and selling mining and corporate assets. Figuratively and literally, it represents a generational shift; its founder, Eike Batista, is the son of the visionary president of CVRD, Eliezer Batista, who led CVRD through its major expansion in the 1970s and 1980s. Although EBX did not by the mid-2000s rank among the top several dozen business groups (and its total revenues at any point in time are hard to ascertain because it acquires and spins off subsidiaries with such rapidity), it is the kind of company that could leverage commodity growth to become one of Brazil's largest groups.

From this section, the answer to the question of why these firms in these sectors is fairly clear. Save for upstarts like JBS and EBX, these firms were among the largest in their respective sectors in the early 1990s, and they took off with the boom in demand and sustained high commodity prices in international markets.

Manufacturing

There are two striking things about this section on manufacturing. The first is its major focus, Embraer, which is one of the amazing stories of business development in Brazil over the last decade. Embraer is the only major commercial aircraft manufacturer from a developing country, and it is one of the few Brazilian firms that are likely to become a household name in developed countries, because so many millions of passengers have flown in Embraer jets. The second striking aspect of this section is that Embraer is the only firm in it. Other emerging MNCs from developing countries are prominent in automobiles, shipbuilding, informatics, electronics, and other manufacturing sectors (especially from Asia), but Brazil has only one huge high-technology manufacturing MNC.[30] Of course, Brazil is a major exporter of a range of manufactured goods, from automobiles (and auto parts) to cellphones, but these exports are produced by foreign-owned MNCs.

---

29. The success of OGX, an oil subsidiary that raised $3.6 billion in an initial public offering in 2008, is due in part to the strategy of hiring exploration engineers from Petrobrás (*The Economist*, June 19, 2008).
30. See Goldstein (2007).

Embraer (Empresa Brasileira de Aeronáutica) is one of Brazil's national champions.[31] By 2007, it had 24,000 employees, up from 7,000 in 1998.[32] It competes head to head with developed-world companies (Bombardier), exports 95 percent of its production, leads Brazil in manufactured exports, and leads the world market for unit sales of regional aircraft.[33] However, fifteen years ago, almost no one would have predicted that this "ugly duckling" would emerge such a champion. In fact, the first time the firm was put up for sale in a privatization auction in the early 1990s, it had to be taken off the block for lack of buyers, and it did not turn a profit until 1998. What saved the firm in the mid-1990s, and catapulted it on to a trajectory of long-term growth, was the coincidental emergence of a rapidly growing market for regional, medium-size jets (i.e., jets with 50–100 seats) in the United States.[34] Since 1996, it has shipped more than 1,000 aircraft to twenty countries.[35]

However, being in a position to fill this new demand depended on several decades of prior institutional development after Embraer's founding in 1969. Two key factors shaped these early decades. First, the firm was created by the Air Force, during military rule, with a clear connection to military goals for national defense, so it had strong backers and clear noncommercial goals. For most of its incarnation as a state-owned enterprise, it was subordinate to the Ministry of the Air Force (rather than the Ministry of Industry and Commerce or the Ministry of Mines and Energy, as with most state-owned enterprises), as well as protected by it from intervention by politicians or outside civilian ministries.

Second, Embraer could draw on skilled personnel from the nearby Instituto Tecnológico da Aeronáutica (ITA) and Centro Técnico da Aeronáutica (CTA).[36] In fact, the training of aeronautical engineers by

31. See Goldstein (2002) and chapter 8 in this volume by Amann.

32. See http://embraer.com.

33. Goldstein (2008, 58).

34. Revenues increased more than tenfold in a decade, from $300 million in 1995 to $4 billion in 2005 (*Newsletter IBGC,* May 2006). Previously, however, Embraer had a long-established presence in markets for smaller turboprop planes. In the 1970s, its nineteen-seat Bandeirante captured nearly half the North American market. The thirty-seat Brasília had a quarter of the world market in the 1980s (Avrichir and Caldas 2005, 48).

35. Goldstein (2008, 58).

36. ITA and then CTA were Air Force initiatives shortly after World War II designed explicitly to promote the transfer and absorption of technology in Brazil. Both programs developed close connections with, and drew heavily on, the aeronautical engineering program at the Massachusetts Institute of Technology (Avrichir and Caldas 2005, 49).

ITA preceded the establishment of Embraer, and Embraer could also later count on ITA for collaboration in R&D.[37] This protection and assistance meant that Embraer could survive for many years on continued subsidies. Among other things, the government, through the BNDES, provided subsidized credit to buyers, taxed competing imports, and offered prepayment on government contracts.[38] By the 1980s, critics were even charging that Embraer in fact subtracted rather than added value, in that the cost of the inputs was greater than the price of the final planes it sold. However, the subsidies and opportunity for learning through trial and error allowed the firm to develop its own models for regional jets, which turned out by the 1990s to be highly competitive in world markets.

Government support for Embraer continued after its privatization, especially for export financing and R&D, and protection from outside takeover attempts. The firm continued to receive funding from the BNDES, as well as the Financiadora de Estudos e Projetos (FINEP) and the Programa de Desenvolvimento Tecnológico Industrial (PDTI) for R&D. Total subsidies to Embraer amounted to R$142 million from 1993 to 2000 (when the real was near parity with the dollar).[39] One of the main reasons Embraer has emerged as a *national* champion is that the government retained a small ownership stake (initially 7 percent) and a golden share that grants it veto power over major ownership changes. Moreover, the government stipulated at the time of privatization in 1994 that foreign ownership of the firm could not exceed 40 percent. Without these protections, Embraer would have been an attractive target for foreign acquisition.

Services

Big businesses in services are divided between long-standing firms, founded mostly in the 1930s and 1940s, in banking, construction, and retail, and newer firms created through privatization (as in telecommunications) or the withdrawal of the state (air transport). These services are essentially nontradable, so these firms were less affected by trade liberalization. However, in other countries of the region, these are sectors where foreign MNCs have been actively acquiring many domestic firms. That these sectors are less denationalized than elsewhere requires an

37. Goldstein (2008, 59).
38. Avrichir and Caldas (2005, 49).
39. Goldstein (2008, 59).

examination of government regulation and promotion, as well as particular group-level obstacles to takeovers.

Engineering and Construction

Brazil's largest three engineering and construction firms—Odebrecht, Camargo Corrêa, and Andrade Gutierrez—were all founded in the late 1930s and early 1940s, and they expanded with a series of government programs that began in the 1950s: investment in infrastructure and a national transportation network, the construction of Brasília, the development of hydroelectricity, and the megaprojects of the 1970s. After the 1970s, and accelerating after the 1980s, all three groups looked to diversify by going abroad and by entering new sectors at home.

Founded in Bahia in 1944, Odebrecht was one of the few large Brazilian firms to come from the North. By the 2000s, it had operations in more than a dozen countries and across a range of sectors, including construction, engineering, petrochemicals, insurance, and private infrastructure development. Its major subsidiaries outside construction revolved around petrochemicals, initially in consortia with MNCs and Petroquisa, the government's state-owned enterprise in the sector. However, the Odebrecht subsidiary in petrochemicals, Braskem, now has a broad range of autonomous ventures. In 2007, Braskem joined a consortium to buy Ipiranga (until then one of the largest business groups in Brazil). Braskem also expanded into other countries of the Americas, including a large joint venture in Venezuela. Total revenues for Braskem in 2007 were more than $12 billion.[40] Camargo Corrêa has been less expansive abroad and more broadly diversified in Brazil. By the 2000s, it had major subsidiaries beyond construction and engineering in cement, electricity generation, textiles, and footwear. In 2005, Camargo Corrêa bought the Argentine cement giant Loma Negra, doubling its capacity from 2 to 4 million tons of cement annually. Overall, however, Camargo Corrêa got less than 25 percent of its revenues from non-Brazilian operations, and it had invested only in Latin America.[41]

Telecommunications

The third major construction company, Andrade Gutierrez, made its major mark outside construction in telecommunications. The govern-

40. Goyzueta and Piedragil (2008).
41. ECLAC (2006, 72).

ment's privatization program in telecommunications in the late 1990s was carefully prepared, costly (or revenue generating, for the seller), and generally viewed as one of the most successful divestitures in the region.[42] The government sought to ensure postprivatization competition, so government planners divided the country into multiple regions and within regions into multiple service segments (e.g., mobile vs. fixed line), and limited the ability of firms to dominate multiple segments and regions. For the most part, the government did not favor domestic investors, though when one firm, Oi (previously Telemar), emerged as the leading Brazilian firm in competition with Mexican and Spanish giants, the government took steps to encourage it. Andrade Gutierrez was one of Oi's major shareholders.[43] In 2008, the government favored Oi's bid to acquire Brasil Telecom. The combined venture would have 70 percent of Brazil's fixed-line market, 40 percent of its broadband Internet services, and almost 20 percent of its mobile market, the largest and fastest-growing segment of the telecommunications market.[44]

Finance

Three banks—Itaú, Bradesco, and Unibanco—dominate private banking in Brazil.[45] Bradesco has long been the largest private Brazilian firm, and all three banks have consistently ranked in the top ten largest groups (see the appendix and table 7A-1 there). In the wake of the banking crisis of 2007–8, Brazilian banks rose in international rankings. By early 2008, Bradesco (already the largest bank in Brazil and in Latin America) and Itaú were among the ten largest banks in the Americas (ahead of Merrill Lynch) and among the top twenty-five worldwide.[46] These banks have been somewhat slower than other large Brazilian firms to expand abroad, and none of them ranked in 2006 among the twenty Brazilian MNCs with the most assets abroad—though Itautec, the information technology

---

42. Castelar, Bonelli, and Schneider (2007).

43. Over the past decades, several of Brazil's largest groups bought minority positions (though always as a part of a controlling bloc) in other large firms—e.g., Andrade Gutierrez in Oi, Odebrecht in Ipiranga, Bradesco in Vale, and Safra in Aracruz. See Aldrighi and Postali (2007) for a full account.

44. Economist Intelligence Unit, *Business Latin America,* May 5, 2008.

45. A full analysis of finance in Brazil would also need to cover the huge public banks: Banco do Brazil, Caixa Econômica, and the BNDES. See Castelar (2007) and Martinez-Diaz (forthcoming).

46. *Gazeta Mercantil,* email synopsis, March 21, 2008.

subsidiary of Itaú, did.[47] Itaú expanded into Chile, almost by accident, when it acquired the Bank of Boston's operations in Brazil.[48] Most private banks in the other large countries of Latin America, especially Argentina and Mexico, have been acquired by foreign banks, mostly U.S. and Spanish based. The Brazilian government opened the banking sector to foreign firms, in principle, but in practice government regulators have been selective in approving entry and thus provide protection for the big three.[49]

Air Transportation

Although not yet among the ranks of the huge, several airlines emerged as some of the most dynamic and fastest-growing firms in Brazil. The airline sector, as well as the air transport system as a whole, has been through a great deal of turbulence, both corporate and logistical, in the last decade. Yet, as the previously dominant carriers, Varig, Transbrasil, and Vasp, went through bankruptcy and restructuring, two new, lower-cost carriers, Tam and Gol, expanded rapidly to meet new demand (with double-digit growth through most of the 2000s) and evolved into a fairly matched duopoly (Tam had 49 percent of the domestic market in 2007, against 43 percent for Gol[50]). Although not yet on the scale of Latin America's largest private carrier, LAN Chile, Gol and Tam have opportunities to continue to grow at a rapid pace (provided problems in Brazil's air traffic control do not slow them down). As in most countries, foreign ownership of domestic airlines is restricted in Brazil, so neither firm faces the threat of foreign takeover.[51]

Retailing

Pão de Açucar is the largest Brazilian firm in retailing. It was established in 1948, and it led the expansion and modernization of retailing in Brazil with supermarkets in the 1960s and hypermarkets in the 1970s, as well as convenience and department stores. In the 1970s and 1980s, it also expanded outside retail operations, but soon after it spun off its nonretail subsidiaries during its crisis and restructuring in the 1990s. Many foreign

47. Fundação Dom Cabral and Columbia University Program on International Investment, "Brazil's Multinationals Take Off," press release, 2007.
48. Interview, Rodolfo Fischer, executive vice president, Banco Itaú, August 3, 2006.
49. Martinez-Diaz (forthcoming).
50. SNA (2008, 1).
51. Davies (2004, 15).

retailers, especially Carrefour, have taken large market shares in Brazil, but Pão de Açucar has survived as the largest Brazilian retailer (though it sold half control to the French Casino Group in the mid-2000s). However, unlike the aggressive Chilean retailers Falabella and Cencosud, Pão de Açucar has few operations outside Brazil.

Summary

In sum, outside commodities, most of Brazil's largest and fastest-growing firms over the last decades have been in services, especially those segments that have seen the most rapid expansion, such as mobile telephony, banking, and air travel. As with big business in other sectors, service firms have also leveraged various forms of past government promotion and continuing government protection to good advantage.

Comparative Overview

Big Brazilian firms are generally more numerous and larger than business groups from the smaller countries of Latin America, which is not surprising, given that they emerged in the largest economy of the region. By 2005, more than 40 percent of the largest firms in the region were from Brazil (figure 7-1). The countries above the diagonal line in figure 7-1 (Brazil, Mexico, and Chile) had proportionally more of the largest firms in the region relative to their share of economic output. Argentina, Colombia, Peru, and Venezuela had proportionally fewer large firms. A first interpretation is that, with the exception of Chile, firms are likely to grow large in larger domestic markets.[52] A more detailed explanation, beyond the scope of this chapter, would likely focus on important policies in Chile, Brazil, and Mexico that favored the growth of large firms, as well as the generally less volatile political and macroeconomic environments in these three countries than in Argentina, Colombia, Venezuela, and Peru.

The domestic private sectors of most developing countries are dominated by huge, family-owned, diversified business groups.[53] Brazil is an outlier in this regard because of the prominence of several huge, institutionally owned, and relatively specialized firms. On the ownership side, one survey of thirty-three of the largest business groups in Latin America

---

52. Santiso (2007, 29).
53. Khanna and Yafeh (2007); Morck, Wolfenzon, and Yeung (2005).

FIGURE 7-1. Percentage of Latin America's Largest Firms
by Percentage of Gross National Income

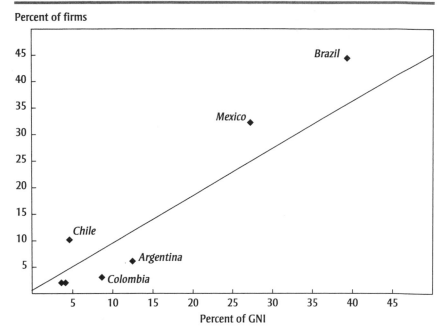

Percent of firms

Sources: Included are all 295 firms with sales over $1 billion in 2005 from seven countries in Latin America—
Argentina, Brazil, Chile, Colombia, Mexico, Peru, and Venezuela, as reported in *América Economia*, July 14, 2006.
This tally of firms also includes some multinational corporations and state-owned firms. Gross national income,
adjusted for purchasing power parity, for these same seven economies is from World Bank (2004, 256–61).
    Note: The countries above the diagonal line (Brazil, Mexico, and Chile) had proportionally more of the largest
firms in the region relative to their share of economic output.

found that more than 90 percent were family owned.[54] For the twenty-
three Brazilian groups listed in table 7A-1 in the appendix, the proportion
is closer to three-quarters.[55] Companies like Vale and Embraer are rare in
developing countries in the absence of family ownership. Privatizations of
similar firms in other countries usually meant acquisition by either MNCs
or family business groups. The key difference in Brazil was the role of
pension funds and the BNDES in facilitating and financing privatization

---

    54. Schneider (2008).
    55. Aldrighi and Postali (2007, 9–10) found a similar proportion—sixteen out of twenty-
six of the largest business groups were family owned—though they also note that family-
owned groups were also prominent shareholders in many of the other ten groups.

to institutional buyers. Of course, other major Brazilian firms, some of which are family owned, have invested major stakes in these firms (e.g., Bradesco in Vale), but they do not have the absolute control characteristic of group acquisitions elsewhere.

Major firms like Vale, Embraer, the big banks, and other new entrants (as in meat and airlines) are also more specialized than large firms in other developing countries.[56] Some of this specialization can be attributed to the fact that these firms were "born" specialized through the process of privatization, and some of them may ultimately evolve into, or be acquired by, more diversified groups. However, even these firms tend to be more diversified than similar firms in developed countries, especially the United States. Vale, for example, has diversified into new minerals and maintains major subsidiaries in transportation, logistics, and energy, though these are all organically connected to core mining activities. At the same time, some new entrants like EBX, as well as long-standing groups like Votorantim or Odebrecht, have successfully managed much broader, and unrelated, diversification. The conclusion, at least for the past several decades, is that the Brazilian economy has accommodated two very different strategies, either specialization or diversification.[57]

Compared with the largest firms in other regions, business groups in Latin America are small. For example, among the 50 largest manufacturing firms from developing economies in 1993, there was only one private firm from Latin America, Vitro in Mexico. The list included six firms in Brazil, but they were all foreign or state owned.[58] In a global survey, the Inter-American Development Bank found that "the largest firms in Latin America are very small in comparison with other regions in the world. Among seven regions, Latin America comes in last in average size in terms of total assets of the countries' 25 largest companies."[59] It found that the three variables that explained 85 percent of the variance were country size, size of the financial sector, and quality of infrastructure.[60] In a study of 100 "global challengers" from developing economies (excluding South Korea, Hong Kong, Singapore, and Taiwan), Brazil had 13 firms, Mexico

56. Schneider (forthcoming).
57. Goldstein and Schneider (2004); Aldrighi and Postali (2007).
58. Amsden (2001, 198–99).
59. IDB (2001, 35, 40).
60. However, the Inter-American Development Bank study looked only at the largest firms, not the conglomerates or groups to which they might belong, so the results might vary if these firms were combined into their relevant groups.

had 7, and Latin America had 22 combined, compared with 41 from China and 20 from India.[61] Last, in a ranking of emerging MNCs from developing countries, only two private Brazilian firms (and only three more from the rest of Latin America) made it into the top 50 (measured by foreign assets), compared with dozens from smaller Asian economies like Singapore, Hong Kong, Taiwan, and South Korea.[62]

Another way to understand differences in size and sectoral distribution is qualitative and historical. Brazil and South Korea had different development strategies and growth trajectories throughout the late twentieth century that profoundly affected the evolution of the large business groups in each country. In the 1960s, South Korea's military regime promoted large firms, and President Park Chung Hee explicitly viewed large firms as "indispensable."[63] By the 1970s, the government was pushing the already-mammoth *chaebol* (business groups) into a variety of new sectors with cheap credit and few limits on borrowing. Moreover, the export push of this period meant that the *chaebol* were not held back by the limitations of the Korean market. In Brazil, in sharp contrast, import-substitution industrialization greatly limited markets. Other policies promoted domestic firms, but with restraint, in that the government wanted to maintain competition in all sectors, and the main source of long-term finance, the BNDES, placed limits on firms' debt/equity ratios.[64]

The other approach to the question of why these firms in these sectors is to ask why not other firms in other sectors. Large firms from Asia are more concentrated in middle- and high-technology manufacturing, such as automobiles, shipbuilding, cellphones, and computers, where none of Brazil's largest domestic firms has a presence. The deeper historical cause is that Brazil, unlike Japan and South Korea, encouraged MNC investment in most manufacturing sectors throughout the late twentieth century.[65] So, though Brazil is a major and growing auto exporter, the exporting firms are all foreign MNCs. More recently, the penetration of MNCs into manufacturing accelerated through a boom in acquisitions since the 1990s.[66] Though Brazilian commodity firms were able to leverage record prices, high profits, and easy credit into takeovers abroad,

61. Boston Consulting Group (2007, 8).
62. Goldstein (2007, 27–29).
63. Amsden (1989, 50).
64. Amsden (2001, 226).
65. Evans (1979).
66. Rocco (2007).

Brazilian manufacturing firms instead became attractive targets for takeovers from abroad. Trade liberalization in the 1990s subjected many manufacturing firms to intense international competition that lowered their prices, squeezed their profit margins, and forced them to adjust, and thereby generally lowered their market value so that they became attractive options for MNCs looking to expand or establish operations in Brazil (often with an eye to using Brazilian operations to enter markets in the Southern Cone). So, most of the mergers and acquisitions bustle in the 1990s and 2000s involved foreign takeovers.[67]

Outward foreign direct investment (FDI) by leading Brazilian firms really took off after 2004 and even exceeded inward FDI in 2006,[68] though the bulk of the investment has run through a handful of firms, notably Vale and Petrobrás. The stock of outward FDI from Brazil grew from $69 billion in 2001 to $112 billion in 2005. As in most major corporate transitions of the past half century, the BNDES stepped in to help support and finance outward FDI by Brazilian firms.[69] However, more than 70 percent of this stock was located in offshore financial centers (*paraísos fiscais*).[70] In terms of strategies for international investment, Brazilian FDI in productive ventures has been predominantly market seeking or resource seeking, rather than efficiency seeking, as is more common among manufacturing firms (Embraer is again the clear exception to this general pattern). More generally for Latin America, "compared to their Asian peers, which leveraged technological prowess and social capital in their foreign expansion, *multilatinas* have invested abroad on the basis of a superior ability to manage the process of economic liberalization."[71] And, with the exception of several billion dollars in greenfield investments by Vale and Petrobrás, nearly all the remaining Brazilian FDI has come through acquisitions.[72]

67. Domestic acquisitions grew 40 percent in 2007 to exceed foreign acquisitions for the first time in four years; *Gazeta Mercantil,* online summary, December 21, 2007. See Aldrighi and Postali (2007). The Brazilian firm Metalfrio, though still not among the giants, is an interesting exception. It is one of the few middle-technology manufacturing firms (freezers mostly) that has thrived in Brazil and expanded through major acquisitions abroad.

68. Fundação Dom Cabral and Columbia University Program on International Investment, "Brazil's Multinationals Take Off," press release, 2007, 15.

69. Goldstein (2007, 98).

70. Corrêa and Lima (2008, 251).

71. Goldstein (2007, 69).

72. Beausang (2003); Fundação Dom Cabral and Columbia University Program on International Investment, "Brazil's Multinationals Take Off," press release, 2007, 11.

TABLE 7-1. Percentages of Employees of Selected Business Groups in Brazil with Primary, Secondary, and Tertiary Education, 2005–06

Percent

Type of business and firm	Sector	Primary education	Secondary education	Tertiary education
Labor-intensive firms				
Camargo Corrêa	Diversified	58	33	9
Andrade Gutierrez	Diversified	62	24	14
Sadia	Meatpacking	58	36	6
Perdigão	Meatpacking	47	42	11
Capital-intensive firms				
Gerdau	Steel	12	68	19
Votorantim (only cellulose)	Pulp and paper	10	54	36
Services				
Unibanco	Banking	2	50	48
Bradesco	Banking	—	17	82
Itausa	Banking	—	53	46
Telemar	Telecommunications	—	25	72

Sources: Firms' annual reports for 2005, 2006, and 2007.

Note: — = negligible. The business groups listed here are the only ones from those ranked in table 7A.1 (appendix) that provide readily available data on employee education. Rows may not sum to 100 due to rounding or missing data.

How do Brazil's leading firms contribute to overall development? There are a number of angles from which to approach this question, including employment, investment, and innovation. In terms of generating high-skill, high-wage employment, the prospects are better for services, and of course for Embraer, than for commodity firms, which have, as noted above, fewer high-skill jobs in research, development, and marketing. Similarly, growth in commodities is extensive (producing more units of the same products), whereas the service sector can continue to grow by adding new products. Among the firms that provide information on the educational levels of their employees (see table 7-1), capital-intensive firms in steel (Gerdau) and cellulose (Votorantim) not surprisingly employ fewer, more-educated workers, whereas labor-intensive firms in construction and textiles (Camargo Corrêa) and food processing (Sadia and Perdigão) employ larger numbers of less-educated workers. The best-educated workforces are in banking and telecommunications. Systematic data are lacking, but it is clear that some of Brazil's leading firms and prominent MNCs rely on relatively unskilled labor.

Rapid expansion abroad raises the question of how outward FDI contributes to the sending country's development. In a short-term, zero-sum view, sending investment resources abroad makes them unavailable for investment at home. Additionally, foreign locations may offer better sites for R&D or management overall. Many of South Africa's largest groups, as well as one of Argentina's largest firms (Bunge y Born), have moved their headquarters (along with some of their best jobs) to London and New York, respectively. But over the longer term, investment resources may flow back, possibly in greater quantity, to the domestic economy, along with the management expertise gained from global operations.[73] It is still too early to tell how these potential costs and benefits will net out, but the provisional hypothesis for now is that Brazilian MNCs would come to resemble the MNCs from other countries with which they compete, and thus have similarly complex and ambiguous effects on Brazil's development.[74]

Although a full discussion of the promise and perils of commodity-led development is beyond the scope of this chapter, it is worth noting some of the conditions for success that were delineated in a major, optimistic study by the World Bank.[75] This study concluded that commodity-led development had been quite successful historically in four now-developed countries—Australia, the United States, Finland, and Sweden—but it explained that the essential accompanying conditions for success were high levels of public investment in education and high levels of private investment in R&D. In essence, these countries transferred rents and income from commodities through both taxation and retained earnings to channel them into human capital and technological innovation, which became the sources of growth and comparative advantage in postcommodity development. So far, such transfers in Brazil have been incipient and partial. Public expenditures on basic education in Brazil have expanded steadily, as has private investment in tertiary education, yet overall levels of education still lag where they should be, given Brazil's level of development.[76] The numbers on overall R&D are even less encouraging.[77] By one study, no country in Latin America spends more

---

73. Beausang (2003).
74. See Moran, Graham, and Blomström (2005); and Cohen (2007).
75. De Ferranti and others (2002).
76. De Ferranti and others (2003).
77. See chapter 8 in this volume by Amann.

than $10 per capita on R&D, compared with more than $200 per capita for countries like South Korea, Australia, and Ireland.[78] In short, there is much to be done to leverage commodity exports into longer-term development.

Conclusions: Between External Demand and Internal Protection

The three main forces acting on the evolution of large, private Brazilian firms over the last several decades have been the state, the growth of the service sector, and shifts in demand in international markets. The state is prior in the sense that it set the terms before and during the 1990s under which firms would enter international markets. Through state ownership, tariff protection, subsidized credit, government contracts, research support, and other means, the government nurtured many of today's giants from the 1940s on. It is also worth noting that in sectors where the government did not promote Brazilian firms but rather invited in MNCs, these MNCs continue to dominate and almost no Brazilian competitors have attempted to enter these sectors. Though the government relinquished most tools of direct intervention into the economy in the 1990s, it retained major protections (especially against foreign takeovers) and major promotional strategies, especially through BNDES financing and share ownership.[79] By 2008, the BNDES's financing exceeded $40 billion, and the market value of its shares in thirty-one listed firms was $34 billion.[80]

The major sectoral shifts of the 1990s were out of manufacturing and into services, where nearly all new jobs were created.[81] Many long-standing business groups in banking, construction, engineering, and insurance were well placed to take advantage of these shifts. In addition, privatization and the expansion of demand in other sectors—especially telecommunications and air travel—opened up new opportunities for growth among newcomer firms. Nearly all these firms also benefited from past and continuing government protections, though less through subsidies than through restrictions on foreign takeovers.

Although few of today's Brazilian corporate giants have not benefited from some major state support in the past, the biggest winners of the

---

78. *América Economia,* April 23, 2007.
79. Boschi (2007).
80. *Valor Econômico,* online summary, June 19, 2008.
81. Stallings and Peres (2000).

2000s have been determined mostly by shifts in world markets and the growing appetite (at least through 2008) for Brazilian commodities—from aluminum to frozen chicken to iron ore. The rate of growth of nearly all the leading firms in Brazil has been dramatic in the 2000s, but it has been truly explosive among commodity firms, which leveraged record prices and profits into major foreign acquisitions. It has been at least a half century since the international market has had such a decisive influence in the evolution of big business in Brazil.

Shifts in international capital markets may also be a major source of future changes in big business, both in corporate governance (and family management) and sectoral specialization. The rapid expansion of equity markets, fueled in large part by the flood of portfolio investment from abroad, sets Brazil's stock markets apart from those in most other countries of the developing world. Moreover, by early 2008, thirty-seven Brazilian companies had listed shares in New York.[82] The long-term effects of this expansion are difficult to gauge at this point, but several likely trends are evident. First, the stock market has become an important source of investment capital for rapidly growing service firms, which should help them grow more quickly than established groups, which have usually financed expansion out of retained earnings with some bank finance. Second, though nearly all firms have controlling shareholders, the expansion of the Brazilian stock markets facilitates shifts in ownership and could promote hostile takeovers (which are as yet almost unheard of) and more mergers and acquisitions, and consequent corporate concentration. Third, as in the United States, new equity investors, especially institutional investors, could increase pressures for specialization and de-diversification.[83]

Appendix: Data Sources on Major Business Groups

Rankings of firms by size in both domestic and foreign markets are increasingly temporary and fleeting and are easily rendered obsolete by a major local or foreign acquisition. Rankings also vary depending on the metric used to determine size: sales, employment, assets, or profitability. Several business publications, including *Exame, Gazeta Mercantil–Balanço Annual,* and *América Economia,* provide annual rankings. These

---

82. Economist Intelligence Unit, *Country Finance: Brazil,* April 22, 2008.
83. Zorn and others (2006).

TABLE 7A-1. The Largest Business Groups in Brazil, 2003

Business group	Sales, 2003 (billions of reais)	Number of employees	Main sectors of business
Bradesco*	47	83,000	Banking
Itaúsa*	28	78,000	Banking, computing
Vale (CVRD)	20	57,000	Mining, smelting, transportation, energy
Telemar/Oi	19	100,000	Telecommunications
Unibanco*	18	33,000	Banking
Odebrecht*	17	59,000	Construction, petrochemicals
Votorantim*	17	32,000	Cement, pulp and paper, aluminium, energy
Gerdau*	16	37,000	Steel
Pão de Açucar*	13	64,000	Retail
Usiminas	11	46,000	Steel
CSN*	8	16,000	Steel, mining, energy, transportation
Camargo Corrêa*	7	57,000	Construction, cement, textiles, energy
Embraer	7	19,000	Aircraft
Sadia*	6	52,000	Meat, processed food
SulAmérica*	5		Insurance
Safra*	5		Finance
Ultra*	5	7,000	Gas, petrochemicals
Perdigão*	4	45,000	Meat, dairy
Suzano*	4		Pulp and paper, petrochemicals
Andrade Gutierrez*	4	13,000	Construction, telecommunications
TAM*	4	20,000	Airline
Copersucar	4		Sugar, ethanol
Klabin*	3	7,000	Pulp and paper

Sources: *Valor Econômico* (2004, 36–43). Employment figures are from various sources, mostly annual reports, and various recent years.
*One or several families have ownership control (see Aldrighi and Postali 2007, 10).

rankings, however, give only a partial picture because they do not include unlisted firms or consider how firms are connected into business groups. For most analytic purposes, business groups, rather than their component subsidiaries, are the relevant unit of analysis. In this sense, *Valor Econômico*'s rankings in *Grandes Grupos,* first published in 2002, is the best source for a more composite view of big business in Brazil. The largest private Brazilian-owned firms from *Valor*'s 2004 rankings are listed in table 7A-1. *Valor*'s rankings for 2005 have virtually the same firms for the top twenty, though the ordering shifted somewhat.[84] Overall, the several

84. Aldrighi and Postali (2007, 23–30).

dozen firms considered in this chapter would certainly figure at the top of most recent rankings of large, private domestic firms. Some smaller firms are also included because their growth trajectory and opportunities for expansion suggest that they may soon be part of the top several dozen firms.

References

Aldrighi, Dante, and Fernando Postali. 2007. "Business Groups in Brazil." Paper prepared for Kyoto International Conference on Business Groups in Emerging Economies, Kyoto, November 26–28.

Amann, Edmund, João Carlos Ferraz, and Germano de Mendes Paula. 2006. "Corporate Governance, Regulation, and the Lingering Role of the State in the Post-Privatized Brazilian Steel Industry." In *Regulating Development,* ed. Edmund Amann. Northampton, Mass.: Edward Elgar.

Amsden, Alice. 1989. *Asia's Next Giant: South Korea and Late Industrialization.* Oxford University Press.

———. 2001. *The Rise of "the Rest": Challenges to the West from Late-Industrializing Economies.* Oxford University Press.

Avrichir, Ilan, and Miguel Caldas. 2005. "Competitividade nas alturas." *GV Executivo* 4, no. 3: 47–51.

Beausang, Francesca. 2003. *Third World Multinationals: Engine of Competitiveness or New Form of Dependency?* New York: Palgrave.

Berger, Suzanne. 2005. *How We Compete: What Companies around the World Are Doing to Make It in Today's Global Economy.* New York: Doubleday.

Boschi, Renato. 2007. "Capacidades estatais e políticas de desenvolvimento no Brasil: tendências recentes." Instituto Universitário de Pesquisas do Rio de Janeiro.

Boston Consulting Group. 2007. *The 2008 BCG 100 New Global Challengers: How Top Companies from Rapidly Developing Economies Are Changing the World.* Boston.

Castelar, Armando. 2007. "Bancos Públicos no Brasil: Para Onde Ir?" In *Mercado de Capitais e Bancos Públicos: Análise e Experiências Comparadas,* ed. Armando Castelar and Luiz Chrysostomo. Rio de Janeiro: Contra-Capa.

Castelar, Armando, Regis Bonelli, and Ben Ross Schneider. 2007. "Pragmatism and Market Reform in Brazil." In *Understanding Market Reforms in Latin America,* ed. José Maria Fanelli. New York: Palgrave Macmillan.

Chandler, Alfred, Franco Amatori, and Takahashi Hikino, eds. 1997. *Big Business and the Wealth of Nations.* Cambridge University Press.

Cohen, Stephen. 2007. *Multinational Corporations and Foreign Direct Investment: Avoiding Simplicity, Embracing Complexity.* Oxford University Press.

Corrêa, Daniela, and Gilberto Tadeu Lima. 2008. "O comportamento recente do investimento direto brasileiro no exterior em perspectiva." *Revista de Economia Política* 28, no. 2: 249–68.

Davies, Kenneth. 2004. "Regulatory Treatment of Foreign Direct Investment in Infrastructure and Public Utilities and Recent Trends: The OECD Experience." Paper presented at OECD India Investment Roundtable, New Delhi, October.

De Ferranti, David, Guillermo Perry, Indermit Gill, J. Luis Guasch, William Maloney, Carolina Sánchez-Páramo, and Norbert Schady. 2003. *Closing the Gap in Education and Technology*. Washington: World Bank.

De Ferranti, David, Guillermo Perry, Daniel Lederman, and William Maloney. 2002. *From Natural Resources to the Knowledge Economy*. Washington: World Bank.

ECLAC (Economic Commission for Latin America and the Caribbean). 2006. *Foreign Investment in Latin America and the Caribbean 2005*. Santiago: United Nations.

Evans, Peter. 1979. *Dependent Development*. Princeton University Press.

Goldstein, Andrea. 2002. "Embraer: From National Champion to Global Player." *Cepal Review* 77 (August): 97–115.

———. 2007. *Multinational Companies from Emerging Economies: Composition, Conceptualization and Direction in the Global Economy*. New York: Palgrave Macmillan.

———. 2008. "A Latin American Global Player Goes to Asia: Embraer in China." *International Journal of Technology and Globalisation* 4(1): 56–69.

Goldstein, Andrea, and Ben Ross Schneider. 2004. "Big Business in Brazil: States and Markets in the Corporate Reorganization of the 1990s." In *Brazil and Korea*, ed. Edmund Amann and Ha Joon Chang. London: Institute for Latin American Studies.

Goyzueta, Verónica, and Piedragil, Andrés. 2008. "Invisibles y globales." *América Economia,* March 24.

IDB (Inter-American Development Bank). 2001. *Competitiveness: The Business of Growth*. Washington.

Khanna, Tarun, and Yishay Yafeh. 2007. "Business Groups in Emerging Markets: Paragons or Parasites?" *Journal of Economic Literature* 45: 331–72.

Martinez-Diaz, Leonardo. Forthcoming. *Waiting for the Barbarians: The Politics of Banking-Sector Opening in the Emerging World*. Cornell University Press.

Montero, Alfred. 1998. "State Interests and the New Industrial Policy in Brazil: The Privatization of Steel, 1990–1994." *Journal of Inter-American Studies and World Affairs* 40, no. 3: 27–62.

Moran, Theodore, Edward Graham, and Magnus Blomström, eds. 2005. *Does Foreign Direct Investment Promote Development?* Washington: Institute for International Economics.

Morck, Randall, Daniel Wolfenzon, and Bernard Yeung. 2005. "Corporate Governance, Economic Entrenchment, and Growth." *Journal of Economic Literature* 43, no. 3: 655–720.

Ocampo, José Antonio. 2008. "El auge económico latinoamericano." *Revista de Ciencia Política* 28, no. 1: 7–33.

Rocco, Roberto. 2007. "Economic Flexibilisation and Denationalisation in Brazil." In *Big Business and Economic Development*, ed. Alex Fernández Jilberto and Barbara Hogenboom. London: Routledge.

Santiso, Javier. 2007. *The Emergence of Latin Multinationals*. Paris: OECD Development Center.

Schneider, Ben Ross. 1991. *Politics within the State: Elite Bureaucrats and Industrial Policy in Authoritarian Brazil*. University of Pittsburgh Press.

————. 2008. "Economic Liberalization and Corporate Governance: The Resilience of Economic Groups in Latin America." *Comparative Politics* 40 (July).

————. Forthcoming. "A Comparative Political Economy of Diversified Business Groups, or How States Organize Big Business." *Review of International Political Economy*.

Siekman, Philip. 2003. "Good Steel Made Cheaply: Brazil Does It Amazingly Well." *Fortune*, May.

SNA (Sindicato Nacional de Aeronautas). 2008. *O transporte aéreo regular brasileiro em 2007*. Rio de Janeiro.

Stallings, Barbara, and Wilson Peres. 2000. *Growth, Employment, and Equity: The Impact of the Economic Reforms in Latin America and the Caribbean*. Brookings.

Valor Econômico. 2004. *Grandes Grupos*. São Paulo.

Votorantim. 1994. *75 Anos*. São Paulo.

World Bank. 2004. *World Development Report 2005: A Better Investment Climate for Everyone*. Oxford University Press for World Bank.

Zorn, Dirk, Frank Dobbin, Julian Dierkes, and Man-Shan Kwok. 2006. "Managing Investors: How Financial Markets Reshaped the American Firm." In *The Sociology of Financial Markets*, ed. Karin Cetina and Alex Preda. Oxford University Press.

CHAPTER EIGHT

Technology, Public Policy, and the Emergence of Brazilian Multinationals

EDMUND AMANN

The explosive growth in outward foreign direct investment (FDI) from emerging market countries is a salient feature of the changing global economic landscape. These emerging markets—long accustomed to being mere recipients of FDI from Europe, North America, and Japan—now increasingly form the home bases for genuinely global enterprises. Brazil has certainly proved no exception to this trend. Across six continents, Brazilian corporations are entering takeover contests, establishing green-field operations, breaking into new export markets, or bidding for resource extraction concessions. The names Embraer, Petrobrás, and Odebrecht are fast becoming as globally recognized in their sectors as Boeing, Shell, and Bechtel. Yet though the profile of Brazilian multinationals has never been higher, comparatively little attention has been paid to the factors driving their emergence as truly global players.[1] It is the purpose of this chapter to contribute to the sum of understanding here. In analyzing the development of Brazilian multinationals, the chapter pays special attention

---

1. In English, very little has been published beyond material appearing in UNCTAD's annual *World Investment Report* and the Economic Commission for Latin America and the Caribbean's (ECLAC's) annual *Foreign Investment in Latin America and the Caribbean*. As might be expected, more has appeared in Portuguese (the key contributions have been cited in this chapter). Still, surprisingly little of this material has appeared in the form of published journal articles or books.

to the critical issue of the accumulation of technological capability and its interplay with public policy. The focus on technology is not arbitrary or accidental. Instead, it reflects the centrality of technology as a driver of internationalization, at least according to the mainstream theoretical literature.

The structure of the chapter is as follows. The first section reviews the theoretical literature concerning enterprises' internationalization and the role of technology. The second section then presents aggregate summary evidence concerning recent Brazilian outward FDI trends and the technological characteristics of internationalizing firms. The third section discusses the public policy environment and the potential channels through which this may have influenced firms both in terms of internationalization and technological strategy. To analyze these processes at the firm level, the fourth section then presents case study evidence relating to the experiences of Embraer, Petrobrás, Odebrecht, and—more briefly—Marcopolo, CVRD (Companhia Vale do Rio Doce; its new name is Vale), and Gerdau. Finally, by way of a conclusion, the key factors driving the internationalization of Brazilian enterprises are summarized and the relevance of technology, in particular, is considered.

Technology and the Emergence of Multinationals: Some Theoretical Perspectives

Over the past forty years or so, a rich theoretical literature has developed about how enterprises expand operations beyond their country of origin. This process—which the literature refers to as internationalization—may involve a series of sequential stages, starting with the export of products, moving on to the establishment of representative offices abroad and then to the setting up of full-fledged subsidiaries (or, possibly, joint ventures), and, finally, leading to the global integration of all operations.[2] Johnson and Vahlne argued that the accomplishment of each stage of internationalization is necessary to gain the information and market knowledge needed to move on to the next.[3] This suggests that the development of multinational corporations is likely to be a relatively long-drawn-out process, involving the transcending of informational barriers through learning and experience.

2. For an example of such a sequence, see Ohmae (1987).
3. Johnson and Vahlne (1977).

In seeking to engage in deeper forms of internationalization (i.e., FDI through the creation of foreign subsidiaries or joint ventures), the enterprise is likely to be motivated by a number of factors, some but not all of which will be related to the theme of technology. According to one of the first and most influential theories—the product life cycle theory propounded by Vernon[4]—any given product undergoes five "life stages," starting with research and development, then moving on to initial market penetration, market growth, and then market saturation and decline. As the product enters the saturation and decline phases, the technology it embodies is increasingly commoditized, meaning that the degree of competition intensifies in its core markets. Transferring production to a peripheral, low-cost market not only allows the intensifying competition to be countered in cost terms; it also enhances access to less mature markets. In such markets, demand for the product in question is more likely to be expanding than entering a phase of saturation or decline. Thus, in Vernon's terms, FDI and the emergence of multinationals can best be understood as a process of spinning out the life of products whose technologies have fallen behind the international frontier.

Building on the work of Hymer, Dunning has elaborated possibly the most comprehensive and influential theory of internationalization—the so-called eclectic paradigm.[5] This paradigm holds that a firm will be in a position to internationalize if it is in possession of some firm-specific advantage. Such an advantage may well center on a proprietary technology (e.g., ownership of a patent) but might equally relate to a distinctive brand or an effective organizational model. Presuming that a firm is in possession of such advantages (sometimes referred to in the literature as "core competencies"), it will have a direct financial interest in exploiting them outside its home market if it believes that its competencies will enable it to gain profitable market share in this domain.

The key question to be faced at this point is whether the competencies in question could best be exploited through exports, through FDI, or simply through the licensing of the advantage to third parties (e.g., through technology transfer or franchising). The answer here depends on a number of factors, including the quality and availability of potential licensees or franchisees, the technical feasibility or commercial desirability of wholesale technology licensing, and so on. Presuming that a

4. See Vernon (1971).
5. Hymer (1968); Dunning (1993).

decision is made to engage in FDI, the question then arises as to where the investment is likely to take place. The eclectic paradigm suggests that decisions here will be guided by three key factors: the availability of healthy markets (the market-seeking motive); the presence of resources, whether in the form of raw materials, ideas, or skills (the resource-seeking motive); or an environment that permits economies of scope or scale and low unit costs of production (the efficiency-seeking motive).

As can be seen, the eclectic paradigm suggests that the development of some technological competence can, in conjunction with some location-specific factors, prove a trigger for internationalization via FDI and thus the emergence of a multinational corporation. Such a developmental trajectory for a multinational corporation would typically be associated with an *asset-exploiting* strategy. However, it can also be true that firms lacking an obvious technological edge might still seek to internationalize.[6] The motive here springs less from the desire to leverage core competencies than to actually obtain them in the first place. The implementation of such *asset-augmenting* FDI has become increasingly significant in recent years.[7] Thus, for example, an emerging-market-based multinational could establish a subsidiary in an economy that belongs to the Organization for Economic Cooperation and Development with the objective of gaining access to frontier technologies or seeking exposure to cutting-edge management techniques. Such developments have recently become commonplace, especially in the information technology sector.

Although the discussion so far has suggested that technology can be a prime motive force in the drive toward internationalization, it needs to be recognized that other factors are also likely to play critical roles. For example, the eclectic paradigm explicitly allows for the seeking of natural resources to be a prime driving force. By the same token, the theory easily accommodates the phenomenon of brand recognition (as opposed to organizational or technological superiority) as a key explanatory factor. The extent to which the emergence of Brazilian multinationals can be viewed as a response to technological forces forms the key question addressed by this chapter. Before engaging with it, however, it is worth setting matters in a broader context by examining recent trends in the growth of Brazilian outward FDI and the concomitant expansion of Brazilian multinationals.

6. This is true provided, of course, that they possess some minimum level of competitive advantage.
7. See UNCTAD (2006, 142).

FIGURE 8-1. Brazil's Inward and Outward Flows of Foreign Direct Investment (FDI), 2002–07

U.S. dollars, millions

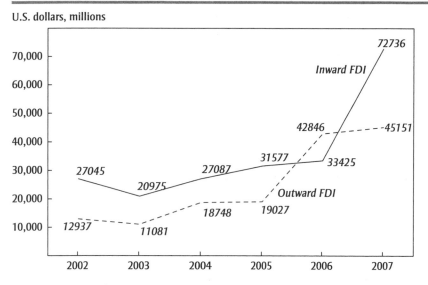

Source: Banco Central do Brasil.

The Emergence of Brazilian Multinational Enterprises: A Brief Quantitative Overview

One of the most striking phenomena surrounding the development of the Brazilian economy in the current decade has been the surge in the growth of outward FDI. As figure 8-1 indicates, between 2002 and 2007 outward FDI flows rose from $12,937 million to $45,151 million, with outward FDI exceeding inward FDI for the first time ever in 2006.[8] The growth in FDI is being driven by the activities of Brazilian multinationals across an array of sectors, ranging from manufacturing to construction to mining. According to data provided by the United Nations Conference on Trade and Development (UNCTAD), the stock of FDI maintained by Brazilian multinationals is the fourth highest among developing or emerging market economies; only China, Singapore, and Taiwan possess (through their enterprises) a greater stock of overseas assets.[9]

8. FDC / Columbia University Program on International Investment (2007, 5).
9. For more details, see Fiocca (2006).

TABLE 8-1. Number of Parent Companies for Selected Developing
Economies, Selected Years

Country	Early 1990s	Year	Early 2000s	Year	Rate of increase (percent)
Brazil	566	1992	1,225	2005	116
China	379	1993	3,429	2005	805
Hong Kong	500	1991	948	2002	90
India	187	1991	1,700	2003	809
South Korea	1,049	1991	7,460	2005	611
Total	2,681		14,762		451
All developed economies	34,280		50,520		47

Source: UNCTAD (2006), 122.

What is perhaps more dramatic than the sheer expansion in outward
FDI flows and stocks is the growth in the number of enterprises generating such investments. Table 8-1 indicates the impressive rate of growth
in the number of parent companies based in Brazil. Although the increase
in numbers is far below that achieved in India and China (two of the
other BRICs—Brazil, Russia, India, and China—the four very large rapidly
emerging economies), it is still very substantial in relation to the developed
countries.

Despite the increasingly important role of Brazilian outward FDI suggested by the data, it remains the case that few Brazilian multinationals in
their respective sectors rank among the very largest worldwide. Ranking
enterprises by revenue in 2005 (or the latest available year), UNCTAD's
2006 *World Investment Report* listed only three Brazilian enterprises
(CVRD, Petrobrás, and Gerdau) among the twenty largest in their respective sectors.[10] Perhaps more surprisingly, ranking the fifty largest non-
financial multinational corporations from developing economies, the 2005
World Investment Report listed only three Brazilian enterprises: Petrobrás, CVRD, and Gerdau.[11] Of the top fifty, no fewer than fifteen multinationals were based in mainland China or Hong Kong, whereas most of

10. The *World Investment Report* is issued by UNCTAD (2006, 123). CVRD ranked as
the fifth largest in the mining sector, Petrobrás the fifteenth largest in petroleum refining, and
Gerdau as the thirteenth largest in steel. No Brazilian enterprise ranked among the twenty
largest multinationals in automobiles, chemicals, electronics, banking, construction, con-
tainer shipping, or telecommunications.
11. UNCTAD (2005, 65). Petrobrás, CVRD, and Gerdau ranked, respectively, eighth,
twenty-third, and thirty-first.

the rest originated in East Asia and Southeast Asia, mainly South Korea, Taiwan, or Singapore. Another interesting feature to emerge from these international rankings is the sectoral specialization of the largest Brazilian multinationals. Though the largest multinationals from East Asia and Southeast Asia tend to be focused on manufacturing (especially electronics) and services, their Brazilian counterparts are strongly connected to natural-resource-based (NRB) activities, specifically oil and gas, and mining and steel.

Moving away from international comparisons and focusing instead on national rankings, the NRB-concentrated sectoral picture begins to fade. Table 8-2 summarizes the results from a recent (2007) survey undertaken by the Fundação Dom Cabral and the Columbia University Program on International Investment (FDC-CPII).[12] This survey ranked enterprises in order of the value of their overseas assets. Interestingly, the table reveals that this bears only an imprecise relationship with the degree of internationalization (in table 8-2, called the "transnationality index," a composite average of foreign assets to total assets, foreign sales to total sales, and foreign employment to total employment). As can be observed, while the NRB-oriented CVRD, Petrobrás, and Gerdau occupy the top three slots (out of twenty), the remaining positions are filled by enterprises from such diverse sectors as aerospace, construction, information technology, and logistics.

Because the data on the international ranking of Brazilian multinationals indicate that the largest are heavily NRB oriented, should this lead one to suppose that strategies of natural resource seeking predominate over those of technology exploitation or acquisition? At least so far as the detailed survey data indicate, the answer here is no. Prochnik and colleagues analyzed a large sample of firms using data provided by the Instituto Brasileiro de Geografia e Estatística (IBGE, Brazilian Geographical and Statistical Institute), supplemented by information from the Central Bank and External Trade Secretariat.[13] These researchers attempted to establish whether there was a link between the internationalization of Brazilian enterprises and their decision to engage in different types of product and process innovation. In the case of enterprises that neither

12. The source here is an FDC-CPII survey; see FDC/Columbia University Program on International Investment (2007).

13. Prochnik, Esteves, and de Freitas (2006). IBGE's PINTEC database, the central reference source used for the study, contained 9,687 enterprises.

TABLE 8-2. FDC-CPII Ranking of the Top Twenty Brazilian Multinationals, Key Variables, 2006

Rank in foreign assets	Rank in transnationality index[a]	Name	Sector	Foreign assets / total assets (percent)	Foreign sales / total sales (percent)	Foreign employment / total employment (percent)	Rank in transnationality index (percent)[b]	Number of host countries
1	2	CVRD	Mining	46	18	24	29	10
2	18	Petrobrás	Oil and gas	12	12	11	12	9
3	1	Gerdau	Steel	39	54	46	46	11
4	6	Embraer	Aviation	45	12	13	23	5
5	24	Grupo Votorantim	Diversified	5	9	4	6	12
6	13	CSN	Steel	18	28	3	16	2
7	9	Camargo Corrêa	Diversified	26	13	18	19	12
8	5	Grupo Odebrecht	Construction and petrochemicals	15	20	47	27	12
9	23	Aracruz	Pulp and paper	19	N.A.	1	7	5
10	7	WEG	Electromechanical	24	30	11	22	12
11	4	Marcopolo	Bus manufacturing	30	30	22	27	7
12	11	Andrade Guiterrez	Diversified	4	7	41	17	8
13	8	Tigre	Construction	27	17	17	20	7
14	31	Usiminas	Steel	1	N.A.	N.A.	0.3	0
15	17	Natura	Cosmetics	22	3	15	14	7
16	15	Itautec	Information technology	19	20	6	15	8
17	19	America Latina Logística SA	Logistics	2	11	23	12	1
18	26	Ultrapar/Grupo Ultra	Diversified	2	2	3	2	2
19	3	Sabó	Auto parts	16	43	27	29	11
20	22	Lupatech	Electromechanical	10	4	7	7	2

Source: FDC-CPII survey of Brazilian multinationals; see FDC/Columbia University Program on International Investment (2007).
Note: N.A. = not available.
a. The "transnationality index" is a composite average of foreign assets to total assets, foreign sales to total sales, and foreign employment to total employment.

exported nor engaged in outward FDI, 69 percent were found not to have undertaken any form of innovative activity. By contrast, more than 80 percent of firms that exported or invested overseas had engaged in product innovation. In the case of process innovation, just 24.7 percent of firms had failed to internationalize, either through exporting or outward FDI.[14] The study also established that the Brazilian enterprises that invest overseas tend to be the most aggressive in pursuing innovation closest to the frontier.

The fact that a positive association exists between innovation and internationalization and the fact that NRB-oriented enterprises are so prominent among Brazilian multinationals are not in any way contradictory. As will be revealed later in the chapter, operating in the natural resources sector—especially at a time when new mineral and oil deposits are ever less accessible—is an increasingly technologically intensive activity. Fortunately for Brazil, its leading NRB-focused multinationals have been highly successful in developing and absorbing cutting-edge technologies. At the same time, it needs to be borne in mind that Brazilian multinationals operate increasingly effectively in other sectors, notably manufacturing. Below, this chapter gives evidence of the close relationship between internationalization and innovation here. Before discussing this firm-level evidence, however, it is worth briefly detailing the domestic policy environment within which firms make decisions to invest in technology and to extend their activities abroad.

The Public Policy Environment and the Internationalization of Brazilian Enterprises

The role of public policy is becoming increasingly recognized as a critical influence in the emergence of multinational corporations from less developed economies.[15] Through both microeconomic and macroeconomic policy interventions, the state can exercise a strong influence on the growth of domestic enterprises, on their investment decisions, and on their technological strategies. In the Brazilian context, in particular, it would be difficult to overestimate the role of the state in the formation of homegrown multinationals. Starting in the 1930s but accelerating

---

14. See Prochnik, Esteves, and de Freitas (2006, 361).
15. See Guedes and Faria (2005) for a wide-ranging discussion of the conceptual issues.

into the 1940s, 1950s, and 1960s, Brazil underwent a program of state-directed, inward-oriented industrialization—an economic program that has become known as import-substitution industrialization (ISI).[16]

The pursuit of ISI led to a structural transformation, resulting in a full-fledged industrialized economy. In its wake, ISI created expanding market opportunities for domestic as well as foreign enterprises and saw the formation of the large domestic economic groups that feature so prominently among the Brazilian multinationals of today. Another notable feature of ISI was the establishment of state-owned enterprises (SOEs), especially in capital-intensive sectors such as steel making, energy, telecommunications, and mining.[17] It is worth noting that two of Brazil's top three multinationals—CVRD and Petrobrás—were established as SOEs, with Petrobrás continuing to be controlled by the state.[18] Former SOEs are also prominently represented in the FDC-CPII list of Brazil's top twenty multinationals.[19] Privatization and the abandonment of ISI in the early 1990s significantly reduced the state's direct role in the economy. Nevertheless, public policy remains a highly significant factor in explaining the growth and internationalization of Brazilian enterprises.

In discussing the contemporary role of the state, it should be acknowledged at the outset that the Brazilian government does not maintain a policy set explicitly designed to encourage domestic enterprises to invest overseas. Instead, it is possible to argue that particular interventions *implicitly* assist Brazilian enterprises in their attempts to expand operations internationally. A critically important channel here is formed by export finance initiatives. Fiocca points to the vitally important role of Brazil's Banco Nacional de Desenvolvimento Econômico e Social (BNDES, National Economic and Social Development Bank) in supporting internationalization via the financing of the country's exports.[20] Between 1996 and 2005, the BNDES's export finance disbursements

16. See Kohli (2004) for a detailed discussion. ISI involved the erection of tariff and non-tariff barriers to foster domestic industrialization. Initially, ISI in Brazil focused on the establishment of a consumer durables sector. By the late 1970s, the strategy had broadened to include the launch of a capital goods sector.

17. See Baer (2008).

18. CVRD was privatized in the 1990s, while Petrobrás continues to be controlled by the state, albeit with substantial private shareholding.

19. Aside from CVRD and Petrobrás, Embraer, CSN, and Usiminas were, at one time, SOEs; see FDC/Columbia University Program on International Investment (2007).

20. Fiocca (2006).

rose from $890 million to $5.86 billion, with particularly strong growth experienced in relation to financing overseas capital goods sales.[21] The BNDES is also becoming very active in financing export sales related to overseas infrastructure projects in which Brazilian construction firms are involved.[22] As was seen above, the intensification of exports represents a vital prior step that enterprises have to take to gain exposure to local market conditions. In this sense, the increased focus on export promotion is creating a favorable environment for increased outward FDI.

The issue of access to finance extends well beyond the granting of lines of credit to export market customers. To achieve international competitiveness in technologically complex industries, a firm is likely to require capital investment on a substantial scale. In the case of the United States and Europe, capital markets have long been broad and deep enough to provide ready access to the necessary resources, enabling medium-size domestic enterprises to grow in size and scope. Such growth has often given rise to internationalization as scale economies have been unleashed on export markets. This process, of course, often precedes outward FDI and the emergence of full-blown multinational corporations. In the Brazilian case, however, historically, capital markets have been relatively thin and interest rates have been high, meaning that enterprises seeking to step up investment have had to resort to state financing, either through the BNDES or, if they were SOEs, directly from public resources. The only real alternatives to borrowing from the state were to take the popular route of financing investment from retained earnings or, rarely, to issue securities on international capital markets. The latter option was only open to those enterprises with substantial foreign-currency-denominated revenues.

In the past fifteen years or so, the financing picture has begun to change quite considerably. Since the implementation of the real stabilization plan in 1993–94, the pursuit of orthodox fiscal and monetary policies has driven annual inflation from quadruple to single digits.[23] This has allowed benchmark interest rates to drift downward over time. At the same time, reforms have improved liquidity and financing conditions in Brazilian

21. Fiocca (2006, 20).
22. Fiocca (2006, 23). Camargo Corrêa, Grupo Odebrecht, and Andrade Gutierrez (which are shown in table 8-2) are heavily involved in overseas construction and would benefit from such financing programs.
23. See Amann (2005).

equity markets.[24] Of these reforms, the two most significant are the launch of the Novo Mercado and the enactment of the Lei das SA (Limited Companies Law). The Lei das SA, enacted in 2001, is designed to improve corporate governance practices in medium-size enterprises with the aim of drawing in additional investment and breathing new life into domestic private capital markets. Through a number of measures, the law strengthens the position of minority shareholders. Perhaps the most significant provision is one guaranteeing minority shareholders at least 80 percent the price per share as majority holders of preference shares in the event of a takeover.[25]

The Novo Mercado, launched by the main BOVESPA stock exchange, similarly guarantees the rights of minority shareholders, not least through a prohibition on the issue of preference shares. The introduction of improved rights for minority shareholders is especially important in the Brazilian context because many of the enterprises involved are majority family owned and outside investors historically have proved reluctant to inject capital, sensing the vulnerability of their position. The sharp recent rise in domestic stock market capitalization and the explosion of listings on the Novo Mercado suggest that these measures are beginning to work. In the longer run, this may well ease the transition of medium-size (often family-controlled) enterprises to multinational status. By the same token, improvements in the regulation of capital markets should also enhance Brazilian enterprises' ability to finance research and development (R&D). The successful conduct of Brazilian macroeconomic policy has also lent support to the real, whose value has substantially appreciated against the dollar and other major currencies since 2002. Such a development is clearly of value to enterprises seeking to pursue foreign acquisitions, to inject capital into existing overseas operations, or to initiate greenfield investments.

Important though these policy features are, the key focus of this chapter is the role that firms' technological strategies may be playing in their decision to initiate or expand operations overseas. In this connection, what role has the Brazilian state played in facilitating innovation among

24. In March 2008, Brazil moved to the top of the emerging market index, a measure based on strong growth in its equity market; see "Brazil's Stock Market: Food, Fuel and Froth," *The Economist*, March 8, 2008. Still, it needs to be recognized that despite reduced benchmark interest rates, interest rate spreads remain high by advanced economy standards.
25. Teixeira (2005).

enterprises? This is a substantial and complex question, and limitations of space do not allow for a detailed treatment here.[26] In what follows, an overview of some of the more salient features of Brazil's technology policy regime is provided. Some additional discussion relating to this theme will also be offered on a firm-by-firm basis below.

Since the 1960s, the Brazilian government has pursued a series of policy initiatives designed to build technological capabilities in both the public and private sectors. The objective here has been to create new comparative advantages in higher-value-added activities, thus diversifying the economic base and improving the terms of trade. In attempting to achieve these goals, successive governments have relied on a variety of initiatives and, in the process, have created a comparatively elaborate policy architecture. Among the key features of this policy framework is a special funding body, Financiadora de Estudos e Projetos (FINEP, Research and Projects Financing), whose function is to distribute financing and grants to public and private sector organizations pursuing research projects. So far as direct public financing of corporate research is concerned, FINEP is far and away the most important funding body. The activities of FINEP are supplemented by the work of Financiamento de Máquinas e Equipamentos (FINAME), which, in association with the BNDES, provides financing packages to support the sale of technologically complex capital goods. Another important element of the policy architecture is formed by universities and publicly funded research institutes, many of which operate in collaboration with enterprises on research projects. Among the most famous examples here would be the Instituto de Pesquisas Tecnológicas (IPT, Institute of Technological Research) at the University of São Paulo and the Embrapa (Empresa Brasileira de Pesquisa Agropecuária) agricultural technology research institutes. The former has been associated with innovation in the engineering sector, and the latter have been closely involved in developing new crop strains.

Another extremely important source of support for corporate R&D over the years have been the in-house research institutes originally founded by the SOEs. Thus, for example, in the case of telecommunications, the former SOE Telebrás established the CPQd Institute, which was responsible for the development of Brazil's first digital telephone

---

26. Those seeking a more detailed treatment of these issues—at least in terms of policy design—would do well to consult Mani (2002).

exchange. In the case of electricity, the SOE holding company Eletrobrás founded the Cepel research institute, which has made a number of
advances in high-tension power distribution. Despite the privatization
of the telecommunications sector and large parts of the electricity sector,
these research institutes remain operational with special lines of funding.

The effective articulation of links between the research institutes and
their corporate "clients" can be an important factor in explaining the
success of those Brazilian multinationals that have progressed to the technological frontier and have enjoyed export success as a result. For example, Embraer has had a long-term relationship with the Centro Técnico
da Aeronáutica (CTA, Aerospace Technology Center).[27] CTA expertise
enabled Embraer to launch its first successful aircraft, the Bandeirante,
in the 1960s, and the CTA has continued to assist in the R&D process
subsequently, being assigned individual development tasks. An important part of the ongoing linkage between Embraer and the CTA lies in
the transfer of personnel. CTA-trained engineers form the nucleus of
Embraer's in-house technological expertise, and one of the CTA's arms is
charged with maintaining technological liaisons with outside industry.
Similarly, in the case of Petrobrás, the in-house CENPES research institute
has played an important part in developing world-class technologies in
offshore oil exploration and production. Again, personnel transfers have
played an important role, though the institutional links between CENPES
and Petrobrás are naturally even closer than those between Embraer and
the CTA.

As important as the role of the research institutes has been, not every
Brazilian multinational has placed extensive reliance on them. For example, Gerdau and Marcopolo have tended to draw more on a mixture of
in-house capability and expertise provided by equipment and component
suppliers. Even in the case of Embraer, in-house capability has been critical, and there is evidence that more extensive recent use has been made
of foreign technology suppliers. This has occurred through a subcon-
tracting process in which development work for key subassemblies has
been carried out in Europe and North America.

Although the institutional architecture supporting corporate R&D
in Brazil may appear well developed, this does not imply that the recent
evolution of public funding has been particularly favorable. As figure 8-2
indicates, in real terms, despite upward fluctuations from time to time,

27. Cassiolato, Bernardes, and Lastres (2002).

FIGURE 8-2. The Brazilian Government's Spending on Science and
Technology, 1991–2004

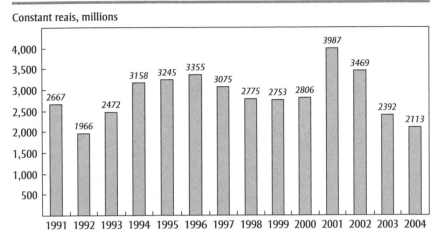

Constant reais, millions

Source: Ministério de Ciência e Tecnologia.

government spending on science and technology was lower in 2004 than
it had been in 1991.[28]

Comparing 2000 with 2004, table 8-3 further indicates the troubling
extent to which public expenditures on science and technology have
come under pressure. The table clearly shows that public spending has
fallen as a proportion of GDP, a development that does not appear to be
compatible with the strategic desire to boost competitiveness and develop
new comparative advantages in technologically dynamic sectors. The
configuration of fiscal policy may help explain this adverse trend. Constrained by the need to generate large primary surpluses and squeezed
between high debt repayments and expenditures on nondiscretionary
items such as pension and social security payments, public sector investment has remained subdued.[29] Against this background, it has been difficult for the Ministry of Science and Technology and other relevant
federal agencies to increase their spending year on year in real terms.
The compression of public spending on science and technology need not
have been so serious in its implications if the private sector had significantly ramped up its expenditures. However, in this regard, table 8-3

28. Such spending, of course, encompasses not only assistance to corporate R&D but
also public investment in basic science within the university system.
29. For a comprehensive analysis, see Amann and Baer (2006).

TABLE 8-3. Spending on Science and Technology in Brazil, 2000–04
Percent of GDP

Type of spending	2000	2004
Public	1.32	1.20
Federal government	0.79	0.71
State governments	0.53	0.49
Business	0.16	0.22

Source: Ministério de Ciência e Tecnologia.

also illustrates another interesting—and disturbing—feature: the subordinate role of business spending on science and technology vis-à-vis that of the public sector. Despite the fact that business spending climbed by 0.06 percentage points of GDP between the two years, it still remains well below that generated by the public sector. Thus, at least reviewing the aggregate data, there is cause for concern surrounding not only the incidence of public sector spending on science and technology but also the tiny proportion generated by business.

Two key factors may help to account for the generally limited role of the private sector as an investor in science and technology. In the first place, and unlike the Brazilian multinationals reviewed subsequently, it is far from always the case that survival (at least in the domestic market) depends on the ability to develop or acquire cutting-edge technologies.[30] Second, even where such innovative activity is more strategically necessary, enterprises' ability to divert resources into R&D ventures is often constrained by a lack of access to capital and a risk aversion borne of years of coping with significant macroeconomic instability.[31] Fortunately, this situation looks likely to change in the future owing to the increasing depth, sophistication, and liquidity of Brazilian equity markets.

The sense that overall spending on innovation in Brazil is "low" is accentuated when one makes international comparisons. Although compared with its Latin American peers, Argentina and Mexico, Brazil's proportionate spending on R&D is impressive, with regard to the nations of Europe, the United States, and other advanced economies, it lags far behind (see table 8-4).[32] This lag is particularly noticeable in relation to

30. Amann (2000).
31. Amann (2000).
32. R&D is a narrower measure of innovative activity than spending on science and technology. It excludes spending on basic science and relates to the development of technologies by both private sector corporations and public sector universities and research institutes.

TABLE 8-4. Research and Development (R&D) Spending: International Comparisons

Country	Year	R&D spending Millions of dollars, at purchasing power parity	Percentage of GDP	Dollars per capita
Brazil	2004	13,494	0.91	74.3
Argentina	2003	1,826	0.41	49.6
Mexico	2001	3,624	0.39	36.2
China	2003	84,618	1.31	65.6
South Korea	2003	24,379	2.64	508.7
Russia	2003	16,926	1.29	118.0
France	2003	37,514	2.19	609.6
Germany	2003	57,065	2.55	691.5
United Kingdom	2003	33,579	1.89	563.8
United States	2003	284,584	2.60	977.7

Sources: Organization for Economic Cooperation and Development; Ministério de Ciência e Tecnologia.

South Korea, a newly industrialized economy to which Brazil is often compared.[33] Though these data present a picture of technological under-investment, they are nonetheless only average indicators. What the data conceal is the fact that—despite currently constrained public funding—some Brazilian corporations have succeeded in developing world-class technologies and have used these as a springboard to internationalization. The nature of this phenomenon and its broader implications form the basis for the next section and the conclusions.

Case Studies of Technology and the Internationalization of Brazilian Enterprises

The growing prominence of Brazilian multinationals over the past few years has been strongly driven by the ability of these enterprises to generate, absorb, and deploy technology in a highly effective manner. As the following case studies indicate, technology has played an important role no matter whether the multinationals concerned operate in product- or process-based industries or in sectors conventionally depicted as "high" or "low" technology. Thus, although one might expect technology to have exercised a critical influence on the emergence of Embraer (an aircraft manufacturer and the first case study), the same can also be said of

33. For a lengthy discussion of these comparisons, see Amann and Chang (2004).

Odebrecht and Vale, both of which operate in longer-established, more traditional sectors.

Embraer

The Brazilian aircraft producer Embraer is one of Latin America's highest-profile enterprises, operating in a sector where the technological frontier has been moving rapidly. Not only has Embraer succeeded in maintaining its products and processes at the leading edge of the frontier; it has also parlayed this achievement into market success. In so doing, it has become one of the world's two leading producers of regional jet passenger aircraft.[34] Having demonstrated its technological virtuosity and commercial viability, it has embarked on a more profound phase of internationalization, launching operations in Portugal and China. As a consequence of this development, it has become a full-fledged multinational corporation. Its progressive internationalization cannot be understood without reference to its technological strategy. At the same time, this technological strategy cannot be understood without reference to the role of the state.

Although Embraer was founded in 1969, its origins can be traced back to the 1940s, with the creation of the CTA by the Ministry of Aeronautics.[35] The CTA was charged with undertaking research on basic aerospace technologies, including aircraft design, engines, and materials. Soon after its founding, the CTA established the Instituto Tecnológico da Aeronáutica (ITA, Technological Institute), whose objective was to train specialized engineers.[36] In the mid-1950s, a further CTA-linked institute—the Institute for Research and Development (IRD)—was set up. Throughout the 1950s and 1960s, these state-directed technological initiatives enabled the accumulation of basic capabilities. These would later prove invaluable in the establishment of a viable national aircraft industry.

The launch of Embraer at the end of the 1960s represented an attempt to capitalize on these capabilities at a time when Brazil was trying to improve its balance of trade position. It was hoped that Embraer would supply the domestic market, lessening the demand for imports,[37] while at the same time driving up exports. In fact, there was a strong emphasis on

34. The other leading producer is Canada's Bombardier.
35. Silva (1999).
36. Cassiolato, Bernardes, and Lastres (2002, 7).
37. In this sense, the launch of Embraer could be seen as part of the ISI strategy (Goldstein and Godinho 2007, 4).

exports from the start, the advantage here being that a focus on external markets would bring longer production runs, greater scope for technical change, and exposure to tough quality and performance standards.[38] Embraer initially targeted the market for smaller propeller-powered civilian aircraft and military trainers. During this period—the early 1970s—some technology was acquired through a cooperative manufacturing agreement with Piper Aircraft of the United States.[39] This allowed the production of very light aircraft for personal transportation and agricultural use. More ambitious—and successful in sales terms—was the larger nineteen-seat Bandeirantes launched in 1973.

During the 1970s and 1980s, Embraer remained an SOE, enjoying a special relationship with the Ministry of Aeronautics and the Brazilian Air Force. This period saw more ambitious attempts to master technologies related to jet aircraft design and production. Thus, in 1980, Embraer embarked upon a program to develop a jet fighter (the AMX), drawing on in-house designers, researchers at the CTA, and technical cooperation from two Italian enterprises, Aeritalia and Macchi Aeronautic. By the end of the 1980s, after two decades of operations, Embraer had carved out a notable niche in the international aerospace market as a designer and manufacturer of regional propeller transports.[40] The enterprise had also grasped the rudiments of jet aircraft design through its experience with the AMX. The acquisition of these capabilities proved a springboard to yet more success as Embraer moved into the emerging market for regional passenger jet transport.

In 1989, Embraer embarked on the design and development of the ERJ-145, a twin-engine, fifty-seat passenger jet designed for use on regional routes. Once again, the project was able to draw on locally acquired expertise centered on the CTA and Embraer itself. The R&D work for the ERJ-145 also relied on extensive cooperation and risk-sharing agreements with major suppliers. Thus, for example, whereas Embraer would perform the overall design function and integrate the various systems, Gamesa of Spain was responsible for wing development and manufacture and Sonaca of Belgium was awarded a contract to develop and manufacture the center fuselage section.[41] Other suppliers in Europe and North

38. Goldstein and Godinho (2007, 5).
39. Cassiolato, Bernardes, and Lastres (2002, 8).
40. The most successful products of this type are the EMB-110 Bandeirante for nineteen passengers and the EMB-120 Brasília for thirty passengers.
41. Cassiolato, Bernardes, and Lastres (2002, 31).

America were responsible for the avionics and the engines, for which Embraer (or other Brazilian enterprises) did not possess the technology. The ERJ-145 program firmly established Embraer as a world-class systems integrator and assembler. This experience was to be put to use in the later development of the larger ERJ-170/190 jet. What both programs did not involve, however, was a concerted attempt to add more value added locally. This was despite the existence of local supplier clusters[42] and, in the late 1990s, increasingly acute trade deficits.

A critical juncture in Embraer's history came in 1994, with privatization.[43] Struggling with losses, its very survival appeared in question. However, the launch of the ERJ-145 at the 1996 Farnborough Airshow and subsequent huge orders from American carriers ensured that, rather than fail, Embraer would go on to spectacularly prosper. Since the mid-1990s, more than 800 ERJ aircraft have been sold, making—for a while—Embraer Brazil's biggest exporter. According to Goldstein and Godinho, more than 95 percent of Embraer's sales are made abroad.[44] Though Embraer may have been privatized, the Brazilian state has nonetheless continued to offer it strong support. Research collaboration persists with the CTA and its satellite institutes, and Embraer is collaborating with state and federal agencies on the creation of enhanced local R&D capabilities.[45] The lingering role of the state has been especially pronounced in relation to exports, where the BNDES has offered special export-financing facilities. The perceived overgenerosity of these triggered a complaint by Canada (where Bombardier is based) at the World Trade Organization.[46]

According to the theoretical material reviewed above, export success may represent a crucial first step toward deeper internationalization.

42. See Bettancourt and others (2005) for a detailed discussion on themes relating to the domestic Brazilian production chain for civil aviation.

43. Foreign ownership was limited to 40 percent. Among the foreign investors came to be a consortium of EADS, Dassault, Thales, and Snecma, with an acquired a total of 20 percent of the voting shares (ECLAC 2005, 73).

44. Goldstein and Godinho (2007, 6).

45. Cassiolato, Bernardes, and Lastres (2002, 46).

46. The dispute erupted in 1996 and centered initially on the Canadian allegation that Brazil's PROEX export finance package breached World Trade Organization (WTO) rules by financing too great a proportion of the value of Embraer's sales over too long a period. In 2001, a WTO ruling obliged Brazil to limit the proportion of export sales value financed to 85 percent over a maximum term of ten years. Brazil, meanwhile, had alleged that Canadian government support for Bombardier also breached WTO rules. In March 2003, the WTO found in favor of Brazil, allowing the latter to impose $248 million in trade sanctions against Canada. See *ICTSD Bridges Weekly Trade News Digest,* July 31, 2001; and Churchwell (2003). At the time of writing, no further Brazil-Canada disputes had erupted.

This, of course, would take the form of outward FDI. It is significant that Embraer's establishment of overseas operations has accompanied its increasing success in penetrating export markets. Initially, foreign investment took the form of the establishment of foreign maintenance facilities.[47] Such investments were a natural concomitant of exporting a complex, maintenance-intensive product. However, in 2002 Embraer announced plans to construct an ERJ-145 assembly line in China.[48] The creation of this first overseas production facility for Embraer was primarily motivated by a desire to gain enhanced access to the Chinese market.[49] In particular, it was thought that by commencing production inside China, Embraer would gain a significant market access advantage over its archrival Bombardier. In December 2003, the first Chinese-assembled ERJ-145 made its maiden flight, triggering a series of orders that have proved more modest than originally anticipated.[50] The decision to invest in China represents, according to the Dunning schema, a classic market-seeking initiative. Having acquired the technology to produce a world-class, market-beating product, Embraer is seeking to capitalize on its initial investment in R&D by maximizing sales. There is no evidence that the decision to invest in China was motivated by a desire to gain access to Chinese technology or know-how.[51]

Embraer's second overseas venture, the acquisition of Portugal's OGMA, also provides evidence of its outward FDI having a market-seeking orientation. OGMA was established by the Portuguese Air Force (FAP) in 1952, specializing initially in the maintenance, repair, and overhaul of the FAP fleet but moving on to limited aircraft production, manufacturing the Auster trainer.[52] In 1994, the same year that Embraer was privatized, OGMA was incorporated, with its shares being transferred to the Ministry of Defense. From 1993 onward, OGMA became an approved maintenance center for the Rolls-Royce AE2100 and AE3007 engines used in the ERJ-145 jet family. However, financial problems generated by managerial mistakes led to worsening financial performance.

47. ECLAC (2005, 73).

48. This was achieved through the establishment of a joint venture (in which Embraer owns 51 percent) with the two SOEs, HAIG and its subsidiary, Hafei Aviation Industry Company.

49. Goldstein and Godinho (2007, 13).

50. Goldstein and Godinho (2007, 14).

51. Quite the contrary; the joint venture agreement provides for technology transfer to the local partners rather than the other way around.

52. Goldstein and Godinho (2007, 16)

This contributed to the decision to privatize in 2003.[53] Of the various bidders in the privatization contest, a joint consortium of Embraer and EADS finally proved successful at the end of 2004.

Two key factors may explain Embraer's decision to acquire the assets of what had been a troubled company. First, OGMA acts as an important service facility for Embraer aircraft in Europe and, as such, its acquisition would enhance Embraer's position to build its position in a key external market. Not only would aircraft sales be supported by such a move, but also access would be gained to a fresh revenue stream: maintenance and overhaul. Second, OGMA acts as a subcontractor to the European military aerospace sector. The acquisition of OGMA and the joint-ownership agreement with EADS potentially offers Embraer enhanced access to the global market for military aircraft.[54] In this connection, Embraer may also be able to benefit from two-way technology transfers because it both transfers its (primarily civilian-based) know-how and also receives potentially valuable technological insights from a key military subcontractor. However, the acquisition of OGMA is still a recent event, and the precise nature of technology transfer processes remains to be seen.

Reviewing the Embraer experience, it becomes clear that internationalization (both in terms of exports and outward FDI) has been conditioned by an ability to master demanding technologies and to incorporate them into commercially attractive products. This mastery could not have been achieved without significant state intervention, whether in terms of the establishment of Embraer as an SOE, the development of a supporting network of R&D institutions, or the provision of export finance. By the same token, Embraer would not have been able to thrive without its ability to forge effective alliances with foreign subcontractors. Indeed, it is possible to argue that it is Embraer's facility as a global systems integrator that lies at the heart of its success. The emergence of Brazilian outward FDI projects in China and Portugal represents, for the most part, an attempt to enhance market access rather than to engage in the acquisition of new technologies. It will be interesting to observe whether, in any future outward FDI, there is any change in this underlying motivation.

---

53. Goldstein and Godinho (2007, 17)

54. The quest toward enhanced access to the military market intensified further in 2004, when Embraer began to make investments in a Florida ex-military base with the eventual intention of establishing aircraft assembly operations (ECLAC 2005, 73). Presuming such an operation ever commences, it would place Embraer in an advantageous position to gain U.S. military contracts.

Petrobrás

The experience of Petrobrás bears some remarkable similarities to that of Embraer. As in the case of Embraer, Petrobrás originated as an SOE.[55] Like its aerospace counterpart, Petrobrás is a leading exporter and has managed to achieve widespread international recognition for its technological excellence. Operating in a technologically demanding and complex field, Petrobrás also benefited from strong links with Brazil's burgeoning network of research institutes. Like Embraer, Petrobrás has used technological competence as a springboard to internationalization through the pursuit of outward FDI.

Petrobrás was founded in 1953 and formed a lynchpin of the state-driven, inward-oriented industrialization drive of the time. As in the case of its Mexican and Venezuelan counterparts, PEMEX and PDVSA, the setting up of Petrobrás as an SOE could be seen as a way of increasing domestic control over national resources. Under the terms of legislation introduced at the time, Petrobrás was granted sole rights over domestic upstream oil production and exploration.[56] It also came to dominate domestic refining activity, although the major foreign oil firms were allowed to retain a role in the downstream distribution sector. For the first two decades of its existence, Petrobrás remained a determinedly domestic player, though it was obliged to gain international experience through its large-scale oil-importation activities. By the early 1970s, change was afoot, however. Substantial rises in the oil price, combined with a desire to guarantee access to foreign oil, led to the establishment of Braspetro.[57] This enterprise sought and obtained foreign exploration and production rights and, famously, discovered the Majnoon oil field in Iraq in 1975. Braspetro was also heavily involved in establishing oil fields in Libya.

Highly competent though Braspetro's exploration capabilities may have been, by the late 1980s Petrobrás had scaled back its overseas investments. This was in large part due to the need to focus its resources domestically, thanks to the discovery of enormous oil deposits in the Campos Basin, off the coast of Rio de Janeiro State.[58] The physical challenges that were posed by the need to develop this new offshore field were

---

55. However, Petrobrás remains one, of course.

56. Unfortunately for Petrobrás, large-scale domestic oil production was not to become a reality until well into the 1980s, by which time market liberalization in this area was close at hand.

57. Antonio and Lara (2005, 12).

58. Antonio and Lara (2005, 12).

considerable. The geology of the basin was not straightforward, and the water depths involved—up to 2 kilometers—were far greater than those encountered in the other great offshore fields of the Gulf of Mexico and the North Sea. With no adequate off-the-shelf solutions available, Petrobrás was obliged to develop its own technologies. Thus, in 1986 the enterprise launched the PROCAP (Deepwater Exploration Systems) program. This ambitious program sought to develop the technological capabilities required to design oil platforms and structures suitable for deep waters.[59]

As in the case of Embraer, the development of these cutting-edge technologies took place not in a corporate vacuum but within a supportive institutional context. Among the most important elements here was the signing of a partnership agreement in 1987 with the COPPE institute based at the Federal University of Rio de Janeiro. Agreements were also later signed with the IPT at the University of São Paulo (mentioned above) and the State University of Campinas (Unicamp).[60] University departments involved in the project were also supported by funding provided by FINEP. Along with drawing on outside expertise, Petrobrás has been able to draw on its own—not inconsiderable—in-house resources. These are centered in a special research institute named CENPES, which was established in 1963 and now employs some 500 people on a site shared with the Federal University of Rio de Janeiro.[61] To a lesser extent than Embraer, Petrobrás has also collaborated with foreign suppliers, notably with the Scottish firm Weir Pumps.

The pursuit of the PROCAP program has resulted in a torrent of groundbreaking deepwater exploration and production technologies, including special deepwater drills, pumps, and semisubmersible platforms. As a result, Petrobrás has been able to operate successfully in ever-deeper waters. Whereas in 1988, two years following the initiation of PROCAP, Brazil's deepest platform operated in 492 meters of water, by 2003 the RO-21 platform was operating in water 1,886 meters deep. Petrobrás has set a number of world records, including, at one point, the record for the world's deepest exploration well (2,853 meters in the Roncador field).[62] Petrobrás has not, of course, neglected more traditional onshore technologies, and it remains a respected exponent in this field.[63]

59. Leite (2005, 81).
60. Leite (2005, 97).
61. Leite (2005, 67–68).
62. World Bank (2008, 62).
63. Leite (2005).

Perhaps not surprisingly, the development of these impressive capabilities has (literally and figuratively) provided a platform from which Petrobrás has been able to engage in an aggressive program of outward FDI. According to the World Bank's *Global Economic Prospects 2008,* Petrobrás "has used its advanced technology to perform exploration and production work in Angola, Argentina, Bolivia, Colombia, Nigeria, Trinidad and Tobago, and the United States and has acquired offshore exploration blocks and interests in Equatorial Guinea, Libya, Senegal and Turkey (Black Sea). It has also recently signed various agreements in China, India, Mexico, Mozambique, and Tanzania."[64]

The trigger for this renewed wave of internationalization is twofold. First, of course, the development of pioneering technology has given Petrobrás an edge on its rivals when it has come to mounting credible bids to gain exploration and production rights in new overseas locations. This edge has become even more telling given current oil prices and the fact that all the easily accessible fields have been claimed. In this sense, Petrobrás has found itself with an especially useful technological lever for engaging in Dunning-esque resource-seeking investments.

Second, in what amounts to a push rather than pull factor, Petrobrás has found itself challenged in the domestic market by the emergence of competition in the exploration and production sector. Since 1997, changes in Brazilian law have deprived Petrobrás of its statutory monopoly in these upstream activities, with the result that foreign oil majors such as Exxon-Mobil and Shell are now operating in the offshore sector. Given this reduced scope for deploying its core competencies at home, it is not surprising that Petrobrás has ventured further overseas.[65]

Odebrecht

Odebrecht, which was founded during World War II in the Northeastern state Bahia, is one of Brazil's longest established and most prominent construction companies. According to the U.S. magazine *Engineering News Record,* in 2002 Odebrecht ranked in twenty-ninth place among global construction groups according to the scale of its international contracts and first among enterprises specializing in hydroelectric projects.[66] Although best known internationally for its work in this field, Odebrecht

64. World Bank (2008, 62).
65. Antonio and Lara (2005, 12).
66. Mazzola and Oliveira (2005, 10).

is in fact quite a diversified group, also being involved in infrastructure and public services, chemicals and petrochemicals, pulp manufacturing, and oil and gas engineering and technical services.[67] Unlike Petrobrás and Embraer, Odebrecht was never an SOE; it was originally established as a family business. However, the state was still to play a crucial role in its evolution and its accumulation of technological capabilities.

The critical growth period for Odebrecht came during the era of import-substitution industrialization, the most dynamic phase of which lasted from the 1950s into the early 1970s. During this period, the state embarked on an unprecedented program of infrastructural investment, with a strong emphasis on highway construction, power generation, and heavy process industries such as steel and petrochemicals.[68] Odebrecht proved highly successful in winning contracts associated with these projects, and it soon moved from being a regional contractor to a full-fledged national player.

It is unlikely that Odebrecht would have achieved the success it did without possessing some core competence unmatched by its less successful rivals. In this regard, there is no doubt that it had a technological and organizational edge thanks to one of the central legacies of its founder, Norberto. This was what Odebrecht terms its Tecnologia Empresarial Odebrecht (TEO, translated loosely as Odebrecht Managerial Technology). The TEO provides a flexible internal organizational structure that devolves as much autonomy—and entrepreneurial decisionmaking—as possible to each manager.[69] Traditional hierarchical structures are eschewed, while the accumulation and transfer of technological knowledge is accomplished through specialized communities of practice within each area of operation.

By successfully winning domestic contracts in infrastructure and heavy industry while deploying this organization model, Odebrecht accumulated considerable technical, planning, and project management skills. Though it can be argued that Odebrecht did not enjoy the same close relationship with the state research institutes and universities as, say, Petrobrás, working hand in hand with such technologically accomplished SOE clients allowed ample opportunity for knowledge transfer and learning by doing.[70]

67. Oliveira (2007).
68. Baer (2008).
69. Mazzola and Oliveira (2005); Oliveira (2007).
70. Leite (2005).

Having accumulated the necessary expertise and experience, it is not surprising that Odebrecht began to embark on a program of internationalization. Such a program would, pace Hymer and Dunning, allow Odebrecht to leverage its core competencies, generating additional returns. In addition, it can be argued that reductions in Brazilian public sector investment from the late 1970s on may have encouraged Odebrecht to look abroad for business opportunities. Thus, perhaps it is significant that it was in 1979 that it commenced international operations with the construction of the Charcani V hydroelectric dam in Peru.[71] This was followed by the launch of further operations throughout Latin America. International expansion continued rapidly, with a subsidiary launched in Angola in 1984, entry into the European market in 1988, and the start of operations in the United States in 1991. Odebrecht's international operations have recently become more diversified and are no longer simply focused on power generation projects. It is now working on rail transportation, airport expansion, water distribution, and highway contracts in countries ranging from Angola to Libya to the United States.[72] This indicates that the enterprise has been diversifying both its expertise and its geographical reach.

Other Experiences

Although a lack of space precludes the discussion of some of Brazil's other leading multinationals in detail, it is nonetheless worthwhile to make brief comments about the experiences of Gerdau, Marcopolo, and Vale (the former CVRD). In the cases of all three, there is evidence that the development and accumulation of technology have played some role in their process of internationalization. For Gerdau, one of Brazil's longest-established steel producers, its overseas investment, especially into North America, has been strongly driven by a desire to gain market access and to circumvent trade barriers.[73] However, the enterprise has distinguished itself throughout its entirely private sector history through its ability to consistently raise productivity and introduce new technology in the enterprises it has acquired.[74] This has obviously assisted its successful drive to

---

71. Mazzola and Oliveira (2005, 11).

72. See the Odebrecht website, www.odebrecht.com.

73. Amann, Ferraz, and Mendes de Paula (2003). Gerdau's North American investment strategy has been strongly driven by acquisitions rather than greenfield projects.

74. Alem and Cavalcanti (2005, 65).

internationalize.[75] Still, the case of Gerdau provides little evidence of a close association with state-linked research institutes or innovation programs. This may in part be due to the fact that this firm was never in the public sector and the fact that many of the core technologies involved are embodied in the capital equipment provided by outside suppliers.[76]

In the case of Marcopolo, a leading player in the international bus and coach market, a senior manager in a 2005 presentation made it clear that the possession of proprietary technology was a key factor facilitating its internationalization.[77] The desire to capitalize on its technology, plus the need to enter markets using knocked-down kits,[78] has led it to establish assembly facilities across Latin America and also in Portugal and South Africa.[79] Another factor helping to explain its internationalization drive has to do with the desire to reduce transportation costs; it has proved more cost-effective to ship components rather than finished vehicles to some locations.[80]

The desire to exploit homegrown expertise on an international scale also characterizes the internationalization of a much larger Brazilian enterprise: the mining giant Vale. Like Embraer, Vale is a former SOE with strong roots in Brazil's ISI era.[81] In common with Petrobrás, Vale was established with the aim of enhancing national control over domestic natural resources. While still an SOE, the firm—then known as CVRD—entered an initial phase of internationalization through minerals exports (especially iron ore). Following its privatization in 1997, the firm now known as Vale embarked on an aggressive path of internationalization through acquisitions and the signing of joint ventures with foreign enterprises. This has involved two paths—one emphasizing the mineral-processing part of the production chain and the other the mineral exploration component.[82] Perhaps significantly, Vale has been rather

75. Alem and Cavalcanti (2005, 65).

76. For a detailed study of the technological trajectory of the steel equipment sector in Brazil, see Amann (2000).

77. The presentation is Martins (2005). The technology centers on windows, bus interiors, coach building, and, like Embraer, systems integration.

78. Shipping in such kits for local assembly often means that high duties on imported assembled vehicles are avoided.

79. Alem and Cavalcanti (2005, 67).

80. ECLAC (2005, 74).

81. Vale is the new name for an enterprise that until recently was called CVRD (Companhia Vale do Rio Doce).

82. Spanazzi de Oliveira and Mendes de Paula (2005, 10–11).

more active in the field of exploration activities,[83] an area in which it has been able to deploy its technological capacities to facilitate a successful resource-seeking strategy.[84] The Vale case demonstrates, once again, how competencies established in the domestic sphere under an inward-oriented industrialization strategy can later be deployed to good effect internationally.

Conclusion

The growing prominence of homegrown multinational corporations has been one of the most striking features of the recent resurgence of the Brazilian economy. This chapter has demonstrated that outward FDI by Brazilian enterprises is being strongly driven by a desire to access markets and natural resources. However, as the theoretical work of Dunning and others demonstrates, such internationalization requires as a precondition the possession of some key competence or advantage. It has been suggested that the development of specific technological capabilities could constitute such an advantage.

From the evidence reviewed, it is clear that certain Brazilian enterprises have developed such capabilities and are now seeking to capitalize on them through accelerated outward FDI. The emergence of these capabilities has been—in many instances—strongly conditioned by the actions of the state. Whether through public ownership (in the case of SOEs), the establishment of R&D institutes, or the initial pursuit of ISI, the state provided an environment in which certain enterprises could build technological competence. However, as was demonstrated above, public spending on technology is now under significant pressure. This must call into question the ability of the state to continue supporting innovation in the productive sector. Significantly, all the multinationals reviewed here "got their technological start" in the ISI period, when the state's financial capacity in this area was stronger than it is today. It will be interesting to see whether a future generation of Brazilian multinationals emerges from the current policy context. Despite the presently restricted ability of the state to assist with the accumulation of enterprises' technological capabilities, there is some room for optimism. In particular, capital market reforms and macroeconomic stabilization

83. Spanazzi de Oliveira and Mendes de Paula (2005, 10–11).
84. Spanazzi de Oliveira and Mendes de Paula (2005, 18–20).

mean that it is now easier than ever to raise (from the private sector) the resources necessary to fund technological development and internationalization. This holds out the possibility that some of today's medium-size enterprises may be able to transform themselves into technologically intensive multinational corporations without the traditionally necessary patronage of the state.

Does the emergence of Brazil's successful multinational corporations from an earlier epoch of state-driven development mean that it is now time to reappraise the earlier period in a more favorable light? Can it really be said that all those years of accelerated public investment under ISI have finally paid off? These are perhaps two of the most profound—and difficult-to-answer—policy questions to spring from the discussion. Though it is difficult to envisage the emergence of Brazil's current crop of homegrown multinationals without the pursuit of state-driven, inward-oriented industrialization, by the same token it is important to recognize the broader efficiency costs and distortions that came as part of the package. These eventually became unsupportable and, arguably, stifled the growth of enterprises without privileged access to state finance or contracts. The end of ISI and Brazil's tortuous exit from it also brought painful adjustment costs. These, too, need to be factored in when appraising the years of intensified state intervention. Still, there is no doubt that, through its legacy of world-class multinationals, the ISI period, in one respect at least, is now paying significant dividends.

References

Alem, A., and C. Cavalcanti. 2005. "O BNDES e o apoio à internacionalização das empresas Brasileiras: Algumas reflexões." *Revista do BNDES* 12, no. 24: 43–76.

Amann, E. 2000. *Economic Liberalization and Industrial Performance in Brazil.* Oxford University Press.

———. 2005. "Structural Reform and Economic Growth in Brazil." *World Economics* 6, no. 4: 149–69.

Amann, E., and W. Baer. 2006. "Economic Orthodoxy Versus Social Development? The Dilemmas Facing Brazil's Labour Government." *Oxford Development Studies* 34, no. 2: 219–43.

Amann, E., and H. J. Chang, eds. 2004. *Economic Crisis and Economic Restructuring in South Korea and Brazil.* London: Institute for Latin American Studies.

Amann, E., J. Ferraz, and G. Mendes de Paula. 2003. "Competitiveness, Export Performance and Corporate Strategy: Some Evidence from the Brazilian Iron and Steel Sector." University of Manchester, Brazilian National Economic and Social Development Bank, and Federal University of Uberlândia.

Antonio, J., and J. Lara. 2005. "Estratégias de internacionalização: O caso de Petrobrás segmento abastecimento." Paper presented at 5th Workshop on the Internationalization of Firms, COPPEAD (Graduate School of Business of the Federal University of Rio de Janeiro), Rio de Janeiro, October 27–28.

Baer, W. 2008. *The Brazilian Economy: Growth and Development.* Boulder, Colo.: Lynne Rienner.

Bettancourt, S., V. Gomes, W. Bartels, J. Lima, M. Pinto, and M. Migon. 2005. "O desafio do apoio ao capital nacional na cadeia de produção de aviões no Brasil." *Revista do BNDES* 12, no. 23: 119–34.

Cassiolato, J., R. Bernardes, and H. Lastres. 2002. *Transfer of Technology for Successful Integration into the Global Economy: A Case Study of Embraer in Brazil.* Geneva: United Nations Conference on Trade and Development and United Nations Development Program.

Churchwell, C. 2003. "Lessons From a Nasty Trade Dispute." *Harvard Business School Working Knowledge,* November 13.

Dunning, J. 1993. *Multinational Enterprises and the Global Economy.* New York: Addison Wesley.

ECLAC (Economic Commission for Latin America and the Caribbean). 2005. "Trans-Latins: An Overview." In *Foreign Investment in Latin America and the Caribbean 2005.* Santiago: ECLAC.

FDC (Fundação Dom Cabral)/Columbia University Program on International Investment. 2007. "Brazil's Multinationals Take Off." Press release, December 3.

Fiocca, Demian. 2006. "O BNDES e a Internacionalização das Empresas Brasileiras." Presentation, Rio de Janeiro, May 29.

Goldstein, A., and M. Godinho. 2007. "Embraer's Internationalization: The Case of Portugal." Organization for Economic Cooperation and Development.

Guedes, A., and A. Faria. 2005. "Internationalization of a Brazilian Corporation: Recognizing Business-Government and Governance-Management Issues." Fundação Getulio Vargas.

Hymer, S. 1968. "The Large Multinational Corporation." Reprinted in *Multinational Corporations,* ed. M. Casson. Cheltenham, U.K.: Edward Elgar, 1990.

Johnson, J., and J. S. Vahlne. 1977. "The Internationalization of the Firm: A Model of Knowledge Development and Increasing Foreign Market Commitments." *Journal of International Business Studies,* Spring: 23–32.

Kohli, A. 2004. *State-Directed Development: Political Power and Industrialization in the Global Periphery.* New York: Cambridge University Press.

Leite, L. 2005. *Inovação: O Combustível do Futuro.* Rio de Janeiro: Qualitymark.

Mani, S. 2002. *Government, Innovation and Technology Policy: An International Comparative Analysis.* Cheltenham, U.K.: Edward Elgar.

Martins, J. 2005. "A Internacionalização da Marcopolo." Presentation given at 5th Workshop on the Internationalization of Firms, COPPEAD (Graduate School of Business of the Federal University of Rio de Janeiro), Rio de Janeiro, October 27–28.

Mazzola, H., and M. Oliveira Jr. 2005. "Gestão do conhecimento em corporações multinacionais Brasileiras: Um estudo de caso na construtora Norberto Odebrecht." Paper presented at 5th Workshop on the Internationalization of Firms, COPPEAD (Graduate School of Business of the Federal University of Rio de Janeiro), Rio de Janeiro, October 27–28.

Ohmae, K. 1987. *Beyond Borders: Reflections on Japan and the World.* New York: Dow Jones–Irwin.

Oliveira, M., Jr. 2007. "Brazilian Multinationals: Competitive Challenges." Presentation, Faculdade de Economia, Universidade de São Paulo.

Prochnik, V., L. Esteves, and F. de Freitas. 2006. "O Grau de Internacionalização das Firmas Industriais Brasileiras e suas Características Microeconômicas." In *As Empresas Brasileiras e o Comércio Internacional,* ed. Araújo DeNegri. Brasília: Instituto de Pesquisa Econômica Aplicada.

Silva, O. 1999. *A Decolagem de Um Sonho.* São Paulo: Lemos.

Spanazzi de Oliveira, T., and G. Mendes de Paula. 2005. "Estratégia de internacionalização da Companhia Vale do Rio Doce." Paper presented at 5th Workshop on the Internationalization of Firms, COPPEAD (Graduate School of Business of the Federal University of Rio de Janeiro), Rio de Janeiro, October 27–28.

Teixeira, N. 2005. "O Mercado de Capitais Brasileiro a Luz de Seus Avanços e Desafios." In *Mercado de Capitais e Crescimento Económico,* ed. E. Bacha and L. de Oliveira Filho. Rio de Janeiro: Contra Capa.

UNCTAD (United Nations Conference on Trade and Development). 2005. *2005 World Investment Report.* Geneva.

———. 2006. *2006 World Investment Report.* Geneva.

Vernon, R. 1971. *Sovereignty at Bay: The Multinational Spread of U.S. Enterprises.* New York: Basic Books.

World Bank. 2008. *Global Economic Prospects 2008.* Washington.

Brazil as an Equitable Opportunity Society

CHAPTER NINE

Income Policies, Income Distribution, and the Distribution of Opportunities in Brazil

MARCELO NERI

During the last thirty years, changes in those Brazilian social indicators that are based on per capita income—such as inequality, poverty, and social welfare—have reflected the marked volatility of the nation's macroeconomic environment. Until 1994, the source of instability was the rise and failure of successive stabilization attempts, though after this period the main source of instability was the impact of external crises. This chapter argues that to understand the mechanics of these sharp macroeconomic fluctuations, as well as their consequences for income-based social indicators, it is crucial to understand the role played by various state-sponsored income policies. During the period of inflationary instability until 1995, income policies were behind both the core of chronic inflation and stabilization attempts. This is to say that they were part of both the problem and of the solutions offered. Anti-inflation plans—such as the Cruzado, Collor, and Real plans—tried to interfere directly with the processes of price formation and income determination through various measures such as price freezes, exchange rate policies, wage de-indexation rules, and currency change. Only the Real Plan was successful in lowering and controlling inflation. Similarly, besides price stabilization, state-sponsored regressive income policies are also key to understand the causes behind high inequality and attempts to fight it in Brazil. In recent anti-inequality policies, income policies have been employed in which the state transfers incomes directly from the public budget. Currently, there is considerable evidence that specific income policies—at least in the short term—have played a direct role in affecting income inequality. This chapter demonstrates that this role offers a diversity of results depending on the specific policies enacted. These effects may also change over time as a function of changes in income policy targets and operation, or changes in the general economic environment.

Brazil is an interesting case study. During the period from 1992 to 2006, there was a fall in poverty levels despite the meager growth observed. Brazil reached the first UN Millennium Development Goal in this period, as the portion of its population earning less than $1 per day (at purchasing power parity) fell 60 percent.[1] The poorest income segments have experienced growth rates on a par with those of China since the beginning of the present decade. The cumulative variation of per capita income of the poorest 10 percent was 57 percent from 2001 to 2006, and, falling monotonically as we reach the top of the income ladder, the figure for the top 10 percent was 6.7 percent.[2] This redistributive movement is noteworthy because Brazil has been notorious for being one of the countries with the highest levels of income inequality in the world. After its steep rise in the 1960s, Brazil's income inequality maintained a high yet stable Gini index for per capita income of about 0.6 between 1970 and 2000.[3] In the period 2001–6, however, inequality was in decline. The fall of inequality observed in this five-year period is roughly 71 percent of the rise observed in the 1960s.[4] This change reflects a combination of labor market improvements seen by low-skilled workers, including increases in educational attainment and the adoption of increasingly targeted official income policies.

The fact is that Brazilian inflation is at its lowest levels in decades and the inequality of per capita incomes is at the lowest level since the Pesquisa Nacional por Amostra de Domicílio (PNAD, the Brazilian National Household Survey) measurements began in 1976. In both cases, an instrumental role has been played by the stability of prices and by the efficacy of income policies such as redistributive programs and anti-inflation plans. The evidence presented here suggests that the speed with which

1. Neri (2006c).
2. Neri (2007b).
3. Hoffman (1989), Bonelli and Sedlacek (1989), Paes de Barros and Mendonça (1992), Ramos (1993), Paes de Barros, Henriques, and Mendonça (2000).
4. Langoni (1973), Fishlow (1972), Bacha and Taylor (1978).

these programs have met with success may be a function of increased targeting of income policies, along with efforts to craft income policies in tune with the electoral cycle.

The former role of stabilization plans is now played by redistributive income policies. President Fernando Henrique Cardoso is credited with stabilizing the currency, and President Luiz Inácio Lula da Silva has continued this process in redistributing the newly stable currency through a structure of social programs initiated under his predecessor. Brazil has slowly come to appreciate the importance of macroeconomic fundamentals for achieving lasting stability, and it must now learn to appreciate the fact that a sustained decrease in inequality depends on other fundamentals, such as the equality of opportunities, represented by the access to stocks of productive assets such as health and education and of physical assets and their impact on work decisions and outcomes.

The main challenge facing the new generation of income policies is to track changes induced in income flows with the high stocks of future productive wealth by the poor. This is the objective of the so-called conditional cash transfers such as Bolsa Família (Family Grant), Bolsa Escola, Bolsa Alimentação, Peti, and so on, and their Latin American counterparts such as Progresa-Oportunidades in Mexico and Praaf in Honduras. The structural side of income policies has yet to be fully understood and perfected in Brazil's social policymaking. Brazil must reinforce the structural side of compensatory policies with individual incentives geared toward the accumulation of productive capital.

In this chapter, I map the impact of income policies on a series of state variables in order to predict the long-term effects of compensatory policies in Brazil. The chapter examines the recent expansion of these benefits between 2004 and 2006 and takes advantage of recent data from the special supplement of the PNAD that covered these social programs during these two years. I use this as a basis for testing how the expansion affected the distribution of opportunity-related social indicators between income strata and also between those low-income individuals who have benefited from the new income transfers versus those low-income individuals who have not benefited. I evaluate the effects of income policies using a difference-in-difference approach to test the effects on elements such as work decisions, fertility, child mortality, education, migration, the accumulation of physical assets, and access to credit.

The chapter summarizes my previous work on the role played by redistributive income policies in Brazil, discussing some of its political economy determinants, its short-run effects on income distribution, and its potential long-run effects that operate through the distribution of opportunities. I also discuss desired upgrades for the next generation of income policies in the country, exploring changes in targeting strategies, the need for imposing new conditionalities, and possible links with the supply of financial instruments. The chapter is organized as follows. The second section discusses the main features of the changes in Brazilian public policy and income distribution in the recent past. The third section discusses the role played by electoral cycles in the adoption of different income policies targeted toward various demographic groups. The fourth and fifth sections describe the principal Brazilian income policies, evaluating their targeting ability and offering a cost/benefit analysis. I devote special attention to conditional cash transfers, noncontributory social security benefits, and minimum wages, studying the close relationship between them. At the end of the fifth section, I discuss the history of how income policies have affected the distribution of income of various age groups. The sixth section takes advantage of recently released data and explores the long-term effects of income policies on a series of state-level variables such as health, education, access to credit, physical assets accumulation, and work decisions. In light of this evidence, in the seventh and final section I propose desirable upgrades of official income policies.

Subjective Well-Being, Poverty, and Income Distribution Trends

This section presents an overview of the recent evolution of a series of objective and subjective social indicators in Brazil. I provide a general background of the main stylized facts of economic policy.

General Background

The Brazilian experience has been quite peculiar in the sense that structural reforms, and in particular trade liberalization, began relatively late in comparison with those of its neighbors. Whereas the other countries of Latin America started opening their economies in the early or middle 1980s, this process started in Brazil only in the early 1990s. The same happened with inflation control; whereas Mexico started its stabilization process in the middle 1980s and Argentina in the early 1990s, Brazil achieved successful price stabilization only after 1994.

Brazil experienced some of the world's highest inflation rates over the period from 1960 to 1995. From at least the beginning of the 1980s, curbing inflation became the focus of public policy in Brazil. Successive macroeconomic packages and three major stabilization efforts have been attempted since then: the Cruzado Plan in 1986, the Collor Plan in 1990, and the Real Plan in 1994. The Real Plan was based on an "exchange-rate-based stabilization" model that led to consumption booms instead of recessions. But the need to support an overvalued exchange rate for stabilization purposes increased the fragility of the Brazilian economy, making it vulnerable to external shocks such as the Mexican (1995), Asian (1997), and Russian (1998) crises.

The 1999 Brazilian devaluation crisis triggered important changes in macroeconomic policy that can be still observed today, including (1) the adoption of floating exchange rates; (2) the adoption of inflation targets; and (3) the implementation of the Fiscal Responsibility Law, which is binding on all government levels and state enterprises alike but has increased the size of the tax burden by about 10 percentage points of GDP from 1995 onward, reaching around 37 percent at the end of 2008. One also has to bear in mind that there were very high real interest rates and an expansion of public expenditures that contributed both to the rise in Brazil's public debt, which reached more than 50 percent of GDP, and also to the slow growth trend assumed. During the 2002 elections, Brazil faced another crisis, which was controlled by the new government in the following year. This was done by means of a so-called confidence shock, which meant keeping the country's previous directions for macroeconomic policy. Following a mild recession in 2003, a boom in the global economy and improved internal fundamentals isolated the Brazilian economy from adverse external shocks. Since 2005, average growth has been higher in Brazil: 8 percent per year on per capita incomes based on the PNAD, which are comparable to the per capita GDP growth rates observed during the economic miracle of 1968–73. According to the new estimates, Brazil became a BRIC, but only in this recent period. (Brazil is often examined alongside three other large and populous emerging economies under the rubric "BRICs"—for Brazil, Russia, India, and China.) During the period from 2004 to 2007, Brazil generated about 10 million new jobs, in particular 6 million formal jobs with no recent labor reforms attached to them. In 2007, employment generation reached 1.6 million new jobs, the new record of the Cadastro Geral de Empregados e Desempregados (CAGED) series since 1992. Despite the economic crisis in the developed countries, during the first five months of 2008, Brazil generated 27 percent more new formal jobs than in the same period in the previous year.

Life Satisfaction

Years ago, when I first wore a pair of eyeglasses to correct my myopia, I began to notice the depth and clarity of things, and I marveled at the subtle shades and hues of the world around me. Similarly, the possibilities of observing nuances in Brazilian society have evolved through the years. An important landmark in this process was the decision made by the Instituto Brasileiro de Geografia e Estatística in 1995 to release its household survey data along with its tabulations and reports. This small but significant step gave individuals the freedom to look at the Brazilian social data from their own perspective, as opposed to a preestablished one. Nowadays, with the release of each PNAD or CAGED report, Brazilian society debates its own achievements and drawbacks with increasing interest and knowledge. The more democratic environment in the political arena and the increasing access to information (enabled by the so-called information and communication era) has contributed to greater transparency and integrity in the public debate. I remember reading in the *New York Times* in 1994—around the same time I began wearing those glasses—an article on social issues, such as the determinants of women's unemployment or the birth weight of children, and I thought how distant Brazilians were from this type of information. At that time, Brazilians would think first and foremost about inflation rates, and this had a distorting effect on the senses and concerns of Brazilians' daily life.

There is a new breed of international surveys, of which Gallup's World Poll is perhaps the best example. This new breed boasts two important innovations. First, Gallup uses the same questionnaire in its research in more than 130 countries, allowing global comparisons and the flexibility enabled by the processing of individual answers (i.e., microdata). The second novelty refers to the type of question that is asked, side by side with traditional survey questions. The respondent is asked directly about individual and collective subjective matters, be they local, national, or global. This feature allows the researcher to delve into the way that people form their aspirations, attitudes, and expectations by inquiring about the interviewees' perceived life satisfaction and their assessments about the national educational system, performance of the local economy, and other topics.

The Center for Social Policies (Centro de Políticas Sociais / Instituto Brasileiro de Economia / Fundação Getulio Vargas, CPS/IBRE/FGV) has been selected along with other Latin American institutions by the Inter-American Development Bank to help analyze and interpret Gallup's global data. This ambitious project will mark the Inter-American Development Bank's fiftieth anniversary by bringing quality of life, as perceived by the respondents themselves, into the debate's center stage.

How do Brazilians' perceived level of satisfaction with life in 2006 compare with the rest of the world? On a subjective scale from 0 to 10, Brazilians stated that their happiness level is 6.61, as compared with a score of 5.25 for the rest of the world and 5.64 for Latin America. Comparatively, U.S. citizens reported a happiness score of 7.09, while citizens of Belgium and India—countries frequently referenced in the Brazilian social debate—rated 7.15 and 5.27, respectively. Denmark holds the world record for happiness with a score of 7.98, whereas Chad ranks last with 3.36. Brazil ranks 23rd among 132 countries.

How has happiness evolved in the last five years in the world? According to Gallup's survey, average global happiness increased from 4.84 in 2001 to 5.26 in 2006. That is, the first five years of the new millennium showed a considerable and consistent advance, concurrent with the expansion of the global economy. When asked about projected happiness in five years' time, the worldwide average was 6.0. In other words, we expect a 25 percent growth in the world level of perceived happiness compared with how we saw ourselves five years ago and how we see ourselves five years ahead. Furthermore, two-thirds of this advance was expected to happen in the second half of the decade. This positive scenario could be at risk, however, given the recent turmoil in markets. But at the moment, Brazilians' expected level of happiness in five years—8.24—exceeds those of all other 130 countries surveyed. In fact, Brazilians believe they will be happier in 2011 than the Danish, whose predicted happiness score of 7.86 ranks them second. The country least optimistic about its future happiness is Paraguay, with 4.08. It is likely that Brazil's results are a reflection of the nation's innate optimism. To control for such cultural aspects, I have compared Brazilians' expected leap in happiness for the next five years with current levels. According to the survey, Brazilians expect to gain 2.56 points in the next five years, exceeded only by 10 countries in the sample, including China's impressive gain of 3.04. On average, Brazil's economic growth is not on a par with China's. What, then, are the determinants of Brazilian optimism? The reduction in inequality since

2001? The 2006 elections? The answers to these questions are explored in the next sections.

Income Changes in 2005 and 2006

In last section, I presented some evidence of the positive expectations of Brazilians. In a 2006 Gallup survey of 132 countries, Brazil was ranked as the most optimistic country with regard to projected levels of happiness in five years' time. Why do Brazilians expect so much if their economic scenario does not rival those of other emerging countries? According to the national accounts statistics, and GDP in particular, Brazil should not be considered one of the BRICs (again, Brazil, Russia, India, and China) or building blocks of future global wealth. Intrinsic cultural optimism helps to explain why the average Brazilian's expectations and reality are out of sync with each other. Swayed by this optimism, a Brazilian's glass is always half full. Nonetheless, even calculating the difference between future expectations and the current reality and accounting for cultural and psychological biases, Brazil's ranking is still remarkable because it nearly equals Chinese rates of expected happiness. If the Brazilian economy is not growing as robustly as the Chinese, however, why do Brazilians experience such a similar feeling of prosperity about their future?

This puzzle can be solved if it is understood that, in fact, Brazil's economic growth parallels China's. Briefly stated, Brazil's national accounts in 2005 and 2006 show an accumulated per capita GDP growth of 3.84 percent. According to PNAD estimates, per capita household income growth, excluding the population growth rate, was 16.4 percent for the same period, or 4.3 times larger than per capita GDP, even after the adjustments made to the national accounts. In any case, either Brazil is growing more than suggested by its GDP, or poverty is not falling as much as suggested by the PNAD figures (23.9 percent in 2005–6).

To reconcile this statistical problem, we could look into the growth of GDP elements that are not captured by the PNAD—that is, consumption movements unrelated to income. The issue here thus concerns the order of magnitude of the observed discrepancy. Another issue is that these explanations increase the paradox, instead of reducing it. In particular, the consumer credit boom points to an increase in consumption expenses that is larger than increases in income. In addition, the BOVESPA index increase of 60 percent between 2005 and 2006 suggests that the Brazilian economy has not undergone a strong reduction of income gains that could explain part of this discrepancy in growth rates.

PNAD income is tabulated from answers to nine direct questions about how much people received from different income sources. The PNAD, however, with its well-balanced sample of more than 400,000 individual answers, has not undergone a single methodological change, nor has the Índice Nacional de Preços ao Consumidor (INPC, National Consumer Price Index) been used in its adjustment. The Chinese-like appearance of the PNAD statistics is reflected in other indicators for 2005–6, such as retail sales (11.8 percent) and job creation (4.6 million jobs created, among which 2.5 million are new formal employment positions).

As demonstrated in the next subsection, Brazil's poorest populations experienced a Chinese-like growth at the beginning of the present decade, but in the past few years, all social groups have had this kind of growth.[5] The recent Brazilian boom is of even a better quality than the Chinese because it is combined with greater equity, while China has increasing inequality—similar to Brazil's rates during the economic miracle of the 1960s. Another parallel with Brazil in the second half of the 1960s is the lack of political freedom in China—whereas Brazilians currently live in a democracy. Growing under a strict political regime is easier in the short term, but not in the long term. In environmental terms as well, China has been noticed as the pollution "black sheep," whereas in Brazil, conservative management by the Ministry for the Environment hampers growth while also making it more sustainable. To sum it up, Brazil's Chinese-like growth of the last couple of years has been better than China's.

Changes in Income Distribution from 2001 to 2006

We move now to the analysis of recent income distribution changes. Figure 9-1 shows that Brazil's poorest (and only they) experienced Chinese-like growth at the beginning of the present decade, but in the past few years all income strata have experienced similar levels of growth. In 2006, Brazil experienced phenomenal growth across the entire income spectrum. According to the PNAD, average individual income increased 9.16 percent in 2006 against a 2.3 percent growth in per capita GDP, even after the methodological revision of national accounts. The first statistic suggests Chinese-like growth, while the second points to Haitian-like stagnation. As shown in table 9-1, in 2006, the average income of the poorest 50 percent of the population increased 11.99 percent against an increase of 7.85 percent for the richest 10 percent and 9.66 percent for the middle

5. See Neri (2007c).

FIGURE 9-1. Accumulated Variation in Income by Per Capita Income Decile, Brazil, 2002–06 Compared with 2005–06

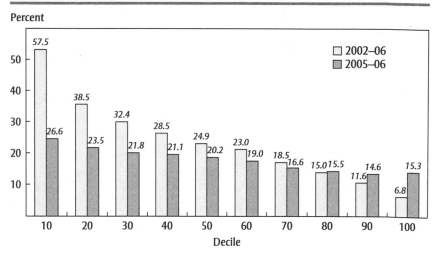

Source: Centro de Políticas Sociais/Fundação Getulio Vargas, processing Pesquisa Nacional por Amostra de Domicílio/Instituto Brasileiro de Geografia e Estatísticamicrodata.

40 percent. These income increases were the largest of any year this decade, including 2004.

Concurrently, as shown in figure 9-2, in 2006 the inequality measured by the Gini index decreased at an intermediate value of –1.06 percent, much lower than values from four previous years: –1.2 percent in 2002, 1 percent in 2003, –1.9 percent in 2004, and –0.6 percent in 2005. The high income inequality seen in Brazil between 1970 and 2000 finally began to relent at the turn of the century. The increasing income equality

TABLE 9-1. Variation in Brazilians' per Capita Income per Year, 2002–06

Percent

Year	Total	50 percent poorest	40 percent intermediate	10 percent richest
2002	0.30	3.65	0.34	−0.68
2003	−5.81	−4.15	−4.67	−7.32
2004	3.14	8.34	4.13	0.68
2005	6.63	8.56	5.74	6.89
2006	9.16	11.99	9.66	7.85

Source: Centro de Políticas Sociais/Fundação Getulio Vargas, from Pesquisa Nacional por Amostra de Domicílio/Instituto Brasileiro de Geografia e Estatística microdata.

FIGURE 9-2. Gini Coefficients on Per Capita Household Income for Brazil, 1992–2006

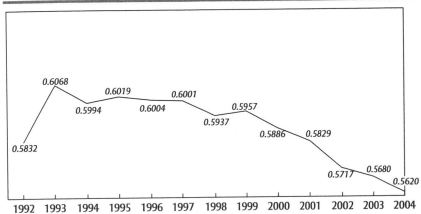

Source: Centro de Políticas Sociais/Fundação Getulio Vargas, processing Pesquisa Nacional por Amostra de Domicílio/Instituto Brasileiro de Geografia e Estatisticamicrodata.

between the years 2001 and 2006 roughly mirrored the rise of inequality observed in the 1960s. Given that this decrease in inequality has occurred since 2001, one may eventually call this era the decade of reduction in inequality, in the same manner as the previous decade could be coined the stabilization decade or the 1980s may be called the redemocratization decade—all of which are part of the same process.

Updating Income Distribution Changes

It is traditional among the research institutions to use data from the Monthly Employment Survey (PME) at individual levels, as opposed to the household levels. Nevertheless, PME is a household survey comparable to the PNAD. It is important to highlight two PME limitations, as follows: It does not consider income unrelated to work, such as income from income transfer government programs and income from interest gains for the groups with a financial wealth stock; it only covers the six main metropolitan areas in Brazil. In short, the research only provides evidence of labor in the metropolitan areas. The main question here is how to improve the monitoring of our population's living conditions in the past eighteen months not covered by the PNAD. The series of mean income, the proportion of poor poverty and inequality captured by the Gini index, is given in table 9-2.

TABLE 9-2. Per Capita Household Income from Work, Six Main
Metropolitan Areas, 2002–08

Date	Mean income (reais)	Gini	Poverty rate (percent)
April 2002	256.56	0.6270	34.93
April 2003	283.24	0.6284	37.13
April 2004	290.68	0.6258	37.17
April 2005	345.03	0.6036	32.58
April 2006	371.27	0.6011	31.61
April 2007	412.31	0.5963	29.09
April 2008	464.09	0.5844	25.16

Source: Centro de Políticas Sociais/Fundação Getulio Vargas, from Pesquisa Mensal do Emprego/Instituto Brasileiro de Geografia e Estatística microdata.

Between April 2006 and April 2008 there is a 25 percent increase in mean per capita earnings income. The Gini index falls from 0.6011 in April 2006 to 0.5844 in April 2008, which once again is considerable given the scale of variation in the index, particularly within the Brazilian context. The same index was 0.6270 in April 2002. Conceptual and geographical differences aside, for comparison purposes, this absolute decrease in six years of 0.0426 is exactly in the same rhythm as in the 1960s. The combination of higher mean and lower dispersion of earnings led to an additional 20.4 percent decline in poverty based on per capita labor earnings. This point is noteworthy given the reduction of the level of activity in developed countries since mid-2007 and the fact that this additional poverty fall occurs on top of declining long-run trends in poverty detailed in the following section. The side effect of this redistributive change was the emergence of a new middle class in Brazil: the C class moves from 42 to 52 percent of the population between April 2004 and April 2008.[6]

Poverty Trends

If long-term poverty movements are measured against the targets set forth in the UN Millennium Development Goals (MDGs), Brazil has succeeded in accomplishing the first goal—and perhaps the most celebrated one—by reducing extreme poverty by 50 percent in less than twenty-five years. In fact, extreme poverty in Brazil has been reduced by 60.53 percent, as figure 9-3 illustrates. Extreme poverty is understood as an individual income level beneath $1 a day. According to MDG calculations, the portion of the

6. See Neri (2008b).

FIGURE 9-3. Cumulative Variation of Extreme Poverty in Relation to the Millennium Development Goals, Brazil, 1993–2006

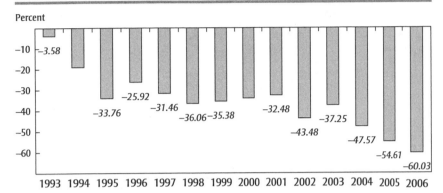

Source: Centro de Políticas Sociais/Fundação Getulio Vargas, processing Pesquisa Nacional por Amostra de Domicílio/Instituto Brasileiro de Geografia e Estatísticamicrodata.
Note: In 1994 and 2000, Pesquisa Nacional por Amostra de Domicílio data were not collected, so these are average values.

population living in extreme poverty fell from 11.73 percent in 1992 to 4.69 percent in 2006, as shown in figure 9-4.

Figure 9-4 points out the dates of presidential elections (1994, 1998, 2002, and 2006), which seem to show reductions that are clear to the naked eye. In the same way that I used the MDGs to consider the long-term trends in poverty, in the next section I use the electoral cycles to explain some of the oscillations in per capita income across different income sources.

Income Policies and Electoral Cycles

This section describes Brazil's political business cycle as captured by the country's social indicators. It discusses the role played by specific income policies in explaining the electoral cycles found in different per capita household income sources.

Description

The literature on electoral cycles describes the behavior of politicians who emphasize or embellish their successes in election years as a way of influencing the result of the elections. According to the political economy literature, the outcomes of elections are determined by the median voter—hence, the option here for the use of median income, which is dated close

FIGURE 9-4. Extreme Poverty in Brazil, 1992–2006

Percentage of population living on less than $1 a day,
at purchasing power parity

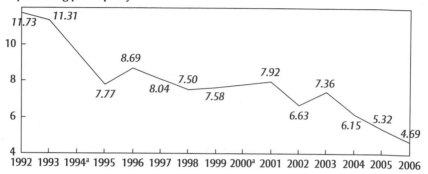

Source: Centro de Políticas Sociais/Fundação Getulio Vargas, processing Pesquisa Nacional por Amostra de Domicílio/Instituto Brasileiro de Geografia e Estatística microdata.
a. In 1994 and 2000, Pesquisa Nacional por Amostra de Domicílio data were not collected, so these are average values.

to the first round of the elections, at the beginning of October, when the PNAD is usually launched. The PNAD did not collect data in 1994 and 2007, so it is not possible to capture the full effects of cycles associated with the two episodes, as table 9-3 demonstrates.

Table 9-3 demonstrates that median per capita household income has increased in all years that preceded a national election for both legislature

TABLE 9-3. Variation in Median Income and Electoral Cycles, 1982–2006

Year	Percent	Year	Percent	Year	Percent
1982	**3**	*1990*	*−2*	2001	2
1983	*−23*	1992	−3	**2002**	**1**
1984	−1	1993	−2	*2003*	*−4*
1985	20	1995	25	2004	6
1986	**53**	1996	0	2005	9
1987	*−27*	1997	3	**2006**	**10**
1988	−11	**1998**	**2**		
1989	**6**	*1999*	*−4*		

Source: Centro de Políticas Sociais/Fundação Getulio Vargas, processing Pesquisa Nacional por Amostra de Domicílio/Instituto Brasileiro de Geografia e Estatística microdata.
Note: Electoral year in bold, postelectoral year in italic. In 1991, 1994, and 2000, Pesquisa Nacional por Amostra de Domicílio data were not collected, so the table gives cumulative values for the following year.

TABLE 9-4. Variation in Poverty Rate and Electoral Cycles, 1982–2006

Year	Percent	Year	Percent	Year	Percent
1982	**0**	1990	1	2001	−2
1983	*19*	1992	0	**2002**	**−3**
1984	−1	1993	0	*2003*	*5*
1985	−13	1995	−21	2004	−10
1986	**−37**	1996	1	2005	−10
1987	*47*	1997	−2	**2006**	**−15**
1988	13	**1998**	**−5**		
1989	**−5**	*1999*	*4*		

Source: Centro de Políticas Sociais/Fundação Getulio Vargas, processing Pesquisa Nacional por Amostra de Domicílio/Instituto Brasileiro de Geografia e Estatística microdata.

Note: Electoral year in bold, postelectoral year in italic. In 1991, 1994, and 2000, Pesquisa Nacional por Amostra de Domicílio data were not collected, so the table gives cumulative values for the following year.

or the presidency since 1980 (i.e., 1982, 1986, 1989, 1998, 2002, and 2006) and that this income has fallen in all postelection years (1983, 1987, 1990, 1999, and 2003). The average variation rate in median income in preelection years was 12.52 percent, versus −11.87 percent in postelection years, when the adjustment account is made. In the most recent elections, this trend was less exaggerated, but still existed: 4.38 percent (1998, 2002, and 2006) during election years, versus −3.68 percent in postelection years (1999 and 2003). Table 9-4 presents a summary of the fluctuations in poverty rates in preelection and postelection years. Similarly, as table 9-4 demonstrates, we observe a general decrease in poverty rates in every year when national elections were held since 1980 (1982 is the exception), followed by increasing rates in all postelectoral years. The average rate of variation in poverty in preelectoral years was −7.69 percent, against 14.05 percent in postelection years.

The data given in figures 9-5 and 9-6 were culled from the PNAD from the years of 1992 to 2006. During this period, the PNAD surveys' questionnaires and income concepts are more comparable. The evidence shows that during this period, election years demonstrated marked poverty reductions and increases in median income. The reduction of poverty between 1993 and 1995 is visible, as a result of the Real Plan in July 1994. The 1998 and 2002 elections display temporary reductions of poverty, that is, poverty reduction beyond the previous trend. In sum, an election year is the time for good illusions, for "inebriating" news, whereas in the following period come the bill and the "hangover." Political cycles have

FIGURE 9-5. Elections and Poverty in Brazil, 1992–2006

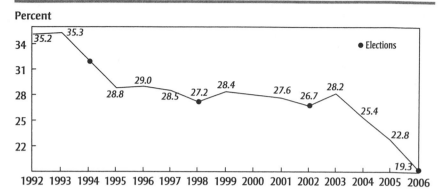

Source: Pesquisa Nacional por Amostra de Domicílio/Instituto Brasileiro de Geografia e Estatísticamicrodata.

become less pronounced as the new Brazilian democracy of 1985 has matured. Now let us further inspect the mechanism that connects elections and income-based social indicators in the Brazilian context.

Mincerian Equations and Electoral Cycles

To study the short-term effects of election year politics on both voters and nonvoters, I examined data from electoral and nonelectoral years.[7] The sample is thus divided into four groups. The interactive effect between the voting age dummy (dV) and the electoral-year dummy (dY) gives us the difference-in-difference estimator. We examined this relationship using a standard Mincerian regression applied to each of the main income sources and to the total sum of sources found in the 1992–2006 PNAD questionnaires using the INPC as the deflator. Mathematically, this difference-in-difference estimator $(D - D)$ can be represented with this Mincerian-type per capita income equation:

$$\text{Ln } Y = g0 + gl * dV + g2 * dY + (D - D) * dV * dY + \text{other controls.}$$

It is useful to detail the income channels of public action that have recently affected mean income in electoral episodes and that have been

7. See Neri (2006a). Neri and Carega (2000) studied the impact of electoral cycles on per capita labor income on longitudinal data for the main Brazilian metropolitan regions. The main channel there was income policies associated with stabilization plans. Neri (2006a) uses the same approach used here.

FIGURE 9-6. **Median per Capita Income in Brazil, 1992–2006**

Constant 2006 reais

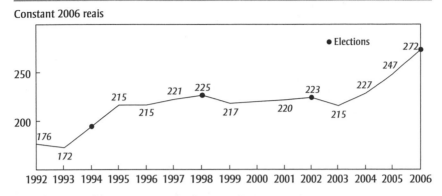

Source: Centro de Políticas Sociais/Fundação Getulio Vargas, processing Pesquisa Nacional por Amostra de Domicílio/Instituto Brasileiro de Geografia e Estatística microdata.

captured by the new PNAD, that is, 1998, 2002, and 2006. Table 9-5 synthesizes the main findings; the data clearly show four results for all income sources (e.g., employment, benefits from social security, and other social programs[8]). First, as expected, per capita income is lower for those above the minimum voting age of sixteen years; this is a common feature across countries. Second, the greatest income differential is found in social security, which is 51.29 percent higher for voters than nonvoters. The smallest differential is in social programs, where income is 28.57 percent higher. Third, income increases were greater in election years, characterizing the electoral cycle. In those years, on average, income from social programs increased the most (22.57 percent), followed by social security (10.51 percent) and general employment (3.16 percent). These numbers further indicate that the use of income transfer programs is tied to the election cycle. Fourth and finally, and most important, despite the per capita household income that smoothes the effects examined here, the income of people of voting age increases more in an election year than the income of children and teenagers who do not participate directly in political contests. This difference-in-difference result is captured by the interaction of the two variables mentioned above. In this case, the main relative gain comes

8. Income from social programs includes Bolsa Família, unemployment benefits, and other public programs, but also the financial income whose main source is also the state. The income from all sources also includes the income from other types of employment, rents, and private transfers between households (maintenance payment, donations, etc.).

TABLE 9-5. Mincerian Equation of the Per Capita Household Income, Various Income Sources

	Income source			
Variable	All sources	Main job	Social security	Social programs
Voters (under 16 years of age)	0.4192**	0.3125**	0.5129**	0.2857**
Electoral Year	0.0611**	0.0316**	0.1051**	0.2257**
Voters*Electoral Year	0.0136**	0.0127**	0.0274**	0.0343**

Source: Centro de Políticas Sociais/Fundação Getulio Vargas, processing Pesquisa Nacional por Amostra de Domicílio/Instituto Brasileiro de Geografia e Estatística microdata.
Note: *Significant at 90 percent. **Significant at 95 percent. Observations: Controlled by sex, ethnicity, head of the household, educational level, size of the city, migration, and state.

from income from social programs. During election years, this income stream increases 3.43 percent more for eligible voters than for children and teenagers below the voting age. Social security follows this trend, with a relative increase of 2.74 percent for eligible voters, followed by the indirect effect of employment income, with 1.27 percent.[9]

Note that in this empirical test carried out using 2005 as the last year, the set of hypotheses given above presented the expected signal, but it was not statistically significant for main work and social security income—which illustrates the potential magnitude of the impact of the last presidential elections for income data. The qualitative smoothing factor that must be applied to the 2006 and 1994 elections, for which data were not collected (1994) or for which data are not yet available (2007, the 2006 postelection), is that the effects seem to last longer than all the remaining election episodes in the the so-called New Democracy in Brazil. In other words, we are talking about expansions of a sustained character to people's lives; hence the expression "real" goes beyond the name of Brazil's monetary denomination and applies to these two episodes. In the Neri, we detail the regressions summarized here.

Trends in Income Policies

The change in poverty levels in the 1993–95 period was associated with the implementation of the Real Plan, but what are the associated features

9. We checked the importance of political cycles directly for work income through raises in the wages of public servants at the three government levels, particularly the municipal level, at the time of voting. In the case of hiring public servants, the effect is negative, perhaps given the electoral year's restriction in job openings.

for changes in poverty levels between 2003 and 2006? What is the role played by income transfer policies sponsored by the state, with the expansion of the Bolsa Família and minimum wage adjustments? What are the specific channels for these policy operations? These are some of the questions I would like to answer, so that the causes and consequences of the recent reduction in inequality can be assessed. I offer a mix of each of these elements by summarizing past research and updating it with new data. I believe that this type of analysis helps to explain the social changes observed in past years, as well as challenges, limitations, and opportunities.

It is true that although other important achievements occurred—such as the universal provision of primary school education in the second half of the 1990s—the turning point for the job market in recent years is associated with greater equity in income, undoubtedly the most marked improvement for a country located on the continent with the most widespread inequality in the world. To reinforce the structural side of compensatory policies with an incentive to demand the accumulation of human capital, it has to be combined with an improvement in the quality of structural policies, for which health and education are important. The Education Development Plan involves sector-specific actions to keep the supply of social services in pace with induced demand increase.[10]

With respect to fighting inequality in the short term, there is no doubt that in Brazil there is a generation of policies better focused and more capable of redistributing income than the policies implemented in the distant past. The problem is that Brazil does not opt for the new generation's policies instead of other less effective policies when attacking inequality and the improvement of welfare. Hybrid, less-focused policies will have a lesser impact than if the resources were allocated today and in the future to more focused policies. Brazil has opted to expand both new and old policies. To paraphrase Ricardo Paes de Barros of the Instituto de Pesquisa Econômica Aplicada, Brazil keeps throwing money out of a helicopter—the difference being that now the doors have also opened over poor corners and slums, which were not targeted by previous policies.

A useful measure in the design of public policies is the income gap (P1). It allow us to calculate how much income is needed on average for the extremely poor to be able to meet their basic needs. Using the Fundação

---

10. Neri and Buchmann (2008b).

Getulio Vargas's extreme poverty line as a basis (R\$125 per month at 2006 São Paulo prices; see Ferreira, Lanjouw, and Neri 2003), the average deficit of each extremely poor Brazilian would be R\$48.52. Because just part of the Brazilian population is below this line, data show that it would be necessary to add R\$9.37 per person on average to alleviate poverty in Brazil, at a total monthly cost of R\$1,717,955,185, or yearly cost of R\$20,615,462,223, around 4 percent of Brazilians' total income, according to the PNAD. This information reveals the minimum amount of transfers needed to lift each extremely poor person up to the basic need level.

This exercise should not be seen as a defense of certain policies but as a reference to the social opportunity cost of adopting nontargeted policies. For example, if universal income maintenance was provided to all Brazilians to eradicate extreme poverty, it would cost 5.6 times more than the minimum cost pointed out above. If we were to use the lower figure of the MDGs, the cost would be 11.1 times higher than the minimum cost.

The fact that inequality reduction has played an instrumental role in Brazil's poverty reduction is reinforced by the Datt-Ravallion methodology.[11] The proportion of extremely poor people in Brazil would fall from 19.3 percent in 2006 to 18.55 percent in 2007, a 3.95 percent drop, if per capita income grows 3 percent in the year. The reduction will be even greater if this growth comes hand in hand with a reduction in inequality. If the 3 percent expansion were combined with a slight decrease in the Gini index (moving from Brazil's to Rio de Janeiro's Lorenz curve, which corresponds to moving the per capita household income Gini index from 0.562 to 0.5605), Brazilian poverty would fall almost twice, or 6.55 percent, which is 2.4 times faster than the first MDG of halving poverty in twenty-five years. The proportion of extremely poor people would be 16.50 percent.

Noncontributory Pensions

During the so-called new Brazilian democracy period that started in 1985, the elderly group was able to achieve substantial gains in income transfers by the state. Apart from the 1988 federal constitution, other more recent social policies have caused changes in the lives of elderly Brazilians. Among these policies, I highlight (1) the 1998 reduction of the minimum age for entitlement from seventy to sixty-seven years (and, more recently,

11. See Datt and Ravallion (1992).

to sixty-five); and (2) the Elderly Statute of 2003, which establishes social rights and promotes equity between the elderly and the remaining members of the population in different fields, increasing their self-esteem and their sense of citizenship.

Concerning income transfers, according to Camarano and Pasinato,[12] following the reduction in the minimum age for eligibility for the Benefício de Prestação Continuada (BPC, Continued Contribution Benefits; under the Lei Orgânica de Assistência Social, known as LOAS)[13] in 1998, the number of beneficiaries increased 253 percent between 1997 and 1999 and 648 percent between 1997 and 2003. If we consider the BPC and the lifetime elderly monthly income, we observe that the number of payment benefits rises 72.9 percent between 1997 and 2003. Apart from an increase in the number of assistance benefits, there was a real increase in the minimum wage deflated by the INPC—an inflation index that informs the calculation of social security benefits—of 22.3 percent between 1997 and 2003. According to the evolution of the real value of all benefits, there was a 44.4 percent increase over the same period. Because the adjustment policies of the social security benefits since 1998 have differentiated benefits payments that are equal to the minimum floor allowed by the 1988 Brazilian Constitution, the effect of the increase of the number of beneficiaries observed rose cumulatively. Besides, in 1998, an income policy was adopted to give higher real adjustments to the floor for social security payments (one minimum wage) that coincides with the BPC and noncontributory rural social security benefits.

Today, Brazil transfers more income to the elderly relative to its GDP than any other country in Latin America.[14] Note that this had started to happen before the country completed its demographic transition. During the last fifteen years, the expansion of noncontributory programs to the low-income elderly population explains a substantial part of this movement. My calculations based on Brazilian national household surveys between 1992 and 2006 show that the elderly population's (i.e., age sixty and above) share in income increased from 7.9 to 9.96 percent. This same age group's share of individual income in the aggregate rose from 13.34 to 17.64 percent, while its share of per capita income in the aggregate rose from 10.8 to 14.51 percent. In per capita terms, the elderly were able to

---

12. Camarano and Pasinato (2004).
13. Lei Orgânica da Assistência Social 8742, Senado Federal Brasília, December 1993.
14. Neri, Considera, and Pinto (1999); Camarano and Pasinato (2007).

get additional income of 172 reais from the state in this period, while children got direct transfers of 17 reais. Even after Bolsa Família was established in 2003, the elderly were able to get higher absolute income gains and relative poverty reductions. Some researchers have argued that the elderly redistribute their incomes within households. Even under this assumption, the poverty level in 2006 was more than 500 percent higher for children compared with the elderly.

Furthermore, Neri, Carvalhaes, and Reis show an improvement of health perceptions much smaller for the indirect beneficiaries of transfers than those observed for direct beneficiaries living in the same households.[15] The fact that the elderly live in smaller families would also diminish the impact of this breadwinner effect (*efeito arrimo de família*). For instance, there were 3.23 household members in families with people over sixty years of age, against 4.98 in the total sample of families in 2003. This may be relevant for policy purposes because people expected that the increasing transfer to the elderly poor in Brazil would generate a sizable externality to other household members' individual welfare levels.

Bolsa Família

Bolsa Família, created in October 2003, is a direct descendent of Bolsa Escola, Bolsa Alimentação, Vale Gás, and other social programs that were designed in the aftermath of the 1999 Brazilian macroeconomic crisis and were gradually implemented during the last years of the Cardoso administration. President Lula integrated these different programs under the name of Bolsa Família and gave it scale. Between the end of 2004 and 2006, there was a sharp expansion of Bolsa Família, moving from 6.5 million to 11 million families, nearly 25 percent of the Brazilian population, at a total fiscal cost of less than 0.8% of GDP.

The common feature of this new generation of income policies is to try to combine speed, targeting, and conditionalities. Families with a per capita income below 50 reais a month were entitled to an unconditional monetary transfer of 50 reais plus a transfer of 15 reais for children between birth and fifteen years of age, up to a maximum of three children, subject to specific conditions, depending on the child's age. Children between birth and six years of age had to undergo vaccinations, whereas children and young teenagers between seven and fifteen years of age had to be enrolled in school with a maximum of 15 percent of days of class

15. Neri, Carvalhaes, and Reis (2008).

missed. Families with incomes between 50 and 100 reais were entitled only to the conditional part of the monetary transfers. Another important feature of Bolsa Família was to elect the mother as the main beneficiary of the transfer, betting on a high degree of altruism.

Inequality and Demographic Trends

As we have seen, the main transfers in terms of social income such as social security and cash transfers are aimed at specific age groups. Social security benefits attempt in principle to smooth living conditions, specifically in old age, whereas the new generation of cash transfer programs in Brazil mostly focuses on children and teenagers. Labor income is also predominantly earned by nonelderly adults. There are, however, exceptions for cash transfer programs included in the other sources of nonlabor income that attempt to provide income to other age groups, such as the continuous assistance benefit, the BPC, for the old and disabled and unemployment insurance, which benefits mostly adults.

Nonsocial income accrues to individuals in very diverse age groups. To make things more complex, these programs are mixed in different income concepts. One way to check the levels and trends of how total incomes affect different age groups in different ranks of society is to compare the per capita growth rates of these groups in the population with their respective pro-poor growth rates (meaning growth rates that are sensitive to inequality changes). Kakwani, Neri, and Son propose a growth and pro-poor growth account methodology that explains the intense and regressive income changes in the PNAD.[16] The pro-poor growth measure comes from a combination of the weights attributed to individuals in a Gini-type social welfare function, whereas the individual welfare follows a logarithmic form. These two forces, in combination, make the pro-poor measure more sensitive than the one implicit in Gini and Theil inequality indexes in isolation.

I have divided the population into three age groups and calculated the levels and trends of the following variables:

—Per capita children and young teenagers in household, between birth and fifteen years of age
—Per capita adults in household, age sixteen to sixty-four years
—Per capita elderly in household, age sixty-five years and over

16. Kakwani, Neri, and Son (2006).

T A B L E 9 - 6 . Demographic Trends 1995–2004: Population Annual Growth Rate

Percent

Period	Unadjusted			Inequality adjusted		
	Per capita, children	Per capita, adults	Per capita, elderly	Per capita, children	Per capita, adults	Per capita, elderly
1995–2004	−1.96	0.83	1.66	−1.64	0.96	−0.67
1995–2001	−1.94	0.90	1.37	−1.60	1.00	−2.03
2001–2004	−2.05	0.70	2.59	−1.81	0.90	2.31

Source: Kakwani, Neri, and Son (2006).

In 1995, children and young teenagers as a group represented 34.7 percent of the population; the corresponding figure goes up to 39.3 percent when we use the inequality-adjusted weighting scheme. This implies that it is more likely to find a child in the lowest per capita income ranks of Brazilian society than elsewhere. Furthermore, as can be seen in table 9-6, the average annual growth rate of the population below sixteen years of age in the 1995–2004 period was −1.96 percent, whereas its inequality-adjusted growth rate was −1.64 percent. This implies a declining trend in the number of children in average households, but with a much slower decline among poor households. Conversely, the number of adults in a household shows an increasing trend. These findings suggest that the cash transfer programs related to children can be further expanded due to the increase in the number of working people in Brazil.

The situation is opposite in all aspects for the old-age group. Its share of the total population is higher than the inequality-adjusted weights, and this gap has increased over the decade. In the 1995–2004 period, the annual per capita growth rate of the elderly was 1.66 percent, against their inequality-adjusted growth rate of −0.67 percent. Overall, the elderly population in Brazil is increasing. This trend, in turn, puts pressure on cash transfer programs targeting the elderly. The good news, however, is that the increase in the elderly population among the poor appears to be slower than among the nonpoor. Hence, the sustainability of cash transfer programs for the elderly in the long term calls for a targeting strategy so that the poor elderly receive greater benefits from the programs compared with nonpoor people.

How Pro-Poor Were Monetary Transfers?

Kakwani, Neri, and Son also apply a growth and a pro-poor growth account methodology to Brazil that explains the intense and regressive changes observed in the different income sources found in the PNAD.[17] The separation of per capita total income into different components allows one to capture the contribution of the main sources of income in the total growth patterns assumed, in pro-poor growth, and in the inequality aspects of social welfare. The interaction between the high nonlinearity of these last two concepts and the additive nature of income sources required the use of a Shapley decomposition to obtain the impact of each income source's contribution to pro-poor growth. I review these results with particular emphasis on social security benefits and conditional cash transfers.

Here, I calculate the ratio between the additional fiscal cost and the benefit in terms of pro-poor growth of expanding the main public cash transfer programs in the period studied. The final objective is to reveal the contribution of each income policy component discussed above to total per capita growth and to pro-poor growth.[18]

Social Security Benefits

Social security is the main component of social income in Brazil, and it is second only to labor earnings among the data on all income sources collected by the PNAD. Social security benefits include a contributory pay-as-you-go system and noncontributory benefits, both of which are subject to the government's discretionary income policies. Given the dominance of the public transfer aspect in this income aggregate, it is useful to observe the ratio of pro-poor growth to total growth contribution. This can be interpreted as an elasticity that shows how many public resources (measured by their share of total income) are translated into social welfare, a type of cost/benefit analysis. The corresponding elasticity of pro-poor growth with respect to total growth (i.e., its fiscal cost), both explained by social security, rose from 0.45 in the 1995–2001 period to 2.82 in 2001–4, demonstrating a marked improvement in the ability of social security

---

17. Kakwani, Neri, and Son (2006).
18. This means growth in social welfare that is very pro-poor using a specification that uses the weights of a function that yields the Gini coefficient and an individual logarithmic welfare function like the Theil Index.

benefits targeting the poorest segments of Brazilian society.[19] After 1998, the government adopted the new policy of setting higher adjustment rates to lower social security benefits. In the entire 1995–2004 period, this elasticity amounted to 0.74. This elasticity makes it possible to compare to what extent different types of public transfers reach the poor.

Bolsa Família

Other nonlabor income sources include very different types of incomes, ranging from cash transfer programs such as the Bolsa Família to capital income such as flows derived from interest rates paid on government debt. The pro-poorness aspects of these items are expected to be very different, despite the fact that both are not only subject to public policy choices but also are mostly mediated by the state.[20] Interest income is largely underestimated by the PNAD data; hence, this income concept is largely explained by public cash transfer programs such as Bolsa Família.

The elasticity of the contribution to pro-poor growth of a particular income transfer with respect to its contribution to total growth is useful for guiding policies aimed at the poorest groups in Brazilian society. The corresponding elasticity of other nonlabor income sources was 14.66 during the 1995–2004 period, which is much higher than the one found for social security benefits. Each percentage point in the share of government transfers in this item bought 19.8 times more pro-poor growth in other nonlabor income than in social security benefits; this result is consistent with the evaluation of conditional cash transfers done in Brazil and elsewhere.[21]

Figure 9-7 synthesizes the main channels affecting mean incomes, social welfare, and inequality growth rates from 2001 to 2005. Because mean growth was rather small, inequality changes are similar to social welfare changes (i.e., equality is equal to pro-poor growth minus growth). Thus, half the inequality reduction is due to labor income change and the other

19. One possibility is to divide the information on social security benefits in two regimes: one with benefits equal to one minimum wage, the constitutional floor, and the rest. Neri (1998, 2001) followed this approach and showed that about 60 percent of social security benefits amounted to one minimum wage, while 80 percent of social security income accrued to benefits above this level. Each additional real spent adjusting the social security benefits floor resulted in 4.5 times more poverty reduction than a uniform adjustment to all benefits.

20. The public debt is the main source of interest gains earned by Brazilian households.

21. Lindert, Skoufias, and Shapiro (2005); Hoffman (2005); Soares (2006), Bourguignon, Ferreira, and Leite (2003); Coady and Skoufias (2004); Suplicy (2002).

FIGURE 9-7. Determinants of Social Welfare, Mean, and Inequality of Per Capita Household Income

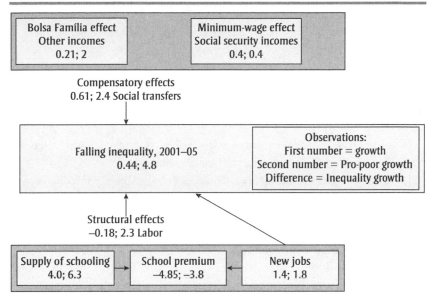

Source: Kakwani, Neri, and Son (2006).

half is due to monetary transfers. Splitting this last term into its components, we find that the Bolsa Família effect is equal to 80 percent of the income policies segment, whereas social security is equal to the remaining 20 percent.

In sum, other nonlabor income sources have played a dominant role in a pro-poor growth pattern that is assumed to have made a minor contribution to total growth and to the Brazilian fiscal accounts. It seems that a small increase in government cash transfer programs had a large impact on poor people's living conditions.

The Impact of Income Policies on Distribution Opportunities

This section takes advantage of the PNAD's 2006 special supplement on social programs, which allows separating the beneficiaries of different official income transfer programs. Because the same questions were also used in the 2004 PNAD, there is an opportunity to test the effects of Bolsa Família using a difference-in-difference estimator like the one used in the section above on electoral cycles. The main advantage of this approach, which compares the relative evolution of the eligible and the ineligible, is that it allows inferences on causality.

I have taken advantage of the richness of the PNAD questionnaire to consider a variety of potential Bolsa Família effects using a series of variables:

—Education conditionalities (enrollment, school assiduity, and the motivations associated with these education elements, such as a lack of income)
—Access to education infrastructure (hours of study, school lunches)
—Child health (infant mortality rates, fertility)
—Communication and information technology (Internet access, cellular telephone)
—Public infrastructure (sewerage, water)
—Housing (access to toilets, house financing, land property rights)
—Durables (e.g., a refrigerator)
—Work decisions (participation, occupation, multiple occupations, hours worked, contribution to social security)
—Labor income (individual earnings, per capita earnings)

Almost all the exercises were performed for the three age groups: children and young teenagers (birth to fifteen years), adults (sixteen to sixty-four), and the elderly (over sixty-five). Here, I emphasize the specific age groups for which the issues discussed are more relevant. For example, in the case of fertility and the risk of losing a child, I consider nonelderly adults. In the case of the youngest group, I further divide them into three subgroups: birth to six years, seven to fifteen years, and sixteen to seventeen years, following the different conditionalities imposed by Bolsa Família on their human capital accumulation.

The focus of the empirical analysis is on the impact of the eligibility criteria to access Bolsa Família with year dummies for 2004 and 2006 indicating temporal evolution and their interaction. This last variable corresponds to the difference-in-difference estimator captured by the relative impact of Bolsa Família's expansion on its potential beneficiaries, with a direction of causality implied in the interpretation of the results. I implement the analysis in two stages, first putting more emphasis in the interpretation by comparing by means of multivariate regressions the relative evolution of eligible and ineligible individuals, where eligibility is defined as per capita income without considering public transfers below

100 reais in real 2004 prices. I put the coefficient (or the odds ratio, in the case of logistic regressions) of the year dummy, the Bolsa Família eligibility dummy plus an interactive term for each of the exercises performed. The first captures differences across time between eligible individuals—that is, per capita household incomes without the social benefits of the program of R$100 or below—and the noneligible population. The regressions use controls such as gender, race, migration, state, city size, age, age squared, and per capita income without social programs. The second type of analysis stems from bivariate tabulations of the same variable but also provides a zoom-in on the eligible group, depending on the size of benefits to which they are entitled.

The second stage of the empirical analysis is a simple bivariate exercise presented in the appendix tables. They allow checking the absolute evolution of the variables of interest and a comparison within the eligible group: that is, the performance of those with per capita income below R$50—those eligible for an additional R$50 per family besides the R$15 for each completed conditionality maximum of three (R$45) within each beneficiary family—and those with per capita income between R$50 and R$100 that receive only the benefits associated with conditionalities. The idea here is to test the effects of discontinuities in the size of benefits on economic behavior.

Human Capital Accumulation

This section examines the effects of Bolsa Família conditionalities on capital accumulation elements such as school permanence, fertility, and child health.

School Permanence

To be eligible for Bolsa Família, children between seven and fifteen years of age must be enrolled in school and must not miss more than 15 percent of classes. There was an increase in this variable among lower income groups. When we compare low-income eligible groups and noneligible children in table 9-7, we see that the former groups tend to present ambiguous effects on relative school permanence, with a relative decrease in school attendance (0.96) but with a substantial reduction in the number of classes missed (0.8313). When we use qualitative data on income insufficiency (or need to work) as the main reasons behind reduction in school permanence, we observe a reduction in these motivations for

TABLE 9-7. Human Capital Accumulation: Education, 7 to 15 Years of Age—Odds Ratio

Logistic model 7 to 15 years

			Enrolled in school	Misses more than 15 percent of classes— enrolled in school	Not enrolled due to lack of income	Misses class due to lack of income— enrolled
Eligibility	Low income		0,9100**	1,2030**	1,2733**	1,2049**
Eligibility	Nonelegible		1,0000	1,0000	1,0000	1,0000
Year	2006		1,1600**	0,7358**	1,8873**	1,1297**
Year	2004		1,0000	1,0000	1,0000	1,0000
Eligibility * Year	Low income	2006	0,9600**	0,8313**	0,8179**	1,0494**
Eligibility * Year	Low income	2004	1,0000	1,0000	1,0000	1,0000
Eligibility * Year	Nonelegible	2006	1,0000	1,0000	1,0000	1,0000
Eligibility * Year	Nonelegible	2004	1,0000	1,0000	1,0000	1,0000

			Eats school lunch	School hours up to 4 hours
Eligibility	Low Income		1,6100**	1,1800**
Eligibility	Nonelegible		1,0000	1,0000
Year	2006		0,9000**	0,8500**
Year	2004		1,0000	1,0000
Eligibility * Year	Low income	2006	1,0100**	0,9700**
Eligibility * Year	Low income	2004	1,0000	1,0000
Eligibility * Year	Nonelegible	2006	1,0000	1,0000
Eligibility * Year	Nonelegible	2004	1,0000	1,0000

Source: Centro de Políticas Sociais/Fundação Getulio Vargas, processing Pesquisa Nacional por Amostra de Domicílio/Instituto Brasileiro de Geografia e Estatística microdata.
Note: *Significant at 90 percent. **Significant at 95 percent.

nonenrollment (0.8179) but a small increase for missed classes above Bolsa Família's 15 percent limit (1.0494). The impact on access to school infrastructure increases somewhat, both measured by the variable indicating the fact that children eating school lunches rose slightly (1.01) and especially by the reduction of daily school hours up to four hours a day (0.97). Nevertheless, among the poorest group, around two-thirds of the children stay only four hours in school. This set of results indicates that the program is not pointing to the achievement of its objectives in terms of school attendance but that children in school have a relative increase in school hours and in their access to infrastructure.

TABLE 9-8. Human Capital Accumulation: Fertility and Child Morbidity, Mothers 16 to 64 Years of Age—Odds Ratio
Logistic model 16 to 64 years

			Is a mother	Had child born dead	Death of kids in childhood (up to one year of age)	Death of kids in childhood (up to six years of age)
Eligibility	Low income		2,2793**	1,2507**	0,8169**	0,8219**
Eligibility	Nonelegible		1,0000	1,0000	1,0000	1,0000
Year	2006		1,0598**	1,0629**	1,1977**	0,9987
Year	2004		1,0000	1,0000	1,0000	1,0000
Eligibility * Year	Low income	2006	0,9806**	1,0264**	1,0624**	1,0078
Eligibility * Year	Low income	2004	1,0000	1,0000	1,0000	1,0000
Eligibility * Year	Nonelegible	2006	1,0000	1,0000	1,0000	1,0000
Eligibility * Year	Nonelegible	2004	1,0000	1,0000	1,0000	1,0000

Source: Centro de Políticas Sociais/Fundação Getulio Vargas, processing Pesquisa Nacional por Amostra de Domicílio/Instituto Brasileiro de Geografia e Estatística microdata.

Fertility and Child Health

A main concern with respect to compensatory policies is the possible effect on fertility. Bolsa Família allows a maximum of three additional transfer conditionalities for children between birth and fifteen years of age and imposes conditionality on prenatal examinations and child vaccinations. Eligibility due to low income from private sources among women sixteen to sixty-four years of age shown in table 9-8 indicates a differential decrease in the fertility for the lower-income groups captured by the odds ratio of the variable indicating if the woman is a mother (0.9806). This may indicate a dominance of the income effect inducing a reduction in fertility over the possible incentive effects of the Bolsa Família program. The program might induce localized incentives for families with fewer than three children between birth and fifteen years of age, which were not tested here. The results on child morbidity (the quality of child health care) is the opposite; for the lower-income groups, there is a differential increase in the percentage of babies born dead (1.0264) and in the death of children in their early childhood up to one year of age (1.0624), but no statistically significant change for children up to six years of age. In sum, the results indicate that the income effect of expanding income transfers is possibly dominating the other incentive effects of Bolsa Família on birthrates but not on the quality of child care.

Consumption Decisions and Physical Assets Accumulation

A differential increase in the purchase of durables, public services, and housing is generally associated with the eligibility criteria for Bolsa Família, as shown in table 9-9. The only exceptions are access to sewerage collection among Bolsa Família beneficiaries and access to housing credits for eligible low-income groups, which suggests that these items became more of a luxury service.

There is an improvement in public infrastructure in the household access to bathroom (1.04), sewerage (nonsignificant), and water (1.0884) that may have a positive impact on health indicators. The access to communication and information technology (cellular telephone, 1.1284; computer with Internet connection, 1.3828) indicates a differential increase in the ability to generate income in the future. The Brazilian government is discussing the possibility of financing the acquisition of new refrigerators by the Bolsa Família beneficiaries in order to induce energy savings and environmental protection. The poor informal access to electricity inhibits the price effects for energy savings. Eligibility criteria and effective access to Bolsa Família are associated with an increase in access to refrigerators (1.07). Finally, although access to housing credit (0.9819) is growing at smaller rates for low-income eligible groups, groups eligible for Bolsa Família are experiencing higher rates of access to land property rights (1.18) than are noneligible groups, which may indicate a future improvement in poor people's ability to access not only housing finance but also other forms of credit. This may be enhanced by explicit credit consignation clauses, as were applied to social security benefits from 2004 onward. I will return to this point in the next section.

Work Decisions and Outcomes

This section examines Bolsa Família collateral effects on work decisions and outcomes. The first subsection emphasizes occupational choices. The second gauges these effects on continuous variables such as individual and per capita earnings and work hours.

Work Decisions

One of the main possible side effects of compensatory policies is a work disincentive effect due to a raise in reservation wages. The results in table 9-10 for the labor market categories will be reinforced in the next item with another log-linear equation of continuous variables presented

T A B L E 9 - 9 . Consumption Decisions and Physical Assets Accumulation, 16 to 64 Years of Age—Odds Ratio

Logistic model 16 to 64 years

			Has available		
			Cellular phone	*Computer with Internet connection*	*Fridge*
Eligibility	Low income		0,4588**	0,9884**	0,5249**
Eligibility	Nonelegible		1,0000	1,0000	1,0000
Year	2006		2,1729**	1,2107**	1,0534**
Year	2004		1,0000	1,0000	1,0000
Eligibility * Year	Low income	2006	1,1284**	1,3828**	1,0700**
Eligibility * Year	Low income	2004	1,0000	1,0000	1,0000
Eligibility * Year	Nonelegible	2006	1,0000	1,0000	1,0000
Eligibility * Year	Nonelegible	2004	1,0000	1,0000	1,0000

			Has available	
			Housing finance	*Property title*
Eligibility	Low income		0.6729**	0.5800**
Eligibility	Other case		1.0000	1.0000
Year	2006		0.9972**	0.9300**
Year	2004		1.0000	1.0000
Eligibility * Year	Low income	2006	0.9515**	1.1100**
Eligibility * Year	Low income	2004	1.0000	1.0000
Eligibility * Year	Other case	2006	1.0000	1.0000
Eligibility * Year	Other case	2004	1.0000	1.0000

			Has available		
			Bathroom	*Sewarage*	*Water*
Eligibility	Low income		0,7100**	0,7086**	1,0345**
Eligibility	Nonelegible		1,0000	1,0000	1,0000
Year	2006		1,0500**	0,9586**	0,9753**
Year	2004		1,0000	1,0000	1,0000
Eligibility * Year	Low income	2006	1,0400**	1,0006	1,0884**
Eligibility * Year	Low income	2004	1,0000	1,0000	1,0000
Eligibility * Year	Nonelegible	2006	1,0000	1,0000	1,0000
Eligibility * Year	Nonelegible	2004	1,0000	1,0000	1,0000

Source: CPS/IBRE/FGV processing PNAD (Household Sample National Survey) 2004–2006/IBGE microdata.

T A B L E 9 - 1 0 . Work Decisions, 16 to 64 Years of Age—Odds Ratio
Logistic model 16 to 64 years

			Labor market participation	Occupied	More than one job	Contributes to social security
Eligibility	Low income		0,6800**	0,5000**	0,7331**	0,3819**
Eligibility	Nonelegible		1,0000	1,0000	1,0000	1,0000
Year	2006		1,0100**	1,0000	1,0541**	1,0284**
Year	2004		1,0000	1,0000	1,0000	1,0000
Eligibility * Year	Low income	2006	0,8900**	0,9000**	0,8655**	0,8889**
Eligibility * Year	Low income	2004	1,0000	1,0000	1,0000	1,0000
Eligibility * Year	Nonelegible	2006	1,0000	1,0000	1,0000	1,0000
Eligibility * Year	Nonelegible	2004	1,0000	1,0000	1,0000	1,0000

Source: CPS/IBRE/FGV processing PNAD (Household Sample National Survey) 2004–2006/IBGE microdata.

in table 9-11. There is an absolute fall in lower-income groups for the main labor activity variables such as participation rates (68.06 percent in 2004 to 65.36 percent in 2006) and occupation rates with respect to the whole population in the age group (53.85 percent in 2004 to 52.37 percent in 2006). The results are mixed when we look to other variables bivariate tables. However, in the controlled tests all results do not allow us to reject the hypothesis of a "Lazy-Effect" possibly induced by Bolsa Família. The numbers below correspond to the odds ratio calculated directly from the interaction coefficients of binomial logistic regressions. This reduction in work activity is valid for all measures used, including participation rates (0.89), occupation (0.9), multiple occupation (0.866), and contribution to social security (0.8889).

Labor Earnings and Hours

This new set of results reinforces the previous conclusions suggesting the operation of work disincentive effects for Bolsa Família shown in table 9-10. The results of a log-linear equation of continuous variables will be reinforced in the next item with other labor market categorical variables, all presented in table 9-10. For the lower-income group that is eligible for higher benefits, we observe the combination of a reduction in real labor earnings and in the workload by the lower-income active-age individuals between 2004 and 2006: per capita labor earnings (from

TABLE 9-11. Work Decisions, 16 to 64 Years of Age—Semi-elasticity

Mincerian equations (log-linear) 16 to 64 years

			Per capita labor income	Individual labor income	Weekly hours worked
Eligibility	Low income		−1,1541**	−0,6254**	−0,1211**
Eligibility	Nonelegible		0,0000	0,0000	0,0000
Year	2006		0,0470	0,0547**	−0,0196**
Year	2004		0,0000	0,0000	0,0000
Eligibility * Year	Low income	2006	−0,0460**	−0,0347	−0,0312**
Eligibility * Year	Low income	2004	0,0000	0,0000	0,0000
Eligibility * Year	Nonelegible	2006	0,0000	0,0000	0,0000
Eligibility * Year	Nonelegible	2004	0,0000	0,0000	0,0000

Source: Centro de Políticas Sociais/Instituto Brasileiro de Economia/Fundação Getulio Vargas, processing Pesquisa Nacional por Amostra de Domicílio/Instituto Brasileiro de Geografia e Estatística microdata.

R\$19.74 in 2004 to R\$16.33 in 2006), individual labor earnings (from R\$40.15 in 2004 to R\$32.67 in 2006), with an opposite movement for the other income brackets. In the case of working hours, the lower bracket also experienced a fall (from 35.22 weekly hours in 2004 to 34.17 in 2006), but it was also observed in the other income groups. To assess the statistical significance of these changes, we move now to controlled difference-in-difference analysis to evaluate the relative fall between eligible and noneligible groups. In this case, the numbers in brackets are the premiums measured directly from the interaction coefficients of the estimated Mincerian equation. To be sure, they correspond to the difference-in-difference of returns between beneficiaries and nonbeneficiaries of Bolsa Família: per capita labor earnings (−0.0347), individual labor earnings (−0.046), and working hours (−0.0312). In sum, all the labor market indicators show a relative deterioration in the working performance of adult individuals who are eligible for Bolsa Família benefits.

Summary of the Empirical Results

During the period between 2004 and 2006, during which there was a marked expansion of Bolsa Família benefits, the overall group of working-age individuals eligible for these benefits saw a relative decrease in all indicators of their labor market activity and performance indicators in comparison with the noneligible group. This may indicate the need to work more on the disincentives aspect in the design of the program. On living conditions, measures showed that an increase in the purchase of durables, access to public services, and housing is generally associated with a differential increase of individuals in the group eligible for Bolsa Família. The only exceptions among Bolsa Família beneficiaries are access to sewerage collection and access to housing credits. The first exception may indicate the need to work with the supply side of sewerage, taking advantage of economies of scale and perhaps direct subsidies to Bolsa Família beneficiaries to allow them to pay water and sanitation service bills. This is justified by both economies of scale and scope and by externalities, with a potential impact on health outcomes, especially for children between one and six years of age.[22] The relative reduction in the access to housing credit and work performance may indicate the convenience of using opportunities, such as access to microfinance, and taking advantage of the program's informational and operational structure.

More specifically, with respect to Bolsa Família conditionalities impact and design, I found that the income effect of expanding income transfers is possibly dominating the other incentive effects of Bolsa Família on birthrates. However, indicators of the quality of childcare, such as prenatal and infant mortality, have shown a differential reduction. Finally, with respect to schooling decisions, the results indicate that the program is not pointing to the achievement of its objectives in terms of school attendance but that children in school have a relative increase in school hours and in their access to educational infrastructure.

Conclusions: The Next Generation of Income Policies

Brazilian social policies combine an old and ineffective regime of income policies with a modern regime geared toward the young and the poorest segments of society. Excessive public expenses from social programs have had the undesired effect of impeding growth through a high tax burden (37 percent of GDP in 2007) and real interest rates (one of the highest in the world). Recently, Brazil has seemingly lived in a paradox: In spite of decreased average incomes, the income of those with smaller purchasing power grew as a result of large income transfers from the state. This combination of economic stagnation and poverty reduction, which resulted in decreased inequality, contrasts with the typical path of Brazil in the past.

22. Neri (2008c).

For instance, from 1967 to 1980, Brazil had high growth rates with grow-ing inequality. In the following period, from 1980 to 1994, it had low growth rates, while inequality remained high and persistent. This newer situation of economic stagnation with poverty alleviation occurred from 1994 to 2005 but was more pronounced from 2001 to 2004 due to the expansion of better-targeted income policies. As we have seen from 2005 onward, Brazil is now growing at a much faster pace, yet inequality is still falling (though at a lower rate than in the previous period). In this more recent period, there has been a remarkable expansion of both well-targeted (Bolsa Família) and not-so-well-targeted income policies (associ-ated with institutional links with minimum wage increases). In the near future, faster growth and trends toward income equality could mean greater levels of poverty reduction, but the current situation demands better-targeted income policies.

The advantage of expanding compensatory policies is, in general, the speed with which their effects are felt. In contrast, the associated metaphor for structural policies is that it is better to teach a person how to fish than to give them a fish. The issue is not whether policies involve income trans-fers or asset stocks but their social implications in the short and long terms. A compensatory action that hinders the productive destructuring—as with the task forces against drought—or that motivates the accumula-tion of capital—like Bolsa Família's attempts—can have persistent effects on poverty. The long-term potential impact of income transfers is com-parable to the transfer of productive assets.

The long-term objective of social policies is to enable individuals to realize their productive potential. This movement can be achieved in var-ious ways, by completing the portfolio of their assets or ensuring their access to markets where they are transacted. These public policies pro-vide an exit from poverty by opening up access to markets. Thus, it is possible to generate welfare gains without fiscal implications, which makes them particularly attractive. Figure 9-8 presents a scheme of reforms based on income policies.

There are three desired upgrades for Bolsa Família. The first desired upgrade would be to *improve targeting*—that is, to seek more effective tar-geting by improving the ability of the program to reach the poor. This, in turn, has three aspects. The first is to *integrate income transfers under the Bolsa Família program's framework*. The targeting objective becomes more difficult as the program expands. But the main conclusion here is to avoid spending additional resources on income transfer—alternatives less

FIGURE 9-8. Bolsa Família Upgrades: Exit Doors

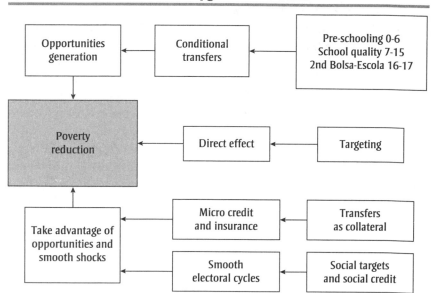

targeted than Bolsa Família, such as those associated with real increases in the value of the minimum wage or the unconditional universal provision of minimum maintenance income. Bolsa Família reaches nearly 25 percent of the Brazilian population and costs less than 0.8 percent of Brazilian GDP, as opposed to the more than 12 percent of GDP spent on social security payments.

The ultimate objective here should be to integrate all noncontributory income transfers in a single program, preferably under the Bolsa Família framework. A first step in this direction was already taken in 2007, when noncontributory social security spending was split from the rest of the social security accounts. This allows better comparisons between the opportunity costs of different income policies. It does not seem equitable to provide income transfers associated with noncontributory transfers that are ten times higher than Bolsa Família benefits.

Complementarily, the Bolsa Família structure could be used to reach nearly 25 percent of the Brazilian population to distribute other services besides monetary transfers. The direct effects vary depending on the target's individual budget constraint or his or her individual welfare paid through direct transfers. One important difference between Bolsa Família and the previous Fome Zero policy was the emphasis given to alternative channels. Fome Zero attempted to direct expenditures through food transfers, leading to allocation inefficiencies. Incidentally, Cedeplar's evaluation of Bolsa Família indicated that a large part of the transfers were directed to food expenses. However, there are situations where economies of scale and economies of scope will allow a better use of the program's structure than just monetary transfers.

The second aspect of effective targeting is to *avoid fragmentation*. Brazil should avoid the temptation to fragment its income policies into different monetary transfer programs according to region, gender, race, and housing conditions (*favelas*, etc.). This fragmentation would make the management of public policy more complex. The binomial income-age provides a straightforward criterion that allows researchers to take into account for the poor population the main phases of the life cycle, such as education, working, and retirement. Our empirical results for the determinants of access to Bolsa Família show an implicit affirmative action in practice: When we compare individuals with identical observable characteristics (gender, region, age, per capita income, etc.), the chances of a black Brazilian gaining access to Bolsa Família benefits are 24 percent higher than those of a white person with the same characteristics. Income transfers from a previous generation, such as BPC, present the opposite results; low-income minorities are underrepresented. A similar effect is observed for those who live in slums (*favelas*). One interpretation is that these marginalized groups' characteristics provide a clearer signal that they are poor, hence favoring their access to a better-targeted program. In sum, the Bolsa Família program in operation—not just design—presents an affirmative action mechanism favoring those groups traditionally associated with lack of opportunities.

The third aspect of effective targeting is *intrahousehold distribution channels*. The evidence found in Neri, Carvalhaes, and Reis shows that BPC transfers to the elderly benefit the health of the recipient more than the health of other household members.[23] Bolsa Família tries to use mothers (in 91 percent of the cases) as the recipients of monetary transfers. This strategy relies on the assumption that mothers will best allocate the resources to reduce intrahousehold inequalities of both opportunities

23. Neri, Carvalhaes, and Reis (2008).

and results. It will be important to study the redistributive and long-term consequences of this strategy.

The second desired upgrade of the Bolsa Família concerns *conditionalities*. Besides the program's ability to reach the poorest segments of the population with monetary and nonmonetary transfers, another improvement of income policies is enhancing its ability to positively affect lives through the imposition of explicit conditionalities—especially for relevant state variables where there clearly are market failures, such as externalities and credit constraints. Most of the current conditionalities of Bolsa Família seem to have a high degree of redundancy in the sense that many of the conditions they impose have already been adopted by the beneficiaries before the start of the program. Let us examine the three specific age groups that are the objects of the conditionalities.

—The first age group includes those from birth to six years of age. The program only demands children's immunization; an experimental evaluation of Bolsa Família by the Cedeplar team has shown no improvement in the vaccination rates of program beneficiaries. This was expected because more than 90 percent of Brazilian children in this age range were already covered before the program started. To provide incentives for preschools and even in nurseries, integrating these demand incentives with new education supply elements, such as the institution of Fundeb, could be more interesting than the current Bolsa Família itself.

—The second age group includes those from seven to fifteen years of age. Similarly, the current conditionality of enrollment and maximum of 15 percent of classes allowed to be missed is redundant.[24] Before the program started in 2001, only 3 percent of the children did not attend school. Good program conditionalities should become obsolete across time, which means the pursuit of higher standards. Second, these conditionalities also present intrinsic implementation difficulties. It is hard for a teacher to signal that his or her poor student is not satisfying the conditions. The teacher may be tempted to benefit a specific student in the short run and harm all students, including this one, in the future by not strictly following the rules of the program. Third, conditionalities tend to increase the tension in the student-teacher relationship. It is perhaps better to avoid the personal student-teacher relationship by delegating the evaluation to a third party. Fourth and finally, we should perhaps be less concerned with

24. Neri (2002); Cardoso and Souza (2003); Schwartzman (2005).

mean indicators such as school attendance and more concerned with end-use indicators such as learning outcomes. The final objective of an education policy is to enable students to learn rather than to attend class. The conjunction of these weak points with the opportunity opened by the implementation of Prova Brasil in 2005 and 2007, and now Provinha Brasil in 2008, lead me to the following proposition: Use these test results at the student level to track the learning process of each student. It is important to note that we are not talking about levels but differences in performance across time. A good school is one that teaches someone who does not know and not one that picks an already good student who keeps performing well during these tests.[25] There are two complementary application possibilities. First, use these scores as an additional monetary reward to the Bolsa Família class attendance standard. This means looking not only at necessary but also at sufficient conditions. The other is to use the test scores to condition the resources provided to schools in the educational budget. In sum, we aim here to improve the quality of education for people, demanding not only quantity but also education quality, creating incentives based on new information sources.

—The third age group includes those from sixteen to seventeen years of age. The need here is to create not an incentive for the first job but, through a second Bolsa Família, to improve the low educational levels observed in all parts of Brazil. This was recently adopted, and it is less subject to redundancy criteria because 18 percent of individuals in this age group are out of school. However, only 25 percent of these students have said that they do not attend school due to income insufficiency.[26]

The third desired upgrade of Bolsa Família concerns *access to markets*. Additional empirical results show that quite a few effects of the Bolsa Família transfers are not subject to explicit conditionalities. The income and liquidity effects of Bolsa Família might explain the differential-increasing share of durables, access to public services and to communication and information technology items, as well as improved housing conditions. Housing credit expanded at slightly lower rates among Bolsa Família beneficiaries; the percentage of households with land titles among its beneficiaries improves the market value of the real estate (in a De Soto–type argument) and the ability of individuals to access credit in

25. Neri and Buchmann (2008a).
26. Neri (2006a).

general. This can improve access to financial markets by the poor. One possibility is to use social benefits as collateral to expand the credit frontier to where it has never been before: to the poor and to informal workers.[27] The possibility of using Bolsa Família's structure to provide access to current accounts in public banks starts to enter the agenda, but the possibility of exploring links with microcredit and microinsurance seems to be more feasible now than it was before Bolsa Família was structured.

A final possible extension of Bolsa Família that has been discussed here is to incorporate targets and incentives at a more aggregate level, such as municipalities that are responsible for selecting Bolsa Família beneficiaries. There is an agenda of incentives provision that uses the accomplishment of social targets to condition the transfers sent to municipalities, following the same spirit of conditionalities to individual families adopted in the current Bolsa Família design. The main lesson provided by this social-targets literature is that one should not set contracts on the level of social indicators but rather on the value added across time.[28] A second point is that one should not use the absolute performance but the relative performance across municipalities, something like the yardstick competition of the economic regulation literature. The combination of these two factors yields a relative value-added criterion that resembles a difference-in-difference estimator. Heuristically, the idea is to create a pseudo-market for social returns, allowing public resources to flow where the returns are higher.

---

27. See "O Efeito-Colateral" and "Alvorada: Um projeto acima de qualquer governo," both published in *Revista Conjuntura Econômica* in 2002. This idea is further developed in Neri and Giovanni (2005) and Neri (2008a).

28. See "Metas sociais para tirar a miséria do país," *Revista Conjuntura Econômica*, March 2000. This idea is explored by Neri and Buchmann (2008a).

Appendix Tables: Eligibility Criteria for Bolsa Família

Human Capital Accumulation: Education, 7 to 15 Years of Age

Percent

Year	Eligibility	Enrolled in school	Misses more than 15 percent of classes	Not enrolled due to lack of income	Misses class due to lack of income	Eats school lunch	School hours up to 4 hours
	PCHI less than 50	93.24	13.06	0.79	2.46	74.38	67.88
	50 < PCHI < 100	95.05	11.32	0.67	1.30	77.67	64.21
2004	Non-eligible	97.11	8.51	0.33	0.85	59.15	50.29
	PCHI less than 50	94.85	8.93	0.78	2.21	80.96	67.71
	50 < PCHI < 100	95.12	7.39	0.70	1.48	81.21	61.72
2006	Noneligible	97.54	6.25	0.39	0.82	60.36	48.30

Source: Centro de Políticas Sociais/Fundação Getulio Vargas, processing Pesquisa Nacional por Amostra de Domicílio/Instituto Brasileiro de Geografia e Estatística microdata.

Note: PCHI = per capita household income.

Human Capital Accumulation: Fertility and Child Mortality
Percent

Year	Eligibility	Mother	Death of children in childhood (up to 1 year of age)	Death of children in childhood (up to 6 years of age)
	PCHI less than 50	78.68	0.36	0.86
	50 < PCHI < 100	78.81	0.36	0.81
2004	Noneligible	65.50	0.26	0.51
	PCHI less than 50	77.87	0.57	1.07
	50 < PCHI < 100	79.90	0.38	0.66
2006	Noneligible	65.86	0.31	0.51

Source: Centro de Políticas Sociais/Fundação Getulio Vargas, processing Pesquisa Nacional por Amostra de Domicílio/Instituto Brasileiro de Geografia e Estatística microdata.
Note: PCHI = per capita household income.

Consumption Decisions and Physical Assets, 16 to 64 Years of Age

Percent

Year	Eligibility in reais	Bathroom	Sewerage	Water	Cellular phone	Has available	Refrigerator	Housing finance	Property title
						Computer with Internet connection			
	PCHI less than 50	75.72	25.40	53.65	19.84	4.03	58.71	1.78	66.74
	50 < PCHI < 100	85.41	25.69	60.53	23.69	0.44	70.87	2.03	67.11
2004	Noneligible	97.38	52.48	84.28	59.16	16.66	93.39	5.02	72.17
	PCHI less than 50	75.18	24.67	55.23	33.46	5.81	60.30	1.54	65.79
	50 < PCHI < 100	85.31	23.51	60.79	41.12	1.21	72.14	2.01	68.10
2006	Noneligible	97.48	51.90	84.49	74.19	22.13	93.81	5.01	71.40

Source: Centro de Políticas Sociais/Fundação Getulio Vargas, processing Pesquisa Nacional por Amostra de Domicílio/Instituto Brasileiro de Geografia e Estatística microdata.

Note: PCHI = per capita household income.

Work Decisions, 16 to 64 Years of Age

Percent, hours, or reais

Year	Eligibility	Participation (employed + unemployed) (percent)	Employed (percent)	Has more than one job (percent)	Makes contributions to the social security and pensions system (percent)	Per capita labor income (reais)	Individual labor income (reais)	Weekly hours worked
	PCHI less than 50	68.03	53.85	2.56	5.50	19.74	40.15	35.22
	50 < PCHI < 100	68.77	58.98	2.49	12.36	62.18	112.07	39.15
2004	Noneligible	75.67	70.08	3.39	38.33	450.01	577.93	42.47
	PCHI less than 50	65.36	52.37	2.51	6.17	16.33	32.67	34.17
	50 < PCHI < 100	68.99	58.91	2.41	11.19	64.25	118.97	37.76
2006	Noneligible	76.18	70.58	3.74	39.52	498.90	632.32	41.89

Source: Centro de Políticas Sociais/Fundação Getulio Vargas, processing Pesquisa Nacional por Amostra de Domicílio/Instituto Brasileiro de Geografia e Estatística microdata.
Note: PCHI = per capita household income.

References

Bacha, E. L., and L. Taylor. 1978. "Brazilian Income Distribution in the 1960s: Tacts' Model Results and the Controversy." *Journal of Development Studies* 14, no. 3: 271–97.

Bonelli, R. P. de, and G. L. Sedlacek. 1989. "Distribuição de renda: Evolução no último quarto de século." In *Mercado de trabalho e distribuição de renda: Uma coletânea*, ed. G. L. Sedlacek and R. Paes de Barros. Série Monográfica 35. Rio de Janeiro: IPEA.

Bourguignon, F., F. Ferreira, and P. Leite. 2003. "Ex-Ante Evaluation of Conditional Cash Transfer Programs: The Case of Bolsa Escola." In *Evaluating the Poverty and Distributional Impact of Economic Policies (Techniques and Tools)*, ed. F. Bourguignon and L. Silva. Washington: World Bank.

Camarano, A. A., and M. T. Pasinato. 2004. "Introdução." In *Os novos idosos brasileiros: Muito além dos 60?* ed. Ana Amélia Camarano. Rio de Janeiro: IPEA.

———. 2007. *Envelhecimento, Pobreza e Proteção Social na América Latina.* Texto para Discussão 1292. Rio de Janeiro: IPEA.

Cardoso, E., and A. P. Souza. 2003. "The Impact of Cash Transfers on Child Labor and School Attendance in Brazil." Departamento de Economia da Universidade de São Paulo.

Coady, D., and E. Skoufias. 2004. "On the Targeting and Redistributive Efficiencies of Alternative Transfer Instruments." *Review of Income and Wealth* 50, no. 1: 11–27.

Datt, G., and M. Ravallion. 1992. "Growth and Poverty in Rural India and Brazil." *Journal of Development Economics* (World Bank) 38: 275–95.

Ferreira, F., P. Lanjouw, and M. C. Neri. 2003. "A Robust Poverty Profile for Brazil Using Multiple Data Sources" (in Portuguese). *Revista Brasileira de Economia* 57, no. 1: 59–92.

Fishlow, A. 1972. "Brazilian Size Distribution of Income." *American Economic Association: Papers and Proceedings*, 391–402.

Hoffman, R. 1989. "A evolução da distribuição de renda no Brasil, entre pessoas e entre famílias, 1979/86." In *Mercado de trabalho e distribuição de renda: Uma coletânea*, ed. G. Sedlacek and R. Paes de Barros. Rio de Janeiro: IPEA/Inpes.

———. 2005. "As transferências não são a causa principal da redução da desigualdade." *Econômica* (Rio de Janeiro) 7, no. 2: 335–41.

Kakwani, N., M. C. Neri, and H. Son. 2006. *Pro-Poor Growth and Social Programmes in Brazil.* Ensaios Econômicos da EPGE 639. Rio de Janeiro: Escola de Pós-Graduação em Economia da Fundação Getulio Vargas.

Langoni, C. 1973. *Distribuição da renda e desenvolvimento econômico do Brasil.* Rio de Janeiro: Fundação Getulio Vargas (3rd ed., 2005).

Levy, S. 2008. *Good Intentions, Bad Outcomes: Social Policy, Informality, and Economic Growth in Mexico.* Brookings.

Lindert, K., E. Skoufias, and J. Shapiro. 2005. *Redistributing Income to the Poor and the Rich: Public Transfers in Latin America and the Caribbean.* Washington: World Bank.

Neri, M. C. 1998. "Análise de Sensibilidade da Relação Custo Fiscal/Benefício Social de Modalidades de Reajustes dos Benefícios Previdenciários." *Boletim Conjuntural do IPEA* 42: 49–52.

————. 2000. "Diferentes histórias em diferentes cidades." In *Soluções para a questão do emprego*, ed. J. P. Reis Velloso and R. Cavalcanti. Rio de Janeiro: José Olimpio.

————. 2001. "Aspectos Fiscais e Sociais de Modalidades Alternativas de Reajuste de Aposentadorias e Pensões Públicas." *Coleção Previdência Social: Previdência, Assistência Social e Combate à Pobreza*, Série Debates 3.

————. 2002. "Projeto Alvorada: Diagnóstico, Impacto e Upgrades Propostos." Secretaria de Estado de Assistência Social, Ministério da Previdência e Assistência Social, Brasília.

————. 2006a. "Eleições e Expanções." Fundação Getulio Vargas, Rio de Janeiro (www.fgv.br/cps/pesquisas/pp2/ [August 2008]).

————. 2006b. "Equidade e Eficiência na Educação: Motivações e Metas" Fundação Getulio Vargas (www.fgv.br/cps/simulador/Site_CPS_Educacao/index.htm [August 2008]).

————. 2006c. "Miséria, Desigualdade e Estabilidade: O Segundo Real." Fundação Getulio Vargas, Rio de Janeiro (www3.fgv.br/ibrecps/RET3/index.htm [August 2008]).

————. 2007a. "A Dinâmica da Redistribuição Trabalhista." In *Desigualdade de Renda no Brasil: Uma análise da queda recente*, ed. Ricardo Paes de Barros, Miguel Nathan Foguel, and Gabriel Ulyssea. Rio de Janeiro: IPEA.

————. 2007b. "Miséria, desigualdade e estabilidade." In *Desigualdade de Renda no Brasil: Uma análise da queda recente*, ed. Ricardo Paes de Barros, Miguel Nathan Foguel, and Gabriel Ulyssea. Rio de Janeiro: IPEA.

————. 2007c. "Miséria, desigualdade e politicas de rendas: O Real do Lula." Fundação Getulio Vargas, Rio de Janeiro (www3.fgv.br/ibrecps/RET3/engl/index.htm [August 2008]).

————, ed. 2008a. *Microcrédito, o mistério nordestino e o Grameen brasileiro: Perfil e performance dos clientes do CrediAMIGO*. Rio de Janeiro: Fundação Getulio Vargas.

————. 2008b. "The New Middle Class." Centro de Politicas Sociais da Fundação Getulio Vargas, Rio de Janeiro.

————. 2008c. "Saneamento e Saúde." Centro de Politicas Sociais da Fundação Getulio Vargas, Rio de Janeiro.

Neri, M. C., and G. Buchmann. 2008a. "The Brazilian Quality of Education Index: Measurement and Incentives Upgrades." Centro de Politicas Sociais da Fundação Getulio Vargas, Rio de Janeiro.

————. 2008b. "Monitoring Dakar Educational Goal: Evaluation of the Brazilian Case" for the UNESCO Global Monitoring Report. *Quarterly Journal of Education* (in press).

Neri, M. C., and J. Camargo. 2001. "Distributive Effects of Brazilian Structural Reforms." In *Brazil in the 1990s: A Decade in Transition*, ed. R. Baumann. New York: Palgrave Macmillan.

Neri, M. C., and F. Carega. 2000. "Eleições, Desemprego e Inflação: O Ciclo Político de Negócios na Nova Democracia Brasileira." In *Desemprego e Mercado de Trabalho Ensaios Teóricos e Empíricos,* ed. Rosa Fontes and Marcelo A. Arbex. Viçosa: Universidade Federal de Viçosa.

Neri, M. C., L. Carvalhaes, and S. Reis. 2008. "Intra-Household Distribution and Health Perceptions." Fundação Getulio Vargas, Rio de Janeiro.

Neri, M. C., and C. P. Considera. 1996. "Crescimento, desigualdade e pobreza: O impacto da estabilização." *Economia Brasileira em Perspectiva* (IPEA, Rio de Janeiro) 1: 49–82.

Neri, M. C., C. P. Considera, and A. Pinto. 1999. "A evolução da pobreza e da desigualdade brasileiras ao longo da década de 90." *Revista Economia Aplicada* 3 (July–September), no. 3: 384–406.

Neri, M. C., and F. Giovanni. 2005. "Negócios nanicos, garantias e acesso a crédito." *Revista de Economia Contemporânea* (Rio de Janeiro) 9, no. 3: 643–69.

Paes de Barros, R., and R. Mendonça. 1992. *A evolução do bem-estar e da desigualdade no Brasil desde 1960.* Texto para discussão 286. Rio de Janeiro: IPEA.

Paes de Barros, R., R. Henriques, and R. Mendonça. 2000. "Desigualdade e pobreza no Brasil: a estabilidade inaceitável." In *Desigualdade e Pobreza no Brasil,* ed. R. Henriques. Rio de Janeiro: IPEA.

Paes de Barros, R., M. N. Foguel, and G. Ulyssea, eds. 2007. *Desigualdade de Renda no Brasil: Uma análise da queda recente.* Rio de Janeiro: IPEA.

Ramos, L. 1993. *A distribuição de rendimentos no Brasil: 1976/85.* Rio de Janeiro: IPEA.

Schwartzman, S. 2005. *Education-Oriented Social Programs in Brazil: The Impact of Bolsa Escola.* Rio de Janeiro: Instituto de Estudos do Trabalho e Sociedade (IETS, Institute for Studies on Labor and Society).

Soares, S. 2006. "Análise de bem-estar e decomposição por fatores da queda na desigualdade entre 1995 e 2004." *Econômica* 8, no. 1: 83–115.

Suplicy, E. M. 2002. *Renda de cidadania: A saída é pela porta.* São Paulo: Cortez Editora and Editora Fundação Perseu Abramo.

Contributors

Edmund Amann is senior lecturer in development economics at the University of Manchester and adjunct professor of Latin American studies at the Paul H. Nitze School for Advanced International Studies at Johns Hopkins University. His research interests center on the economics of Latin America, especially on issues of industrial competitiveness and technological change in industry. He is the author of numerous articles in academic journals. His recent books include *Regulating Development: Evidence from Africa and Latin America* (Edward Elgar, 2007); and, coedited with Ha Joon Chang, *Brazil and South Korea: Economic Crisis and Restructuring* (Institute for Latin American Studies, 2004). He holds a PhD from the University of Manchester.

Geraldo Sant'Ana de Camargo Barros is professor of economics and director of the Center for Advanced Studies on Applied Economics at the University of São Paulo. His current research interests include macroeconomics, agrobusiness, agroenergy, trade, agrarian policy, and international economics. He has also served as a consultant for the World Bank, the Food and Agriculture Organization, the National Confederation of Cattle Breeding and Agriculture, and the Brazilian Mercantile and Futures Exchange. He was formerly president of the Brazilian Society of Agricultural Economics. His recent publications include the essay "Sanitary and Phytosanitary Requirements in Agricultural Trade," cowritten with

271

Heloisia L. Burnquist, Silvia H. G. de Miranda, and Joaquim H. da Cunha Filho, in *Agricultural Trade Liberalization: Policies and Implications for Latin America,* edited by Marcos S. Jank (International Monetary Fund, 2004); and *Determinants and Implications of the Growing Scale of Livestock Farms in Four Fast-Growing Developing Countries,* cowritten with Christopher L. Delgado, Clare A. Narrod, Marites M. Tiongco, and others (International Food Policy Research Institute, 2008). He holds a bachelor's degree in agronomy and a master's degree in agrarian economics from the University of São Paulo, a PhD in economics from North Carolina State University at Raleigh, and a postdoctoral degree from the University of Minnesota.

Mauricio Mesquita Moreira is head of research for the integration and trade sector at the Inter-American Development Bank. He previously held a position in the Research Department of the Banco Nacional de Desenvolvimento Econômico e Social (Development Bank of Brazil) and taught at the Federal University of Rio de Janeiro. He is the lead author of, among other studies, *Unclogging the Veins of Latin America and The Caribbean: A Report on The Impact of Transport Costs on the Region's Trade* (Inter-American Development Bank, forthcoming); *Regional Integration: What Is In It for CARICOM?* (Inter-American Development Bank, forthcoming); "Fear of China: Is There a Future for Manufacturing in Latin America?" (published in *World Development,* 2007); "Regional Integration and Productivity: The Experiences of Brazil and Mexico," in *FTAA and Beyond: Prospects for Integration in the Americas,* edited by Antoni Estevadeordal, Dani Rodrik, Alan Taylor, and Andrés Velasco (Harvard University Press, 2004); and "Exports and Trade Finance: Brazil's Recent Experience," in *The Ex-Im Bank in the 21st Century: A New Approach?* edited by Gary Hufbauer and Rita Rodriguez (Peterson Institute for International Economics, 2001). He received a PhD in economics from University College London.

Pedro da Motta Veiga is a director of the Centro de Estudos de Integração e Desenvolvimento and a partner at EcoStrat Consultores, Rio de Janeiro, working on trade negotiations as well as trade and industrial policies issues. He is a permanent consultant to the Confederação Nacional da Indústria of Brazil, regional adviser for the Swiss Agency for Cooperation and Development, coordinator of the Latin American Trade Network in Brazil and a member of its Steering Committee, and a member of the Advisory Board of the Working Group on Mercosur–EU Negotiations. He has been a consultant to many international institutions, including the United Nations Conference on Trade and Development, the Comisión Económica para America Latina y el Caribe, the Inter-American Development Bank, the World Bank, the Organization for Economic Cooperation and Development, and the Asociación Latinoamericana de Integración. He holds a BA from the Pontifícia Universidade Católica do Rio de Janeiro and an MSc from the Instituto Alberto Luiz Coimbra de Pós-Graduação e Pequisa de Engenharia, Universidade Federal do Rio de Janeiro. He edited *Comércio e Política Comercial no Brasil: Atores, interesses e estratégias* (Singular, 2007) and published the essay "El Régimen Internacional de Inversiones: Un status quo problemático y un futuro incierto," in *Después de Doha: La agenda emergente del sistema de comercio internacional,* edited by R. Bouzas (Marcial Pons, 2007).

Thais Narciso holds a bachelor's degree in international relations from the London School of Economics and Political Science. She has worked as project manager at Prospectiva, a Brazilian consulting firm focusing on international affairs, and is currently undertaking graduate studies in international political economy as part of a degree program offered jointly by Sciences Po, Paris, and the London School of Economics and Political Science. She coauthored "Brazil in Africa: Another Emerging Power in the Continent?" with Alexandre Barbosa and Marina Biancalana (*Politikon: South African Journal of Political Studies,* forthcoming) and collaborated with Alexandre Barbosa on *The Impact of Free-Trade Agreements Signed between ALADI Member Countries on Employment* (Asociación Latinoamericana de Integración/Securities and Exchange Commission, 2008).

André Meloni Nassar is the director-general of the Instituto de Estudos do Comércio e Negociações Internacionais (Institute for International Trade Negotiations) in Brazil since 2003. He has served as a leading agricultural economist on various projects, including the Brazilian Technical Group for the Doha Round agricultural negotiations, coordinated by the External Relations and Agriculture ministries of the Brazilian government, and on a Group of Twenty expert committee commissioned by the Brazilian government to study world agricultural markets. From 1999 to 2002, he was a senior researcher at the Fundação Instituto de Pesquisas Econômicas (Economic Research Foundation) and an associate faculty member at the PENSA Agribusiness Studies Program of the University of São Paulo. In 2001, he was a visiting scholar at Georgetown University's School of Foreign Service. His recent publications include "The Expansion of Agriculture in Brazil and Its Agricultural Policies," coauthored with Flavio Soares Damico, in *U.S. Agricultural Policy and the 2007 Farm Bill: Promoting the Economic Resilience and Conserving the Ecological Integrity of American Farmlands,* edited by Kaush Arha, Tim Josling, Daniel A. Sumner, and Barton H. Thompson (Woods Institute for the Environment, 2006); and "Tariff Spikes and Tariff Escalation," coauthored with Zuleika Arashiro and Marcos S. Jank, in *Handbook on International Trade Policy,* edited by William A. Kerr and James D. Gaisford (Edward Elgar, 2007). He also writes a monthly article on agriculture, trade, and sustainability in the daily *O Estado de São Paulo.* He earned a BS in agronomy from the Escola Superior de Agricultura Luiz de Queiroz (Luiz de Queiroz School of Agriculture) of the University of São Paulo and an MS and PhD from the School of Economics and Business at the University of São Paulo.

Marcelo Côrtes Neri is director of the Centro de Políticas Sociais (Center of Social Policies) tied to the Brazilian Institute for Economics and professor in the Graduate Program in Economics at the Escola de Pós-Graduação em Economia, both affiliated with the Fundação Getulio Vargas. He coordinates the Network on Education, also at the Fundação Getulio Vargas. His main research areas are the evaluation of social programs, the measurement of poverty and inequality, and microeconometrics. He publishes regularly in both national and international journals. His paper "Think Global, Act Local: Social Credit," based on the Millennium Development Goals, was presented at the Global Network Meeting in Dakar in 2005. His most recent books are *Microcrédito, o Mistério Nordestino e o Grameen Brasileiro* (Microcredit, the Northeast Mystery, and the Brazilian Grameen) (coedited; Fundação Getulio Vargas, 2008); *Ensaios Sociais* (Social Essays) (Fundação Getulio Vargas, 2003); *Retratos da Deficiência no Brasil* (Portrait of the Disabled in Brazil) (Fundação Getulio Vargas, 2003); and *Cobertura Previdenciária: Diagnóstico e Propostas* (Social Security Coverage: Diagnosis and Proposals) (Ministério da Previdência e Assistência Social, Coleção Previdência Social, 2003). He is actively involved in proposing and evaluating public policies in Brazil and has also implemented qualitative and quantitative fieldwork in more than fifteen countries in the last five years. He organized the Brazilian chapter of the Network on Inequality and Poverty during 2000 and two international seminars on education during 2005 in Rio de Janeiro. He participates in the public policy debate, writing twice a month in *Valor Econômico* and the magazine *Conjuntura Econômica*. He holds a PhD in economics from Princeton University.

Ben Ross Schneider is professor of political science at Northwestern University. His teaching and research interests fall within the general fields of comparative politics, political economy, and Latin American politics. His books include *Politics within the State: Elite Bureaucrats and Industrial Policy in Authoritarian Brazil* (University of Pittsburgh Press, 1991); *Business and the State in Developing Countries* (Cornell University Press, 1997); *Reinventing Leviathan: The Politics of Administrative Reform in Developing Countries* (North-South/Lynne Rienner, 2003); and *Business Politics and the State in 20th Century Latin America* (Cambridge University Press, 2004). He has also written on topics such as economic reform, democratization, technocracy, the developmental state, and comparative bureaucracy. His current research centers on two longer-term projects, the first on the political economy of market reforms (quasi-markets) in health care and education; and the second on the institutional foundations of capitalist development in Latin America, with particular attention to corporate governance, business groups, foreign investment, and worker training. He holds a BA from Williams College, an MA from Columbia University, and a PhD from the University of California, Berkeley.

Ricardo Ubiraci Sennes is partner director of Prospectiva, a Brazilian consulting firm focusing on international affairs, and professor of international relations at the Pontifícia Universidade Católica de São Paulo. He is a member of the Editorial Board of *Foreign Affairs Latinoamérica*. He was formerly coordinator of the Centro Brasileiro de Relações Internacionais (Brazilian Center for International Relations) in São Paulo. He has also conducted research for the International Relations Center at the University of São Paulo, for the Woodrow Wilson International Center for Scholars in Washington, and for the Iberian and Latin American Studies Center at the University of California, San Diego. His areas of specialization are the economic and politic scenarios of Latin America, with projects in the areas of trade in services, infrastructure, and financial integration. He is the author of *As mudanças da política externa brasileira nos anos 80: Uma potência média recém industrializada* (Brazil's Foreign

Policy Changes in the '80s: A Newly Industrialized Middle Power) (Editora da Universidade Federal do Rio Grande do Sul, 2003), and he has written a number of articles for institutions and academic journals. He holds a bachelor's degree in economics from the Pontifícia Universidade Católica de São Paulo, an MA in political science from the University of São Paulo, and a PhD in international relations.

Index